Create Your First Web Page

In a Weekend™

Revised Edition

STEVEN E. CALLIHAN

PRIMA PUBLISHING

To my sister and brother, Darlene Gadley and Don Callihan

Prima Publishing and colophon are registered trademarks of Prima Communications, Inc. In a Weekend is a trademark of Prima Publishing, a division of Prima Communications, Inc., Rocklin, California 95677.

Publisher: Matthew H. Carleson
Managing Editor: Dan J. Foster
Acquisitions Editor: Deborah F. Abshier
Project Editor: Kevin W. Ferns
Technical Reviewer: Bo Williams
Copy Editor: Hilary Powers
Interior Layout: Shawn Morningstar
Cover Design: Prima Design Team
Indexer: Katherine Stimson

Prima Publishing and the author have attempted throughout this book to distinguish proprietary trademarks from descriptive terms by following the capitalization style used by the manufacturer.

Information contained in this book has been obtained by Prima Publishing from sources believed to be reliable. However, because of the possibility of human or mechanical error by our sources, Prima Publishing, or others, the Publisher does not guarantee the accuracy, adequacy, or completeness of any information and is not responsible for any errors or omissions or the results obtained from the use of such information. Readers should be particularly aware of the fact that the Internet is an ever-changing entity. Some facts may have changed since this book went to press.

ISBN: 0-7615-1388-4
Library of Congress Catalog Card Number: 98-65715
Printed in the United States of America
98 99 00 01 BB 10 9 8 7 6 5 4 3 2 1

CONTENTS

SATURDAY MORNING
The Basic HTML Tutorial 39

SATURDAY AFTERNOON
The Intermediate HTML Tutorial 109

Contents v

SUNDAY MORNING
Planning Your First Web Page 217

SUNDAY AFTERNOON
Creating Your First Web Page 251

ACKNOWLEDGMENTS

Many thanks to Kevin Ferns, Bo Williams, Hilary Powers, Tom Barich, Debbie Abshier, and others at Prima for their strong efforts and very real contributions to this new edition.

ABOUT THE AUTHOR

Steven E. Callihan is a freelance writer from Seattle. He is the author of *Learn HTML In a Weekend*, also published by Prima Publishing.

INTRODUCTION

You live in a busy world in which time is at a premium. You've surfed the Web and wondered what it would take to start creating your own Web pages. It seemed as if you had to become an expert on HTML (*Hypertext Markup Language*), and somehow you just never managed to find the time. But you don't have to wait anymore! Even if you know absolutely nothing about HTML, you can create your first Web page in just one weekend! You also don't have to become an HTML expert—the Saturday HTML tutorials tell you everything you need to know about HTML to create a wide variety of Web pages.

Anyone who has a basic understanding of HTML and the right tools can create the majority of the sites you see on the Web. That's exactly what this book is about. After you create your first Web page, this book also tells you everything you need to know to put your page up on the Web.

Who Should Read This Book

What is so liberating about the Web is that you don't have to be a computer expert to take advantage of its benefits. Everyone has interests besides computers. Computers, the Web, and HTML are tools that enable people to do stuff, not ends in themselves. The Web, via HTML, should

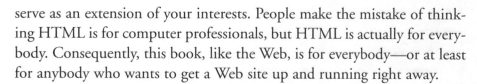

serve as an extension of your interests. People make the mistake of thinking HTML is for computer professionals, but HTML is actually for everybody. Consequently, this book, like the Web, is for everybody—or at least for anybody who wants to get a Web site up and running right away.

HTML isn't something you learn first and do later. It's more like riding a bicycle–you learn by doing. Don't worry about making mistakes, which are merely experimental results by another name. Play around with it and experiment. That's the only way you're going to truly learn.

What You Can Do in a Weekend

I'm not going to promise that you'll be able to learn HTML and develop a full-blown multi-page Web site in a single weekend. But you can learn the most useful features of HTML and apply them to a number of different types of Web pages.

One of the most common pages on the Web is the personal page, where you can tell the world about yourself. You might want to create a page for your family, your fraternity or sorority, or your church or club. If you're interested in getting a job or advancing your career, you might want to create an online version of your résumé.

If you have a product or service to offer, you might want to create an online brochure or business card. You might want to put up a description of your project, organization, or community. You might want to create an informational page, such as a page on which you offer your own special expertise on a subject of interest, or share perspectives with others and get feedback. You could devote this page to a hobby or something you've researched. Basically, the page could be about anything.

If you know quite a bit about a particular subject, you might want to create a glossary or a FAQ (Frequently Asked Questions) page. If you are helping to run an organization or a social club, you might want to create a calendar of upcoming events. If you're creative, you could put up a page of your poetry, a short story, or a gallery of your drawings, paintings, or photographs. If you're a student, teacher, or professor, you might want to publish an online version of a paper, abstract, thesis, dissertation, or book review. You could publish your own page of movie reviews, or a newsletter or journal. Your options are virtually unlimited.

You may not set up the whole site in just one weekend, but you could definitely get its development off to a substantial start. The idea isn't to create just one Web page, but by the end of the weekend to have enough hands-on experience with HTML to be able to create any kind of page mentioned here, or any other type of page you might dream up.

Of course, you don't have to do all the sessions in one weekend. You could just as easily do the five main sessions over a period of five evenings, Monday evening through Friday evening. Or you could do them over a period of a week if you want to include the bonus sessions. It's entirely up to you.

What You Need to Begin

You don't need to be a techie or computer nerd to use this book, but you should have a working knowledge of basic Windows operations (3.1 or 95), such as using File Manager or Windows Explorer to create, copy, move, and delete files or folders.

This book is written under the assumption that you already know how to use a Web browser and navigate on the Web. It mentions quite a few resources available on the Web, so you should know how to download a file or program. Because many programs on the Web are in compressed format (ZIP or TAR), you should know how to decompress files using utilities such as PKUnzip or WinZip.

Although a CD-ROM comes with this book, you don't need to have a CD-ROM drive to complete all the tasks. Web addresses (URLs) are provided for all the software programs, Web art, and reference materials included on the CD-ROM, so you can download them even if you can't use the CD. Sample Web pages and graphics created for this book are available for downloading at `http://www.callihan.com/create2/`.

The examples furnished and techniques demonstrated in this book have all been tested using Windows 3.1 and Windows 95. You don't need Microsoft Windows to use this book—you can create HTML files on any platform—but you do need to find equivalents on your platform for any programs, utilities, or tips and tricks referenced herein.

Besides a computer, of course, you need only three things to create a Web page:

1. **A graphical Web browser connected to the Internet.** Most current graphical Web browsers should be fine for doing the Basic HTML tutorial and creating a basic Web page. For the Intermediate HTML tutorial and creating an intermediate Web page, I recommend you use one of the later versions—3.0 or greater—of Netscape Navigator or Microsoft Internet Explorer. The illustrations in this book feature Navigator 4.02 and Internet Explorer 4.01. You'll probably want to download and install both of these browsers to verify that your Web page is attractive and functional in either one. For links to sites that offer the latest Web browsers for downloading, see Appendix B, "The Web Resources Directory."

 NOTE If you're connected to the Internet through an online service such as CompuServe or America Online, you may not have your choice of browser, and you might not be able to run it offline. Check to find out if you have these capabilities. Even if the answer is no, you can still do the tutorials and exercises in this book—you just have to do them online.

2. **A text editor.** I recommend you use Windows Notepad, which comes with both Windows 3.1 and Windows 95, rather than a word processor or an HTML editor. Notepad is perfectly suited for creating HTML files and offers several advantages over larger, more cumbersome programs, and many professional HTML coders prefer Notepad. A couple of other Notepad-like HTML editors, Aardvark Pro and Gomer HTML Editor, are also well-suited for HTML coding, and both are included on the CD-ROM. Avoid starting

out with one of the WYSIWYG-type HTML editors. Learn some HTML first, then try out some of the fancier tools (a large selection of which are included on the CD-ROM).

3. **A graphics editor capable of creating GIF files.** Any of the commercial draw or photo-paint programs can create GIF files, but some excellent graphics programs for creating and working with GIF files are also available on the Web. In case you don't already have a graphics editor capable of working with GIF files, both LView Pro and Paint Shop Pro are included on the CD-ROM.

How This Book Is Organized

The book is divided into five main sessions designated for Friday evening, Saturday morning, Saturday afternoon, Sunday morning, and Sunday afternoon. Also two bonus sessions for Saturday evening and Sunday evening are included that you can do if you have the time. Each of the main sessions should take no more than three to four hours to complete, while the bonus sessions should take no longer than a couple of hours or so, but I've tried to take different learning styles into account and build in as much flexibility as possible. The Saturday Afternoon session and both bonus sessions are optional, to be done only if you have time (you can always come back and do them later). I've also included a number of appendixes, including a Beginner's Guide to Style Sheets, a Resource Directory, the CD-ROM contents, a table of special characters, and instructions on how to put your Web page up on the Web. Here are some details of what's included in the book:

○ **Friday Evening: Getting Started.** This session covers essential background information and the minimum requirements necessary to do the two Saturday HTML tutorials. It also includes an optional section on tools and resources that can help you create your Web page.

○ **Saturday Morning: The Basic HTML Tutorial.** Here you have a step-by-step tutorial that covers the basic HTML codes most commonly

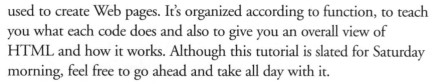

used to create Web pages. It's organized according to function, to teach you what each code does and also to give you an overall view of HTML and how it works. Although this tutorial is slated for Saturday morning, feel free to go ahead and take all day with it.

- **Saturday Afternoon: The Intermediate HTML Tutorial.** If you speed through the morning session, you can run through this optional tutorial. It covers some more features of HTML, mostly codes originally introduced as Netscape Extensions but now incorporated into HTML 3.2. You don't need this information to plan and create your first Web page on Sunday. Do whatever suits your schedule or interest level.

- **Saturday Evening: The Tables Tutorial (Bonus Session).** Take on this optional tutorial only if you have the time and energy. It covers all the essentials you need to know to effectively use tables in your Web pages.

- **Sunday Morning: Planning Your First Web Page.** This is a hands-on session that guides you in planning your Web page, including defining an objective, doing an outline, and assembling or creating the different pieces or components that will make up your page. It includes writing your text, creating a banner graphic, and gathering any Web addresses you want to use as hypertext links. It also furnishes some models that you can follow in assembling or creating these components.

- **Sunday Afternoon: Creating Your First Web Page.** Here you actually create your first Web page based on the decision tree you designed during the morning's planning session. You also choose whether to use basic HTML or intermediate HTML to create your page.

- **Sunday Evening: The Graphics Tutorial (Bonus Session).** This optional tutorial can be done after you create your first Web page. It shows you how to use Paint Shop Pro to create banner, button, and icon graphics for your Web pages.

Once you've created your first Web page this weekend, you can check out the appendixes in this book for additional resources to further assist your Web publishing efforts. Here's a short rundown on what is contained in the appendixes:

○ **Appendix A: The Web Resources Directory**. This is a comprehensive guide to HTML and Web publishing resources on the Web. You'll find links to HTML tutorials, style guides, forms, frames, image maps, Cascading Style Sheets, and more. You'll also find many links to graphics resources on the Web, including interlaced and transparent GIF images, background images, and Web art libraries.

○ **Appendix B: The Web Tools Directory**. Look here for a comprehensive guide to HTML and Web publishing software tools. You'll find links to Web browsers, HTML editors and converters, and software utilities for adding advanced HTML features to your Web pages such as frames, forms, image maps, GIF animations, style sheets, Java applets, and more.

○ **Appendix C: Special Characters**. You are not stuck with using characters from the keyboard when creating Web pages. Look here for a comprehensive listing of all the special (non-keyboard) characters you can include in your Web page, along with the HTML codes you need to include them.

○ **Appendix D: Putting It Up on the Web**. Once you've created your first Web page, you are going to want to put it up on the Web! Look here for information on finding a Web host for your pages and using WS-FTP LE, a great freeware FTP client that is available on the CD-ROM.

○ **Appendix E: What's on the CD-ROM**. Look here for information on how to use the CD-ROM.

What's New in the Revised Edition

HTML is like a layer cake. As new developments occur, they are layered onto the already existent body of HTML. The earlier layers of the cake, the basic and intermediate HTML, remain just as good and tasty as when they were the newest thing. They will remain the heart and soul of HTML for quite some time. In fact, by learning HTML with the graduated approach applied in this book, you will be even better prepared to understand the newest developments in HTML and integrate them into your Web publishing efforts. Wherever relevant, I've included information on incorporating the latest HTML developments into your Web pages, including HTML 4.0, Cascading Style Sheets, and Dynamic HTML.

The bonus sessions for Saturday and Sunday evenings are also new. These are entirely optional sessions that present tutorials on using tables and creating Web graphics. They are shorter than the other tutorials in the book and should take no longer than a couple of hours to complete.

Finally, the Resource Directory in the first edition has been entirely updated, and is now present as two appendixes, Appendix A, "The Web Resources Directory," and Appendix B, "The Web Tools Directory." Use these appendixes as your own personal guides to the latest Web publishing resources and tools that are available on the Web.

Special Features of This Book

This book contains a number of conventions to make your job easier as you work through the sessions. You'll find that these conventions offer helpful and informative tidbits about the topics covered, and they sometimes provide valuable insight into the more complicated aspects of Web page construction.

Notes are food for thought as you work through the tutorials. They will help you to begin thinking about some of the finer points of organizing and creating your Web page.

Tips offer helpful hints, tricks, and ideas to apply as you progress in the creation process.

Cautions warn you of possible hazards and point out pitfalls that typically plague beginners.

Buzzwords are terms and acronyms that you should be familiar with as you journey into the land of Web page designers.

This icon denotes trialware included on the CD-ROM that comes with this book. For more information on CD-ROM contents, see Appendix E, "What's On the CD-ROM."

I have set up the *Create Your First Web Page in a Weekend* Web site at `http://www.callihan.com/create2/`. At the Web site, you will find a list of affordable Internet presence providers (IPPs) that you can use as a starting point in your search for a server to host your Web page. There are also continually updated lists of Web publishing resources and tools, links to readers' pages, Web page templates, and other information. Additionally, all sample Web pages and graphics used in the book are available for download.

It's Friday evening—at least if you're following the schedule. Yes, for the purposes of this book, Friday evening constitutes part of the weekend. Okay, maybe that is fudging a bit, but if you're going to create your first Web page in a weekend, you need to get this little reading assignment out of the way first.

The first sections of this Friday evening session include general background information on the Internet, the World Wide Web, HTML, and Web pages. You really should have some grounding in the medium you plan to use before you start the HTML tutorials on Saturday morning or begin to plan and create your first Web page on Sunday. Of course, if you're already very familiar with something, feel free to skip it.

The second section, "Getting Set Up," covers selecting and setting up the tools you'll need to complete the HTML tutorials and plan and create your first Web page. This will include selecting a Web browser, a text or HTML editor, and a graphics editor for creating custom graphics for your first Web page.

What Is the Internet?

It could be said that the Internet is the most valuable legacy left over from the Cold War. It originally came into being as the ARPANet, which was founded by the U.S. Defense Department's Advanced Research Projects Agency (ARPA) to link academic research centers involved in military research.

Today's Internet has grown far beyond its original conception. Originally linking just four university research centers, it has become an international and global system consisting of hundreds of thousands of *nodes* (servers). In many ways, it has become what Marshall McLuhan called "the global village," in that every node is functionally right next door. You can just as easily communicate with someone in Australia as you can with someone two blocks down the street—and if the person down the street isn't on the Internet, it's actually easier to communicate with the bloke in Australia. That is the premise, even if the original founders didn't realize it, and today it has become an increasingly pervasive reality.

◀ ◀

BUZZ WORD A *client* is a computer that requests something from another computer. A *server* is a computer that responds to requests for service from clients.

◀ ◀

An internet is a network of networks, a kind of meta-network. Simply put, the Internet is a set of protocols (rules) for transmitting and exchanging data between networks. In a broader sense, however, it is a worldwide community, a global village, and a repository of global information resources.

◀ ◀

BUZZ WORD TCP/IP *(Transmission Control Protocol/Internet Protocol)* is the standard rule set for Internet communication. The essence of the Internet is not the wire, but the means for sending and receiving information across the wire. It doesn't matter what type of systems are connected to the Internet, be they mainframes, minicomputers, or Unix, Macintosh, or MS-DOS computers. All that matters is that they all use the same protocol, TCP/IP, to communicate with each other.

◀ ◀

What Is the World Wide Web?

The World Wide Web, also called the WWW, W3, or simply the Web, dates back to 1989, when it was proposed by Tim Berners-Lee, often called its inventor. Many others have been critically involved, but

Berners-Lee gets the credit for originally proposing and evangelizing the idea as a way to facilitate collaboration between scientists over the Internet.

On the original Web page for the World Wide Web Project, posted on the CERN (The European Laboratory of Partical Physics, birth place of the World Wide Web) server in 1992, Tim Berners-Lee described the World Wide Web as "a wide-area hypermedia information retrieval initiative aiming to give universal access to a large universe of documents." Today he is more liable to describe the Web as the "universal space of all network-accessible information." Ted Nelson, inventor of the concept of hypertext, wrapped all this up in a wonderfully apt term, describing the Word Wide Web as a "docuverse."

Like the Internet, the Web is essentially defined by a set of protocols, as follows:

❖ **HTTP (Hypertext Transfer Protocol)** is used to exchange Web documents across the Internet. When you request a Web document from a server, the protocol used for the request is HTTP.

❖ **HTML (Hypertext Markup Language)** enables users to present information over the Web in a structured and uniform fashion. It is used to mark up documents so that a Web browser can interpret and then display them. See "What Is HTML?" later in this session for more information.

❖ **URLs (Uniform Resource Locators)** are addresses that identify a server, a directory, or a specific file. HTTP URLs, or Web addresses, are only one type of address on the Web. FTP, Gopher, and WAIS are other types of addresses you'll find fairly often on the Web. Until recently, there were still more FTP and Gopher servers on the Internet than HTTP servers. See "What Is a URL?" later in this session for additional related information.

❖ **CGI (Common Gateway Interface)** serves as an interface to execute local programs through a gateway between the HTTP server software and the host computer. Thus, you can include a hypertext link in a Web document that will run a server program or script to process input from a customer request form.

Although other mediums of exchange on the Internet share the same cyberspace, the Web has come to epitomize the new paradigm. In fact, Web browsers can access not only Web or HTML documents, but the entirety of the Internet, including Gopher, FTP, Archie, Telnet, and WAIS, as well as Mail and News servers. The Web's tendency to embrace and incorporate all other mediums and operate as a universal medium is its most revolutionary character.

A LITTLE HISTORY

The beginnings of the Internet go back at least as far as 1957, to the founding of the Defense Department's Advanced Research Projects Agency (ARPA) in response to the Soviet Union launching *Sputnik*. In 1963, ARPA asked the Rand Corporation to ponder how to form a command-and-control network capable of surviving attack by atomic bombs. The Rand Corporation's response (made public in 1964) was that the network would "have no central authority" and would be "designed from the beginning to operate while in tatters." These two basic concepts became the defining characteristics of what would eventually become the Internet. The Internet was conceptualized as having no central authority and as being able to operate in a condition of assumed unreliability (bombed-out cities, downed telephone lines); that is, of having maximum redundancy. All nodes would be coequal in status, each with authority to originate, relay, and receive messages.

What happened between this first military initiative and the Internet we know today? Plenty. Here are some of the highlights:

1965: Ted Nelson invents the concept, and coins the term, of hypertext.

1969: ARPANet, the forerunner of the Internet, commissioned by the Department of Defense, links nodes at UCLA, Stanford, UC Santa Barbara, and the University of Utah. Within two years, the number of nodes increases to 15, including MIT, Harvard, and NASA/Ames.

1972: Telnet is introduced.

1973: The first international connections to the ARPANet occur from England and Norway. FTP (File Transfer Protocol) is introduced.

1977: E-Mail is introduced.

1979: News groups (USENET) are introduced.

1982: ARPANet adopts TCP/IP (Transmission Control Protocol/Internet Protocol), the real beginning of the Internet.

1984: Domain Name Server (DNS) is implemented, allocating addresses between six basic "domains" (gov, mil, edu, com, and org for government, military, educational, commercial, and noncommercial hosts, respectively).

1986: NSFNet is formed by the National Science Foundation (NSF) using five supercomputing centers to form the first high-speed "backbone," running at 56 Kbps. Unlike ARPANet, which is focused on military or government research, the NSFNet is available to all forms of academic research.

1987: 10,000 hosts make up the Web.

1988: The Web backbone is upgraded to T1 (1.544 Mbps).

1989: Tim Berners-Lee proposes the invention of the Web, leading to the creation of the World Wide Web.

1990: The ARPANet closes down. Archie is introduced on the Web. The World (world.std.com) becomes the first commercial provider of dial-up access to the Internet.

1991: Gopher is introduced. The World Wide Web is released at CERN (European Laboratory for Particle Physics) in Switzerland. The Web's Backbone is upgraded to T3 (44.736 Mbps).

1992: The Internet Society (ISOC) is formed. Viola, the first English-language graphical Web browser, is released. Veronica is introduced to the Web. 1,000,000 hosts are present on the Web.

1993: Marc Andreesen's Mosaic for X (X-Windows, a Unix GUI) is released by NCSA, followed shortly by versions for PC/Windows and Macintosh. The White House goes online. The HTML 1.0 draft proposal is published.

1994: Mosaic Communications, later to become Netscape Communications, is formed by Marc Andreesen and James Clark, ex-president of Silicon Graphics. The first meeting of the W3 Consortium is held at MIT. The first cybermalls form. The HTML 2.0 draft proposal is published.

1995: Netscape goes public. The NSFNet is replaced by a network of providers for carrying U.S. backbone traffic. NSFNet reverts to a research network.

1996: Bill Gates and Microsoft jump into the game with the Internet Explorer browser. Proposed recommendation for HTML 3.2 is released in May by the W3C (World Wide Web Consortium). The recommendation for Cascading Style Sheets, level 1 (CSS1), is released in December.

1997: The final recommendation for HTML 3.2 is released in January. The working draft for the Document Object Model (DOM), a key element in the future direction of Dynamic HTML, is released in September. The final recommendation for HTML 4.0 is released in December.

1998: The proposed recommendation (last step before final release) for MathML (Mathematical Markup Language) and the final recommendation for XML 1.0 (Extensible Markup Language) are released in February. The proposed recommendation for Cascading Style Sheets, level 2 (CSS2), and an updated working draft for the Document Object Model (DOM) are released in March.

What Is Hypertext?

You could say the Web is a graphical, platform-independent, distributed, decentralized, multiformatted, interactive, dynamic, nonlinear, immediate, two-way communication medium. The basic mechanism that enables all of it is actually quite simple. This is the *hypertext link,* a kind of jump point that allows a visitor to jump from a place in a Web page to any other Web page, document, or binary data-object (a script, graphic, video, etc.) on the Web. Not only can you jump to another Web page, but you can jump to another place, either in the same Web page or another Web page. A link can connect anything, anywhere, that has an address or URL on the Net. When Ted Nelson originally coined the term *hypertext* in 1965, he conceptualized it as "non-sequential writing." In other words, any link can go to any object anywhere (anything with an address) within the "docuverse," or "universal space of all network-accessible information," (Tim Berners-Lee). See Figure 1.1 for a general representation of how hypertext links work.

Figure 1.2 illustrates some of the different kinds of data objects to which you can link from a Web page. Note the difference between an inline image, which appears as part of the Web page, and other graphics, which your browser or viewer can link to and display separately.

Figure 1.1

Using hypertext links, you can jump from one Web page to another Web page, or to another place in a Web page.

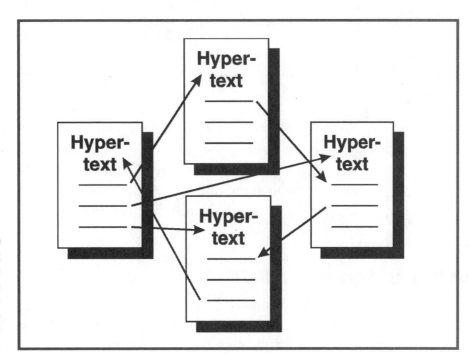

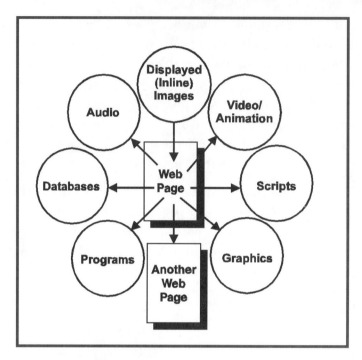

Figure 1.2

A Web page can
link to many other
kinds of data
objects besides just
other Web pages.

A hypertext link, also referred to as an *anchor,* actually works much like a cross-reference in a book, except that you can immediately click on and go to it, whether it's a link within the same document or to a page halfway around the world. You don't have to thumb through the book or go down to the local library to find the reference. Anything that has an address on the Web can be linked, including Gopher documents, FTP files, and Newsgroup articles.

What Is Hypermedia?

Given that hypertext linking occurs within and between documents, it makes sense that hypermedia (a term also coined by Ted Nelson) refers to connecting with other nontext (binary) media such as graphics, audio, animation, video, or software programs. Many pages on the Web are now generated on the fly from scripts, programs, or database queries. Increasingly, Java applets are being used to generate dynamically interactive Web sites. Over time, the Web will evolve from a system composed of primarily static hypertext Web pages to one composed of dynamically interlinked hypermedia, within which text is just another medium.

For now, the Web mainly consists of documents, or pages, and you can still think of hypermedia as a subcategory of hypertext.

What Is HTML?

HTML, Hypertext Markup Language, is a subset of SGML *(Standard Generalized Markup Language)*. SGML was developed to standardize the *markup,* or preparation for typesetting, of computer-generated documents. HTML, on the other hand, was specifically developed to mark up, or encode, hypertext documents for display on the World Wide Web.

An HTML document is a plain *ASCII* (text) file with codes (called *tags*) inserted in the text to define elements in the document. HTML tags generally have two parts, an on-code and an off-code, which contain the text to be defined. A few tags don't require an off-code, and I'll note those as they arise. You can represent a tag in the following way, where the ellipsis (. . .) represents the text you want to tag:

```
<Tagname> . . . </Tagname>
```

For instance, the following is the tag for a level-one heading in a Web document:

```
<H1>This is a level-one heading</H1>
```

The most important thing to keep in mind about HTML is that its purpose isn't to specify the exact formatting or layout of a Web page, but to define the specific elements that make up a page—the body of the text, headings, paragraphs, line breaks, text elements, and so on. You use HTML to define the composition of a Web page, not its appearance. The particular Web browser you use to view the page controls the display of the Web page. For instance, you can define a line using the <H1> . . . </H1> tag, but the browser defines the appearance of a first-level header line.

One browser might show H1 lines as 18-point Times Roman text, while another might show H1 lines in a totally different font and size.

To understand why this is the way it is, you need to understand how HTML-coded Web pages and Web browsers work together. To display a Web page on your computer, a Web browser must first download it and any graphics displayed on the page to your computer. If the Web page were to specify all the formatting and display details, it would increase the amount of data to be transmitted, the size of the file, and the amount of time it takes to transfer. Leaving all the formatting and display details to the Web browser means that the size of HTML documents sent over the Web can remain relatively small since they're just regular ASCII text files. It's rare to have an HTML file that exceeds 30KB (not counting any graphics that it may contain).

However, this means that every Web browser has its own idea about how to best display a particular Web page. Your Web page may look different in Netscape Navigator than it does in NCSA Mosaic. That's why you may want to test your completed page on more than just one browser. Some Web browsers support the display of tables, which was part of the proposed HTML 3.0 standard and has since been incorporated into HTML 3.2. But most current graphical Web browsers support HTML 3.2. In the Intermediate HTML Tutorial scheduled for Saturday afternoon, I'll show you how to effectively incorporate HTML 3.2 features into your Web pages.

The advent of the new HTML 4.0 specification adds more complications to the mix. The current versions of Netscape Navigator and Internet Explorer support parts of HTML 4.0. While the latest version of Internet Explorer is fully compliant with the Cascading Style Sheets standard, the latest version of Navigator does not. Neither browser has yet to support the latest proposed standard, Cascading Style Sheets, level 2.

Most of HTML 4.0 will be supported soon, as well as most of the new Cascading Style Sheets standards (CSS1 and CSS2). Anyway, trying to prognosticate the future of HTML is sort of like trying to predict the weather. Stay tuned for the nightly report, because that is exactly how fast things will be changing. Remember that the more things change, the more they stay the same—most of what is being added to HTML now is frosting on the cake. The cake is still composed almost entirely of HTML 2.0 and HTML 3.2 elements and attributes.

If you are concerned with compatibility with the majority of current graphical Web browsers, it may be wise to stick with HTML 3.2 elements and attributes, at least until HTML 4.0 is more fully supported. If you want to incorporate any of the new HTML 4.0 features, you should thoroughly check your pages in both of the main Web browsers. Other Web browsers may ignore unrecognized tags, and a Web page that looks fantastic in a Web browser supporting HTML 4.0 may look pretty crummy in one that doesn't. It's probably not a bad idea to keep an older Web browser installed on your system so you can check this. Saturday's sessions ("The Basic HTML Tutorial" and "The Intermediate HTML Tutorial") include several examples of how the same HTML coding can have quite different results depending on the Web browser used to view it.

NOTE As HTML has evolved, it has become more descriptive, allowing you more freedom to design your page rather than schematicize it. The more attention you give to designing your page to have a particular appearance, the less likely it is that all browsers will display your page consistently and accurately. The Basic and Intermediate HTML Tutorials show you how different browsers can display the same element. Also, many of the designer features that have been added to HTML require a Web browser that is up-to-date enough to display them.

Basic HTML encompasses most of what was HTML 2.0 (the HTML standard prior to HTML 3.2). I cover this level of HTML in the Saturday Morning session. Most graphical Web browsers should support this level of HTML.

Intermediate HTML encompasses most of what is included in HTML 3.2, as well as a few tidbits from HTML 4.0. I cover this in the Saturday Afternoon and Saturday Evening sessions ("The Intermediate HTML Tutorial" and "The Tables Tutorial"). Most current graphical Web browsers should fully support HTML 3.2, although support for it from earlier browser versions may be quite sketchy (HTML 3.2 is largely a pastiche of what were previously called "Netscape extensions" and proposed elements that were supposed to be included in the failed HTML 3.0 proposal).

Advanced HTML includes HTML 2.0, HTML 3.2, and HTML 4.0 tags, as well as other advanced features such as Cascading Style Sheets and Dynamic HTML. These features require considerably more experience than a beginning Web publisher is likely to have, or require more space and time to properly explain than is available for this book. You can find links, however, to many resources, tutorials, and tools for including advanced features in your Web pages in Appendix A, "The Web Resources Directory," and Appendix B, "The Web Tools Directory." I've also included Web page templates on the CD-ROM to assist you in creating your own two-frame and three-frame Web sites, as well as a template for including an image map navigation bar on your Web pages. For more information on the Web page templates included on the CD-ROM, see Appendix E, "What's on the CD-ROM."

What Is a URL?

A URL (*Uniform Resource Locator*) identifies the address, or location, of a resource on the Internet. Every Web page has its own unique URL. If you know the URL of a Web page and access is not restricted, you can connect to it and view it in your browser. Resources other than Web pages also have URLs, including FTP, Telnet, WAIS, Gopher, and Newsgroups.

A URL may consist of the following parts:

- ⚙ **Service.** The service designator specifies the service being accessed: http (for WWW), ftp, gopher, wais, telnet, or news.

- ⚙ **Host.** The host designator specifies the domain name of the server being accessed, such as the following: `www.myserver.com`.

- ⚙ **Port number.** The port number only needs to be specified if it is a nonstandard port number for the service being accessed—most URLs don't require port numbers (the default port number is 80 for Web servers, 21 for FTP servers).

- ⚙ **Resource path.** The resource path specifies the directory path and often the file name of the resource being accessed. At minimum, you should probably include a "/" here to indicate the root directory of a domain (although most Web browsers let you get away with leaving this off following a domain name): `http://anywhere.com/` rather than `http://anywhere.com`, for instance. You can exclude the file name here if you use the default file name for index files specified by the server, which may be INDEX.HTML, INDEX.HTM, or DEFAULT.HTM, depending on the actual server. If you don't use the default file name for index files, then you must include the actual file path and name of the Web page. For instance:

`http://anywhere.com/myfolder/mypage.html`

Figure 1.3 shows a diagram of a URL. Because most Web addresses don't use port numbers, this illustration leaves out the port number.

Figure 1.3

A Uniform Resource Locator (URL) is the address of a resource on the Internet.

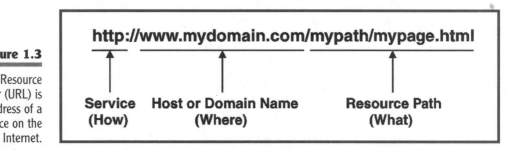

A URL is actually an instruction or request from an agent such as a Web browser to a server on the Internet that specifies the following three things:

- **How?** This is the protocol for the transaction. For Web pages, this is HTTP. Essentially, it tells the server what software it needs to run to manage the transaction. More than one server can reside on the same computer—for instance, a single computer can function both as an FTP server and as an HTTP (or Web) server.

- **Where?** This is the address where the transaction is to take place. For instance, `www.mydomain.com/mypath/` would specify the domain name and location within that domain of what is to be transacted.

- **What?** This is the name of what is to be transacted. For instance, `mypage.html` would specify the actual HTML document, or Web page, that is the subject of the transaction.

NOTE   If you link to a file or data object that resides within the same directory structure as the referring page, you don't have to supply the full URL for it, just as you don't have to dial the area code for a local phone call. When a link is local and uses abbreviated information, it's known as a *relative URL,* while standard (full) URLs are known as *absolute URLs.* The advantage of using relative rather than absolute URLs to reference local files is that if you later want to move your Web pages and their attendant files, you don't have to redo your local URLs as long as the directories in which they reside retain the same names and relations. See "Using Relative URLs" in the Saturday Morning session for a fuller explanation of this concept.

CAUTION   Most Web pages reside on Unix servers. Unlike MS-DOS and Windows systems, Unix systems use case-sensitive file paths and file names. So if you see a path and file name like MySite/HOMEPAGE.html, you should type it exactly as it appears—changing the capitalization to "Mysite" will get you somewhere else entirely or nowhere at all.

What Is a Domain Name?

Every Internet server has a numerical IP *(Internet Protocol)* address, which usually consists of four numbers between 0 and 255 separated by periods (something like 185.35.117.0, for instance). Computers prefer numeric addresses of this type because they're precise. Unfortunately, humans have trouble remembering numbers—they prefer meaningful text addresses, like www.mysite.com. That's what a domain name is: a text alternative to an IP address. You can usually use the two interchangeably. If you know the domain name, you don't have to know anything about the IP address. You will sometimes run into an odd URL on the Web that specifies the IP address rather than the domain name (and there is nothing forbidding a server from having an IP address, but no domain address).

Most servers have applied for and received a domain name from Inter-NIC (the *Internet Network Information Center*), which handles domain name registrations. As long as your Web pages are located on a server that has a domain name, you can use that domain name in the addresses, or URLs, for those Web pages. You don't have to have your own server to have your own domain name. You can also set up a Web site on someone else's server and use your own domain name in what is often referred to as a *virtual host* arrangement—to the outside world it looks just like you have your own server.

NOTE

Registering domain names used to be free, but this led to a free-for-all somewhat similar to the Oklahoma Land Rush, as companies and individuals scrambled to grab up domain names before anyone else could claim them. And because an organization or individual could claim an unlimited number of domain names, speculative trading in (scalping) domain names evolved. For these reasons, as well as to help fund the costs of registering rapidly increasing domain name requests, the InterNIC charges a fee of $50 per year for registering and maintaining a domain name.

A domain name represents a hierarchy, starting with the most general word on the right and moving to the most specific on the left. It can include a country code, an organization code, and a site name. For instance, myname.com.au, reading from right to left, specifies the name of a site in Australia ("au") in the commercial (com) subcategory, called "myname." Every country connected to the Internet has its own code, such as "uk" (United Kingdom), "ca" (Canada), "fr" (France), "nz" (New Zealand), and so forth. The country code for the United States is "us." Most sites in the United States don't include the country code, however, because the Internet began in the United States and the country codes were created later, after the Internet went international. The organization codes are:

✿ **EDU for "education."** Schools and universities use the EDU organization code.

✿ **GOV for "government."** Various governmental departments and agencies use the GOV organization code.

✿ **MIL for "military."** The Internet was, after all, originally a U.S. Defense Department initiative (the ARPANet).

✿ **NET for "network."** NET can refer to a network connected to the Internet. In practice, you usually run into NETs with ISPs (Internet Service Providers) that are offering public access to the Internet.

✿ **COM for "commercial."** This code was created to accommodate commercial usage of the Internet by business enterprises.

✿ **ORG for "organization."** This code is for noncommercial, nonprofit organizations.

Figure 1.4 gives you a graphical representation of the domain name system.

NOTE There may soon be seven new top-level domain name categories available: ".firm," ".shop," ".web," ".arts," ".rec," ".info," and ".nom." Currently, businesses, organizations, and individuals are already preregistering these new domain categories.

Figure 1.4

Internet domains have been organized into categories such as COM for commercial, EDU for educational, and so on. CA and UK are international domains for Canada and the United Kingdom.

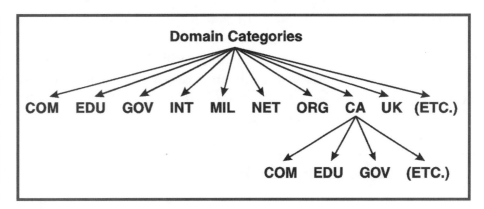

What Is a Web Page?

A Web page is a hypertext (HTML) document contained in a single file. To have more than one Web page, you must have more than one file. Despite the connotation of the word *page,* a Web page can be any length, although most Web pages display no more than two or three screens of data.

A Web page is simply a plain text document. All codes are entered into the document as ordinary text, with none of the binary-level formatting a word processor would embed in it. When you mark some text as italic in a word processing document, you don't see the actual computer code that causes the text to appear or print in italics. In HTML, you have to do it all yourself. There's no underlying program code to translate what you type as you go. You type in "<I>" where you want the browser to turn on italics and "</I>" where you want it to turn them off. This cuts down on the computer overhead, allowing Web pages to remain small but still pack quite a punch.

When a browser displays a Web page, the page may appear to contain special graphical elements like logos or buttons. These graphics don't reside in the HTML file itself; they're separate files that the HTML file references. For instance, you might see a line like this in the HTML file:

```
<IMG SRC="mylogo.gif">
```

The code places the graphic into the version of the page that a browser displays. When a browser displays the page, the reference opens and inserts the graphic in the specified spot. You can include a banner or logo, buttons, icons, separator bars, navigational icons, and more. See Figure 1.5 for a graphical representation of a Web page that contains these different kinds of elements.

What Is a Web Site?

The term *Web site* has a couple of different meanings. Servers often are called Web sites (sites on the Web), but any grouping of related and linked Web pages sharing a common theme or subject matter may also be called a Web site. To avoid confusion, in this book, I'll always refer to a collection of related Web pages as a *Web site*, and to a Web server as a "Web server," or alternatively as a *Web host* (a Web server that hosts Web sites).

Figure 1.5

Graphic elements such as banners or logos, images, icon bullets, horizontal rules, and navigational buttons are actually separate files linked to and displayed as part of your Web page.

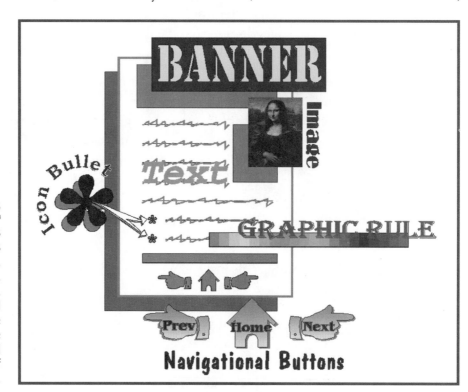

Your service provider (the company or organization that provides you access to the Internet) may give you space for a personal, noncommercial Web site at little or no cost. If you're a student, you may be able to have your pages hosted by your school's server. Many online services, such as CompuServe or America Online, also host Web pages at a reasonable cost. If you want to create a commercial Web site that offers a product or service, or you want to create a more sophisticated Web site that requires more space, higher traffic allowances, more technical support, and a wider range of features than your ISP will give you, you may need an *Internet Presence Provider (IPP)*—a company that specializes in Web space and can offer a fuller menu of services aimed specifically at Web publishers. A presence provider can also register and maintain a domain name for you, usually at a reasonable cost.

What Is a Home Page?

The term *home page* can have a number of different meanings. When you start your browser, it loads whatever Web page you designate as its home page (including a page on your own hard drive). Most browsers have a Home button or command that takes you back to the home page. Usually, this home page is your access provider's home page, or possibly Netscape's, Microsoft's, or NCSA's home page, depending on which browser you use. The home page is sometimes referred to as a start page. Figure 1.6 shows the home page I've designated in Netscape Navigator, which happens to be a city directory for Seattle (my home town) that has been put up by my Internet access provider. I could designate any other Web page located on the Web or on my local hard drive as my home page.

A home page can serve as an entry point (or front door) to a Web site, or group of linked and related Web pages. The term *home page* serves to designate any Web page that stands on its own (in keeping with the front door comparison, you could think of a stand-alone Web page as a one-room shack). The diagram in Figure 1.7 shows the relationship between home and Web pages.

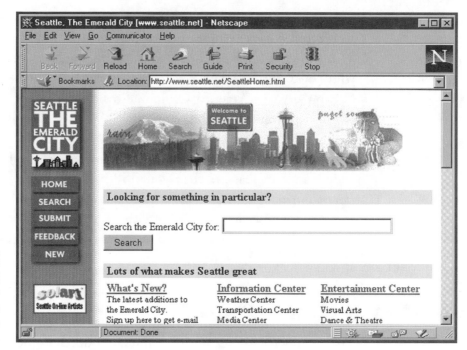

Figure 1.6

I have designated this page as my default home page when using Navigator.

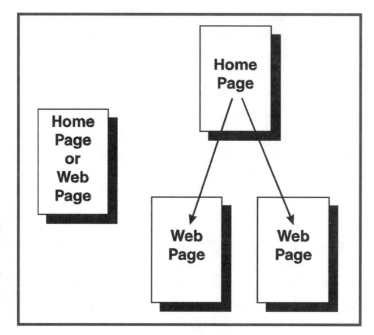

Figure 1.7

A home page can be either a stand-alone Web page or an entry point (index file) or front door to a Web site.

Most servers let you create a default home page, most often "index.html," that loads automatically without having to specify the file name in the URL. This allows you to have `http://www.myserver.com/mydirectory/` as your URL rather than `http://www.myserver.com/mydirectory/index.html`.

Home pages used as entryways are generally kept small, often serving simply as menus or directories to the Web pages that make up the rest of the Web site. The idea here is that a viewer need only display the home page, which is relatively small, and then decide what else to view in the remainder of the Web site.

Having a Web site go deeper than three or four levels is rare, but the number of levels of Web pages you might want to have appended as subpages off of your home page is technically unlimited. The deeper a Web page is (a subpage of a subpage of a subpage of a subpage of your home page), the less accessible it will be to visitors to your site. See Figure 1.8 for an illustration of a multi-level Web site.

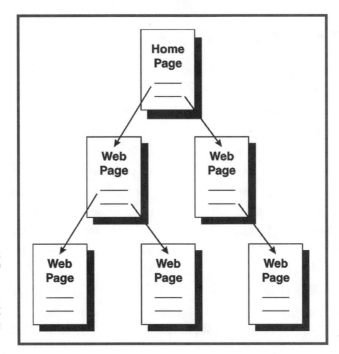

Figure 1.8

A Web site can have several levels, although it is best to keep it to three or fewer levels.

You can also create a home page that links together multiple home pages. You might, for instance, have a series of Web sites that are relatively autonomous, share a common theme, are produced by the same department, or are part of a larger project. Or you may want to link pages together to get increased visibility on the Web—as with the various cybermalls increasingly prevalent on the Web.

Take a Break

If you're short on time, please feel free to skip ahead to the "Getting Set Up" section in this session. You don't need to read the "Where's HTML Going?" section that follows to do the HTML tutorials and plan and create your first Web page. You can come back and read the "Where's HTML Going?" section later.

Relax and stretch a bit. Fix yourself a cup of tea or get a glass of juice. I'll see you back here in five minutes or so for the remainder of this session.

Where's HTML Going?

With HTML, the only constant is truly change. The Web and HTML form a new medium that continues to evolve. Nearly a decade ago, neither the Web nor HTML even existed. In the meantime, HTML 1.0 has come and gone and the standard, HTML 2.0, is definitely getting creaky—even though it has been around for only a couple of years. HTML 3.0 was the draft proposal for the next standard for HTML, but it was recently abandoned in favor of a more incremental advance, HTML 3.2. The ink on the final recommendation for HTML 3.2 (January 1997) was hardly dry before the *draft* specification for HTML 4.0 was announced (July 1997). Lo and behold, less than six months later, the stamp of approval was put on the new HTML 4.0 specification (December 1997). Proposed recommendations for Cascading Style Sheets, level 1 and level 2 (CSS1 and CSS2), MathML (Mathematical Markup Language), and XML 1.0 (Extensible

Markup Language) followed in quick succession. HTML is constantly changing, growing, and expanding, while still trying to keep firm contact with its roots.

The W3C (World Wide Web Consortium), the organization that is responsible for HTML and Web development, has committed itself to maintaining the character of HTML as "a language which the ordinary person can use" and its accessibility to individuals who "still find value in writing their own HTML from scratch." So, if you are worried about the world of HTML being taken over by the likes of FrontPage 98 or PageMill, leaving all the hand-coders and Notepad-niks in the dust, you need not worry. While new developments are occurring monthly, the essential core of HTML will remain largely the same.

Netscape and Microsoft Extensions

Both Netscape and Microsoft have developed their own special HTML codes, or extensions, for use in their browsers. These can be used in any Web document, but they translate into special formatting only when a user views the Web page in the particular browser for which they were created (unless the other browser's manufacturer provides support for the extensions, too).

Most of the extensions to HTML that Netscape pioneered have been incorporated into either HTML 3.2 or 4.0. The only purely Microsoft extension to be included in HTML 4.0 is the FACE attribute for the FONT tag, although Microsoft supported a number of proposed HTML 4.0 elements in its Internet Explorer 3.0 browser prior to the release of HTML 4.0. There are still extensions, such as Microsoft's MARQUEE tag or Netscape's BLINK tag, that can only be displayed in one or the other of these browsers. Unless everybody in your target audience uses the same browser, it is a good idea to avoid using HTML that will only work in one browser.

Still, there are Netscape extensions that haven't been incorporated into either HTML 3.2 or 4.0, but are also supported by Microsoft. There are some Microsoft extensions to HTML that Netscape has chosen to support. In the tutorials and other relevant sections of this book, I'll do my best to keep you updated on what is officially sanctioned HTML versus the more loose *ad hoc* standard for HTML, which is simply what is supported by the latest versions of *both* Netscape Navigator and Microsoft Internet Explorer.

Probably the most noteworthy of Netscape's recent innovations is the FRAME tag. Frames are rapidly proliferating on the Web, compelling other Web browsers to follow suit and incorporate the display of frames in their repertoire. Frames have since been incorporated into HTML 4.0 despite a certain amount of controversy. As usual on the Web, it is what Web publishers use that matters, and on that score the vote is in—a qualified thumbs up. The primary objections to frames are two-fold: a purist objection that they don't conform to SGML (of which HTML is supposed to be a subset) and a functional objection that they make it difficult to link into a subpage within a frameset.

◀ ◀

A page using frames is defined using the FRAMESET tag, so a collection of Web pages defined by a FRAMESET tag is often referred to as a *frameset*. Every Web page that uses frames starts from an initial frameset, although further framesets may be nested inside of the initial frameset.

◀ ◀

Microsoft has introduced a number of extensions to HTML that have remained unique to its Web browser. These include the capability to automatically play background sounds (you can add background sounds to Navigator, but only by using an entirely different method). More recently, Microsoft introduced scrollable background images (when you scroll down through the text, the background image remains fixed), but this can now be done using Cascading Style Sheets. Microsoft's addition of the FACE attribute to the FONT tag has since been supported in Navigator 4.0 and has been included in HTML 4.0.

HTML 3.0

HTML 3.0 was the proposed draft for the next HTML standard. Tables, not part of the HTML 2.0 standard, were proposed as part of HTML 3.0. However, all current major graphical Web browsers have incorporated the HTML 3.0 specification for tables, with some variation (Netscape has introduced a number of extensions beyond what was proposed as part of HTML 3.0). Other proposed HTML 3.0 elements that have gained the favor of Web browsers to one degree or another are superscripts and subscripts, font size changing (with the BIG and SMALL tags), and underlining. Those parts of the proposed HTML 3.0 standard that have been most widely implemented in current Web browsers have since been incorporated into HTML 3.2. Additionally, even more tags that were proposed for HTML 3.0 have been added to HTML 4.0, including tags for marking insertions and deletions, acronyms, and quotations.

HTML 3.2

In May 1996, the W3 Consortium announced HTML 3.2 as its new specification for HTML. The final recommendation for the HTML 3.2 specification was delivered in January 1997. HTML 3.0, which was the previous draft proposal for the next HTML standard, was abandoned, largely because the differences between HTML 2.0 and HTML 3.0 were too large to achieve consensus and agreement. HTML 3.2 was a more modest step up from HTML 2.0 and had been carefully crafted and developed in cooperation with industry leaders, including IBM, Microsoft, Netscape, Sun Microsystems, and others. Here are some of the primary features included in the HTML 3.2 standard:

- Tables
- Applets (for Java and JavaScript)
- Background images
- Background, text, and link colors
- Font sizes and colors

✪ Flowing of text around images

✪ Image borders

✪ Height and width attributes for images

✪ Alignment (left, center, or right) of paragraphs, headings, horizontal rules, and the CENTER tag

✪ Superscripts and subscripts (the SUP and SUB tags)

✪ Strikethroughs (the STRIKE tag)

✪ Document divisions (the DIV tag)

✪ Client-side image maps (the MAP tag)

✪ Provisions for style sheets (the STYLE tag), left otherwise undefined

It isn't surprising that a large part of the new HTML 3.2 specification is a rubber stamping of what originally were Netscape's unofficial and ad hoc extensions to HTML. The rest of the HTML 3.2 specification covers features of HTML 3.0 that already have gained wide acceptance and implementation—tables, for instance. HTML 3.2 really offered little that hadn't already been widely implemented.

HTML 4.0

HTML 3.2 had the code-name "Wilbur," and HTML 4.0 was code-named "Cougar." Cougar has since been officially released in the form of the draft specification for HTML 4.0. HTML 4.0 is the officially recommended specification for HTML. However, you should be aware that it may be some time before full browser support for HTML 4.0 is available. Those who want to play it safe should probably stick with HTML 3.2 for at least a little bit longer. Here are some of the primary features included in HTML 4.0:

✪ Frames, including inline frames.

✪ Cascading Style Sheets, Level 1 (CSS1).

✪ New form elements, including the BUTTON element, which allows the creation of graphical form buttons.

- New table elements, including the ability to apply formatting to column and row groups.

- New text-markup elements, including the INS (Insert), DEL (Delete), Q (Quote), S (Strikeout), and SPAN elements.

- Microsoft's FACE attribute has been added to the FONT element, allowing specifying font faces that can be used when displaying text marked by the FONT element.

- New universal attributes (ID and CLASS) that can be used to apply styles to individual instances of tag elements, as well as additional "intrinsic event" attribute handles that can trigger the activation of scripts from such events as passing the mouse over an element, clicking on an element, and so on.

I cover a few of the new HTML 4.0 features in the Intermediate HTML and Tables Tutorials that are scheduled for Saturday afternoon and evening. For information on other HTML 4.0 features, see Appendix A, "The Web Resources Directory," and Appendix B, "The Web Tools Directory," for links to resources and tools that can assist you. Also, you'll find a couple Web page templates on the CD-ROM that you can use to easily create a two-frame or a three-frame Web site.

What's in Store for HTML?

There are currently many initiatives afoot to expand HTML. These include:

- Expansion of the Cascading Style Sheets (CSS) standard beyond the rather simple style sheets currently approved as part of HTML 4.0.

- The Dynamic Object Model (DOM) is the keystone for the full implementation and development of Dynamic HTML, allowing the dynamic addressing of any objects in a Web page by scripts or programs.

- Mathematical Markup Language (MathML), providing complex formatting capabilities for equations and formulas.

- Extensible Markup Language (XML), which is not actually an extension of HTML, but an implementation of Standard Generalized Markup Language (SGML) for the Web. This promises to allow different Web communities to define their own markup languages.

Several other widely anticipated features were proposed as part of HTML 3.0 but haven't been included in HTML 3.2 or HTML 4.0. The academic community expects support for footnotes. The NOTE tag was promised for notes, warnings, and cautions. The BANNER tag was supposed to facilitate the display of company banners or logos. The FIG tag for displaying figures was supposed to replace the IMG tag. A TAB tag was promised for setting and inserting tab stops.

How soon will you see any of these features? Many of them are of particular interest to the academic and scientific communities, but what really drives the development of HTML today (for now, anyway) is its commercial potential. The emphasis is switching more from distributing ideas to selling products, with visual appeal currently being on the front burner than more prosaic document annotation features. So cross your fingers, keep your ear to the ground, listen for distant drumbeats, and watch for smoke signals. Hopefully, before too long, a clearer idea of what's in store will crystallize.

Getting Set Up

This section covers getting set up so you can do the HTML tutorials on Saturday and plan and create your first Web page on Sunday. It includes the following:

- Minimum requirements
- Selecting your text editor
- Selecting your Web browser
- Setting up for offline browsing
- Selecting your graphics editor

The minimum requirements for doing the Basic HTML Tutorial and creating your first Web page are that you have either Windows 3.1 or Windows 95 and a graphical Web browser already set up or installed. To be able to do the Intermediate HTML Tutorial, you'll need an HTML 3.2-compliant Web browser (Netscape Navigator 2.0 or greater or Microsoft Internet Explorer 3.0 or greater). Everything else you need either comes with Windows or is available on the CD-ROM.

Selecting Your Text Editor

You don't need anything fancy to create HTML files. Since HTML files are straight ASCII text files, any plain and ordinary text editor will do. I recommend that you stick to using Windows Notepad, which comes with both Windows 95 and Windows 3.1, as your text editor. Notepad has a number of advantages that make it the tool of choice for many professional Web publishers:

- ✿ You already have it.
- ✿ It's a small, efficient program, so it can easily remain in memory with your Web browser without hogging precious system resources. New Web browsers are known to be resource hogs.
- ✿ Because Notepad is a text editor rather than a word processor, you can have an HTML file open in both Notepad and your Web browser at the same time. You can't do that with Write, Word, WordPerfect, and most other word processing programs.

Using an HTML Editor

You can also use an HTML editor to do the HTML tutorials and create your first Web page. My recommendation is that you don't get bogged down trying to learn the ins and outs of an HTML editing program when you need to focus on learning HTML itself (that is, if you want to get your first Web page created in a weekend). Learn HTML first, and then investigate what HTML editing programs can do for you.

You also need to gain a code-level familiarity with HTML. Only then can you stick your head under the hood if something doesn't work right. That means typing in your HTML codes the old-fashioned way, and not just inserting them from a drop-down menu or toolbar.

Once you've done the HTML tutorials and planned and created your first Web page, feel free to experiment with some of the different HTML editors that are available. You'll find several HTML editors on the CD-ROM.

ON THE

CD

Aardvark Pro is an HTML editor that allows you to create your HTML files just like you would with Windows Notepad—typing the codes in from scratch. An added bonus is that you don't have to turn Word Wrap on every time.

Using a Word Processor

I don't recommend that you use a word processing program for the tutorials in this book. That's because you cannot keep the same file open in both your word processor and your Web browser, which means you won't be able to dynamically debug your HTML files.

Selecting Your Web Browser

You will need to use a Web browser to preview your work as you do the HTML tutorials and create your first Web page. I'll show you how to hop back and forth between your text editor and your Web browser to be able to dynamically update your work as you go. For the Intermediate HTML Tutorial, you'll need to have an HTML 3.2-compliant Web browser installed for Windows 3.1 or Windows 95. I recommend either Netscape Navigator 2.0 or greater or Microsoft Internet Explorer 3.0 or greater.

ON THE

CD

In case you don't already have a Web browser installed, an excellent Web browser, Opera, has been included on the CD-ROM.

Setting Up for Offline Browsing

As I mentioned, you'll want to be able to switch back and forth between your text editor and your Web browser as you work through this book, updating your Web page as you go. You'll want to do this offline so you don't run up your Internet bill and hog bandwidth just to edit and preview local HTML files. Even if you have unlimited access to the Internet, it is wasteful to hog an Interent connection just to be able to preview local HTML files.

Offline Browsing in Windows 95 with Netscape Navigator

The following is the quick-and-dirty way to run either Navigator Gold 3.0+ or Navigator 4.0+ offline. It's a bit clunky, but it's pretty simple, and it works:

1. Run Navigator Gold 3.0+ or Navigator 4.0+.

2. At the Connect To dialog box, which prompts you to make a dial-up connection to the Internet, click on the Cancel button (to avoid connecting to the Internet).

3. You'll get an error message that reads "Netscape is unable to locate the server." This is just Navigator or Communicator trying to tell you it tried to connect to the Internet but couldn't. Click on the OK button.

4. Navigator Gold or Communicator will display a copy of its default home page if it can be loaded from the cache. Otherwise, it will display a blank page.

5. To open and display a local Web page (HTML file) from your hard drive in Navigator Gold 3.0+, choose File, Open File in Browser. In Communicator 4.0+, choose File, Open Page, Choose File.

You haven't actually created any HTML files yet, but if you want to try loading a local HTML file into Navigator, you can use Navigator's bookmark file, BOOKMARK.HTM. The location of this file depends upon the version of Navigator: to find where it is stored, click on the Start button on the Windows 95 toolbar, then select Find, Files or Folders, and do a search for "bookmark.htm."

Offline Browsing in Windows 95 with Microsoft Internet Explorer

If you are using a version of Internet Explorer earlier than version 3.02, I recommend that you download and install the latest version of Internet Explorer from Microsoft's Web site if you want to run it offline.

 Just in case you don't want to take the time this weekend to download and install the latest version of Internet Explorer, I've included a page at the Web site for this book, at `http://www.callihan.com/create2/`, titled "Tips for Offline Browsing" that includes details on what you need to do run Internet Explorer 3.0 or 3.01 offline.

The following is the quick-and-dirty way to run Internet Explorer 3.02 or greater offline. As with Netscape, it's a bit clunky, but it's pretty simple—and it works:

1. Run Microsoft Internet Explorer 3.02 or Internet Explorer 4.0 or greater.

2. At the Connect To dialog box, which prompts you to make a dial-up connection to the Internet: in Version 4.0 or earlier, click on the Cancel button; in Version 4.01 or greater, click on the Work Offline button.

3. In Versions 4.0 and earlier, the message "Internet Explorer cannot open the Internet site http://home.microsoft.com" is displayed. Just click on the OK button. In Version 4.01 or greater, the message

"Unable to retrieve Webpage in Offline mode" is displayed in the browser window.

4. Internet Explorer Version 4.0 and earlier will display its default start page if it can be loaded from the cache. If the default start page is not available in the cache, Internet Explorer 3.02 and later will load a local blank HTML file. Version 4.01 simply displays the message quoted in Step 3.

5. In all versions, to open and display a local Web page (HTML file) from your hard drive, select File, Open, and Browse. Go to a folder where a local·HTML file you want to use is stored and then double-click on it to open it. Click on OK to load the file into Internet Explorer.

NOTE Unlike Netscape Navigator, Microsoft Internet Explorer does not conveniently create a bookmark file in HTML format that you can use to test loading a local HTML file. To actually test loading a local HTML file in Internet Explorer, you'll need to wait until you create and save a file tomorrow morning (unless you've also got Netscape Navigator installed).

Seamless Offline Browsing in Windows 95

At the Web site for this book, located at `http://www.callihan.com/create2/`, you can find a page called "Tips for Offline Browsing" that includes instructions on how to set up both Netscape Navigator and Internet Explorer for seamless offline browsing. Included are instructions on how to get rid of the log-on prompt and how to specify a blank or local HTML file as your default home or start page. I recommend that for the time being you stick to using the quick-and-dirty methods outlined here. Later, after you have created your first Web page, feel free to check out the steps required to set up your Web browser for seamless offline browsing.

Offline Browsing in Windows 3.1

Unfortunately, setting up your Web browser for offline browsing in Windows 3.1 is not anywhere near as easy as it is in Windows 95. Running Netscape Navigator offline requires downloading and setting up MOZOCK.DLL (available at the Web site for the book) because Internet Explorer won't run offline. There is, however, a quick-and-dirty method for running both Netscape Navigator and Internet Explorer in what I'll term here "quasi-offline" mode. Here's what you do:

1. Log on to the Internet.

2. Run either Netscape Navigator or Microsoft Internet Explorer as you normally would.

3. Log off of the Internet. To do this, hold down the Alt key, then press the Tab key to select your winsock dialer application, and then execute the commands you normally use to log off the Internet. (From now on, I'll refer to this type of action as "press Alt+Tab.")

4. Return to your Web browser (by pressing Alt+Tab to select your browser) and load a local HTML file. For Navigator versions earlier than 4.0, select File, Open File. For Navigator version 4.0 and higher, select File, Open Page, and Choose File. For all Internet Explorer versions, select File, Open, and Browse.

5. Before exiting either Navigator or Internet Explorer, use Alt+Tab to hop out to Program Manager and log back onto the Internet.

CAUTION

❖❖

When you're using the quasi-offline browsing method, if you exit your Web browser before logging back onto the Internet, your winsock dialer application may hang up when you try to log off. If that happens, it's no biggy, but you'll need to rerun Windows before being able to log back on to the Internet.

❖❖

Seamless Offline Browsing in Windows 3.1

Seamless offline browsing in Windows 3.1 is not possible with Microsoft Internet Explorer. If you are using any version of Internet Explorer for Windows 3.1, you'll need to stick to the quasi-offline browsing method detailed earlier.

However, if you are using any version of Netscape Navigator, running it seamlessly offline is possible, although it takes longer to set it up. If you want to find out how to do this, I've included instructions on my "Tips for Offline Browsing" page that is located at the Web site for this book at `http://www.callihan.com/create2/`.

Running Other Browsers Offline

If you use a browser other than the ones discussed here, you need to check its documentation, help files, or online technical support for the preferred method of running it offline. In most cases, however, some version of the quick-and-dirty or quasi-offline browsing methods should work for almost any browser.

Selecting Your Graphics Editor

If you want to create your own customized graphics for your first Web page, you'll need to have a graphics editor capable of creating GIF and JPG format graphics. I've included what I consider to be the best share-ware graphics editor, Paint Shop Pro, on the CD-ROM. I've also created an optional bonus tutorial scheduled for Sunday evening that shows you how to use Paint Shop Pro to create various graphics special effects, including transparent backgrounds, shadows, fill-effects, and 3-D buttons. There are also a number of excellent commercial graphics editors that do a great job of creating Web graphics. The best known, and the choice of many graphics pros, is Adobe PhotoShop. Another excellent choice is Corel PhotoPaint.

You don't need a graphics editor to do the HTML tutorials that are scheduled for Saturday, since I've already created all the graphics used in those tutorials for you. Optionally, if you don't already have a graphics editor installed that can create GIF and JPG graphic files, you may want to install Paint Shop Pro from the CD-ROM in order to create a custom banner graphic for your first Web page. But there is no need to install a graphics editor right now. The earliest you might need a graphics editor is for the Sunday Afternoon session, "Creating Your First Web Page," although I provide some sample graphics that you can use until you get around to creating your own custom graphics.

What's Next?

Having finished the first session, you should now have a grounding in the basics of the Internet and the World Wide Web. You should have a good grasp of URLs, hypertext, HTML, and Web pages. You should also be all set up with the tools and example files you'll need to do the HTML tutorials and create your first Web page. So get a good night's sleep, and be ready for the Basic HTML Tutorial tomorrow morning.

The Basic HTML Tutorial

- ✪ Anatomy of a Tag
- ✪ Starting Your Page
- ✪ Creating Paragraphs and Line Breaks
- ✪ Creating Lists

Last night you read up on the Internet, the Web, hypertext, HTML fundamentals, and Web pages. You should now know what Web publishing is all about. Additionally, in the "Getting Set Up" section, you chose the Web browser and text editor you are going to be using to do the Basic HTML Tutorial this morning and the Intermediate HTML Tutorial this afternoon. I recommend using the latest version of either Netscape Navigator or Microsoft Internet Explorer as your Web browser and Notepad as your text editor.

You won't need a graphics editor for today's HTML tutorials, so if you haven't installed your graphics editor yet, that's okay. However, you'll probably want to have a graphics editor for when you get around to planning and creating your first Web page on Sunday.

This morning's tutorial walks you through a top-down approach to learning HTML, organized according to function. Just start from the beginning and continue to the end, and by then you'll know enough HTML to create a wide range of Web pages.

HTML contains many more tags for defining document elements than most people could learn in an entire week, let alone in a weekend, let alone on a Saturday morning. But fear not, because this tutorial only covers basic HTML, which includes the most useful of the HTML 2.0 tags. All current graphical Web browsers should fully support HTML 2.0, which until recently was the standard for HTML. The optional

Intermediate HTML Tutorial that is scheduled for this afternoon covers many of the HTML 3.2 and 4.0 tags.

Everyone has his or her own learning style and speed. Although the Basic HTML Tutorial was designed to be completed in a single morning, you may take more or less time to complete it. The most important thing is to work at your own speed without feeling rushed. If you want to take the whole day to do the tutorial, do so. So relax, sit back, and have some fun.

Creating Your Working Folder

First, you need to create a working folder on your hard drive. This folder will hold all the files you'll be using while doing the tutorials in this book, as well as all of the example files that are used in the tutorials. I suggest that you create a C:\HTML folder for this. You can use a different drive and folder name, if you wish, but I'll refer to your working folder as C:\HTML. Use Windows Explorer in Windows 95 or File Manager in Windows 3.1 to create your C:\HTML working folder.

Installing the Example Files

On the CD-ROM, I've included example graphic files for you to use in the HTML tutorials. You can use the interface on the CD-ROM to install these files by doing the following:

1. Insert the CD-ROM in your CD-ROM drive.

2. For Windows 3.1 only:

   A. Run File Manager, then select File, Run to open the Run window.

   B. In the Command Line text box, type **D:\primacd.exe** (where D:\ is the CD-ROM drive)

3. At the opening screen of Prima's CD-ROM interface:

   A. Click on Book Examples.

   B. Click on Tutorial in the center menu.

4. The Install radio button should already be selected. Click on OK to install the example graphic files for the tutorials.

5. At the WinZip Self-Extractor window, click on OK.

6. In the Unzip to Folder text box, enter **C:\HTML** as your working folder. Click on Unzip. Click on OK when told the files have been unzipped, and then click on Close.

 NOTE   If you don't have a CD-ROM drive, all the example graphic files for the HTML tutorials are available for download from this book's Web site at `http://www.callihan. com/create2/`. Just unzip the tutorial example files into C:\HTML.

A Quick Word About HTML

Before you begin to do the tutorial, a quick reminder about the nature of HTML might save some unnecessary confusion. The philosophy behind HTML is to specify the framework of a page, not its actual appearance or display. How a Web page looks onscreen is determined by the browser used to view it.

Actually, you do have a good deal of control over how most browsers present your page. Today's graphical Web browsers allow you to include not only inline graphics, but interlaced and transparent graphics, background images and colors, image maps, forms, tables, font size and color changes, animations, streaming audio and animation, and more.

Although most current graphical Web browsers support most of these enhancements, HTML 2.0 specifies only some of them. Many facilities for more complete control over how Web page will be displayed have been incorporated into HTML 3.2 and HTML 4.0, the latest versions of HTML.

NOTE   A very real concern in HTML is backward compatibility and universal access to one's documents. Old Web pages need to be displayed properly in new browsers, just as new Web pages, in most cases, should be coded in such a fashion that they won't break old browsers. Unless you wish to cater only to those with a certain browser, you should make your page accessible to everyone. In this afternoon's Intermediate HTML Tutorial, I'll show you how to use many of the new HTML 3.2 and HTML 4.0 features without breaking older browsers.

The Basic HTML Tutorial sticks to HTML 2.0, which should be compatible with all Web browsers. If you don't have time to get to the Intermediate HTML Tutorial today, don't worry. The Basic HTML Tutorial covers everything you need to know to plan and create your first Web page on Sunday. You can always come back and do the Intermediate HTML Tutorial after you create your first Web page.

The model that the tutorial employs resembles a "scratch pad" approach. Think of your text editor as a scratch pad. As you do the Basic HTML Tutorial, enter the suggested tags and text as though you were jotting them down on a scratch pad; in other words, you don't have to clean the slate each time you move on to a new section. Just move on down the page, leaving everything you have already done in place. Doing so also leaves you with a sample file to which you can return and reference later.

Dynamically Updating Your Work

As you work through the basic tutorial this morning, you will want to *dynamically update* things as you go, or switch back and forth between your text editor and your Web browser to see your results.

Only by being able to make on-the-fly changes to your HTML files can you tell exactly how your page is going to look in a browser while you are still in the process of creating it.

NOTE

If you use a word processor such as Word for Windows, WordPerfect, Windows Write, or WordPad to edit your HTML files, you can't dynamically update your HTML files by switching back and forth between your word processor and your browser. If an HTML file is open in your word processor, you can't display it in your browser at the same time. You can still use your word processor to edit HTML files that are too large to fit in Notepad, although very few HTML files should require this.

To dynamically update changes to your HTML files, you must switch back and forth between your text editor and your Web browser. (See the "Windows Navigation Tips" sidebar if you don't know how to switch between applications in Windows.) To make this hop, take the following steps:

1. Run Notepad (or whatever text editor you're using) and load an HTML file and edit it. Save those changes, but don't exit or clear the window. In Windows 3.1, hop out to the Program Manager. In Windows 95, minimize the current window to reveal the Desktop.

2. Run your browser, preferably in offline mode, and open the HTML file you just edited in Notepad. It will be displayed in your browser, showing the changes you just made. Now switch back to your text editor.

3. In your text editor, make more changes to your HTML file, and save those changes. Switch back to your browser.

4. Click on the Reload or Refresh button to display your HTML file again, showing the changes you just made.

NOTE

In Netscape Navigator, the Reload button loads the updated version of your HTML file, and *Reload* is the term used in this book to describe the reload operation. In Internet Explorer, this is the Refresh button. In both Navigator and Internet Explorer, you can also press Ctrl+R to do the same thing.

WINDOWS NAVIGATION TIPS

In this book, the words *switch* or *hop* refer to switching between open applications. You can switch among the open applications in several ways, so choose the method that works best for you:

⚙ Alt+Tab. Hold down the Alt key while tapping the Tab key to cycle through all currently open applications. This works in both Windows 3.1 and Windows 95. When you see the application you want, release the Tab key to bring that application to the foreground.

⚙ Alt+Esc. This works very similarly to Alt+Tab. It toggles among the open windows, one by one. Hold down the Alt key and tap the Esc key until the window you want comes to the foreground.

⚙ Ctrl+Esc. In Windows 3.1, doing this brings up the Task List window, allowing you to select from a list of currently open applications. In Windows 95, Ctrl+Esc displays the Taskbar at the bottom of the screen—the one that shows buttons for all your open applications—and opens the Start menu.

⚙ Control Menu. In Windows 3.1, you can select Switch To from the Control Menu of any windowed application currently in the foreground. Just click on the button in the upper left corner of the window and select Switch To. It's actually the same as simply pressing Ctrl+Esc, so it can only be recommended to the dedicated keyboard-a-phobe. In Windows 95, the Switch To option is not included in the Control Menu, so this is a Windows 3.1-only feature.

Repeat these steps as often as necessary. As you work through the tutorial, illustrations show you what each tag looks like in a browser. These illustrations may not exactly match what you would see in the particular browser you are using, so you should use them as cues to hop over to your browser to have a look.

NOTE While doing the Friday Evening session, you should have created your working folder (C:\HTML was recommended) and copied (from the CD-ROM or this book's Web site) all the example graphics used in the HTML tutorials to your working folder. If you haven't done this yet, you should go back to the "Getting Set Up" section of the Friday Evening session now and read the instructions on how to copy the example files.

Running Your Web Browser and Text Editor

Run your Web browser so you'll be able to check the results of your work while doing this tutorial. If you're using Windows 95 to run your browser offline, click on Cancel when prompted to log on. If you're using Windows 3.1 to run your browser offline, you'll need to use the "quick-and-dirty" method for browsing offline (logging on to run your browser, then logging off while browsing your local files) that I detailed in the Friday Evening session. For further information on how to do seamless offline browsing, see my "Tips for Offline Browsing" page at the Web site for this book.

Run the text editor you want to use to edit HTML files. As mentioned earlier, I recommend using Notepad until you master the fundamentals of HTML. In Windows 3.1, you can usually find Notepad in the Accessories window in Program Manager. In Windows 95, you can find it on the Start Menu, under Programs and Accessories.

NOTE When you first open Notepad, Word Wrap is not turned on. If you type a line of text without hitting Enter, it will just keep right on going without wrapping. To turn on Word Wrap, just select Edit, Word Wrap (so that it is checked). Unfortunately, you must reset this option every time you use Notepad if you want Word Wrap on.

Save your "scratch pad" file that you'll be using in this morning's tutorial. In Notepad, select File, Save As. Change the folder where you are going to save your file to C:\HTML, and then save your file as SCRATCH.HTM.

Words and codes that you should type in are formatted as **bolded and monospaced** text. Text that is shown for example purposes, but shouldn't be typed in by you, or text that you have already typed, is formatted as monospaced.

Anatomy of a Tag

The words *tag* or *tag element* refer to the HTML codes that define the elements in an HTML file—the headings, images, paragraphs, lists, and whatnot. There are two kinds of tags: *containers*, which bracket or contain text or other tag elements, and *empty tags*, which stand alone. A container tag element actually consists of two tags, a start tag and an end tag, which bracket the text they affect. An empty tag functions as a single standalone element within an HTML document, and thus doesn't bracket or contain anything else.

HTML tags are inserted into a document between lesser than (<) and greater than (>) symbols (also referred to as left or right angle brackets). For instance, a start tag of a container tag or an empty tag element looks like this:

```
<tagname>
```

You always precede an end tag of a container tag element with a forward slash (/) to distinguish it from a start tag:

```
</tagname>
```

To tag a section of text, you contain it within the start and end tags of a tag element. For instance, text contained in a level-one heading tag would look like this, where <H1> is the start tag and </H1> is the end tag:

```
<H1>This is a Level-One Heading</H1>
```

Whenever I refer to "a level-one heading tag," I'm referring to both the start and end tags. When I want to specifically refer to a start tag or an end tag, I'll use "the start tag" or "the end tag." Note, however, that a few tags look like empty tags, but actually are container tags that have implied end tags.

It is convenient to type tag names in ALL CAPS. It helps distinguish HTML tags from the remainder of the text being tagged. As a rule, this book presents tag names in ALL CAPS.

Tag Attributes

Attributes allow you to specify how Web browsers should treat a particular tag. An attribute is included within the actual tag (between the left and right angle brackets), either within a start tag or an empty (stand-alone) tag. End tags can't contain attributes. Most of the tags covered in this tutorial don't use attributes, but you'll use them to include images or hypertext links in a Web page toward the end of this tutorial.

Most attributes are combined with a value to allow you to specify different options for how a Web browser should treat the attribute. Here's the format for including an attribute value in a tag:

```
ATTRIBUTE="value"
```

For instance, to specify that the middle of an image should be aligned with the line of text it is on, you would include the following attribute value inside the IMG tag:

```
ALIGN="middle"
```

Tag attributes are usually typed in ALL CAPS, with any values assigned to them typed in lower-case. You don't have to do it this way, but it does make it easier to pick them out. In most cases, you can get away with omitting values between quotation marks, but there are enough instances where it won't work that you should consider keeping them in all cases.

Nesting HTML Tags

You should always *nest* HTML tags, and never overlap them. For instance, always do this:

```
<B><I>Always nest tags inside each other.</I></B>
```

Notice that the <I>...</I> pair is nested within the <B>...</B> pair. Never overlap tags so that the outer one ends before the inner one:

```
<B><I>Don't overlap tags, like this.</B></I>
```

HTML operates in a hierarchical, top-down manner. A tag element may have other tag elements nested in it or be nested within other tag elements. If you overlap two tags, a browser can't tell what should fall inside of what, and the browser may not be able to display your file at all. Be kind to your browser and those of your potential readers.

Starting Your Page

All HTML files should include these tags:

- The HTML tag
- The HEAD tag
- The TITLE tag
- The BODY tag

The HTML Tag

Recall that a tag defines a structural element within an HTML document. The HTML tag defines the topmost element, the HTML document itself, identifying it as an HTML document rather than some other kind of document. The HTML tag is a container tag that has a start and end, and all other text and tags are nested within it. For example:

```
<HTML>
Your HTML document's contents and all other tags . . .
</HTML>
```

In your "scratch pad" file in Notepad (or other text editor), type the start and end HTML tags, putting a single hard return between them, like this:

```
<HTML>
</HTML>
```

NOTE The HTML start tag (<HTML>) must remain at the very top of your file, while the HTML end tag (</HTML>) must remain at the very bottom of your file. Everything else must fall between these two tags.

The HEAD Tag

The HEAD tag contains information about your HTML file. It may also contain other tags that help to identify your HTML file to the outside world. The HEAD tag is nested within the HTML tag. Type the HEAD tag inside the HTML tag as follows:

```
<HTML>
<HEAD>
</HEAD>
</HTML>
```

Usually, the only tag contained within the HEAD tag is the TITLE tag. Other tags can also be contained within the HEAD tag, but of these, only the META, BASE, and LINK tags are useful. I'll only be covering the TITLE tag here, but if you want to see how to use the META, BASE, LINK, and other elements that can be nested in the HEAD tag, you'll find several links to HTML references in Appendix A, "The Web Resources Directory."

The TITLE Tag

The TITLE tag is nested inside of the HEAD tag. It identifies your page to the rest of the world. For instance, a search engine like Yahoo! or Webcrawler might display the text included in your TITLE tag as a link to your page. The tag also displays on your browser's title bar, but it doesn't appear as part of the page. Make the title descriptive, but keep it under 50 characters, if possible. Try to use a short title followed by a brief description. Someone else should be able to tell what your page is about simply by looking at the title. Think of it as your welcome mat. Type the TITLE tag inside the HEAD tag.

NOTE   If you want to substitute a title of your choosing for the generic title supplied in the following HTML code, go ahead. Don't bust your noggin right now trying to come up with the perfect title. Sunday morning, when you get around to planning your first Web page, you'll spend more time figuring out what contributes to a good title.

```
<HTML>
<HEAD>
<TITLE>Your Title: Describe Your Title</TITLE>
</HEAD>
</HTML>
```

Officially, the TITLE tag is a required element that you should include in each HTML document. In practice, however, most Web browsers let you get away with not including a TITLE tag. Still, you should include a TITLE tag in your HTML document. If you don't include a title, the title of your page appears in some browsers as "Untitled," while in others, the URL for the page appears on the browser's title bar. If you want the page to show up without a title, nothing stops you from including a TITLE tag and leaving it blank. But that defeats the whole purpose of including the tag in the first place.

The BODY Tag

The BODY tag is the complement of the HEAD tag and contains all the tags, or elements, that a browser actually displays as the body of your HTML document. Both the HEAD tag and the BODY tag are nested inside the HTML tag. Note that the BODY tag comes after the HEAD tag; they denote separate parts of the HTML document.

NOTE   The HEAD and BODY tags are the only tags that are nested directly inside the HTML tag. Other than the TITLE tag, which you inserted within the HEAD tag above, you should nest all text and tags you enter in this tutorial inside the BODY tag. Keep both </BODY> and </HTML> end tags at the bottom of your HTML file.

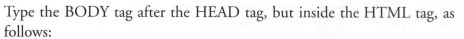

Type the BODY tag after the HEAD tag, but inside the HTML tag, as follows:

```
<HTML>
<HEAD>
<TITLE>Your Title: Describe Your Title</TITLE>
</HEAD>
<BODY>
</BODY>
</HTML>
```

You have started your HTML file. All HTML files begin the same way; only the titles are different. What you have typed so far should look like this:

```
<HTML>
<HEAD>
<TITLE>Your Title: Describe Your Title</TITLE>
</HEAD>
<BODY>
</BODY>
</HTML>
```

Saving a Starting Template

If you want, you can save this as a starting template for creating HTML files. Save it as C:\HTML\START.HTM, for instance. After you save the file as START.HTM, save it again as C:\HTML\SCRATCH.HTM (or whatever working title you want to give it) so you won't accidentally save over your starting template later.

If you hop over to your browser and load this file, it would display nothing but the title in the title bar, as shown in Figure 2.1.

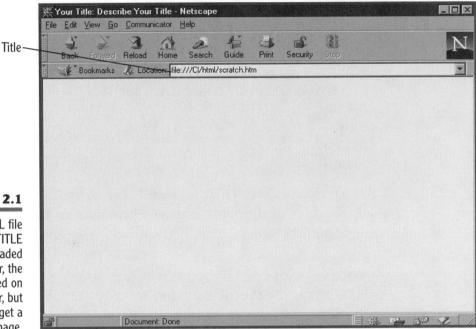

Title

Figure 2.1

When an HTML file
with only a TITLE
element is loaded
into Navigator, the
title is displayed on
the title bar, but
otherwise you get a
blank page.

NOTE You've probably noticed that many Web pages have a four-letter file name extension: .HTML. This is the conventional extension for HTML files that are stored on Unix Web servers. Windows 3.1 and DOS only recognize a three-letter file extension. (Windows 95 can recognize long file names, including four letter extensions.) Luckily, most Unix Web servers can also recognize the .HTM file extension as indicating an HTML file. Because this book addresses both Windows 95 and Windows 3.1 users, I've stuck to using .HTM as the extension for any HTML files. The majority of Web servers support using either extension.

Using Heading Level Tags

You use headings to organize your Web page into hierarchical levels. The top-level heading (denoted by the H1 tag) is the title that will be

displayed at the top of your Web page. (Don't confuse this with the title that appears in the browser's title bar, which you just set up using the TITLE tag.) Because the H1 tag functions as the title for a Web page, each Web page should have only one H1 tag. (This is the conventional use for this tag. Otherwise, nothing forbids including multiple H1 tags in a Web page.)

You use a second-level heading (denoted by the H2 tag) to define a major division in your page, and a third-level heading (using the H3 tag) to define a sub-level division within a major division. Most browsers support up to six different heading levels. Within the BODY element that you typed earlier, type six heading level tags, like this:

```
<BODY>
<H1>This is a top-level heading</H1>
<H2>This is a second-level heading</H2>
<H3>This is a third-level heading</H3>
<H4>This is a fourth-level heading</H4>
<H5>This is a fifth-level heading</H5>
<H6>This is a sixth-level heading</H6>
</BODY>
```

As a practical matter, you probably will seldom use more than four heading levels. Displayed in a browser, different level headings appear as different size fonts, from large to small, although each browser decides which fonts to use. Figure 2.2 shows how a Web browser displays different heading levels.

Just because a tag displays similarly or identically in Navigator and Internet Explorer doesn't mean that it will be displayed similarly or identically in other Web browsers, such as NCSA Mosaic, Sun HotJava, and so on. NCSA Mosaic 2.0, for instance, displays H1 through H6 in a normal, nonboldfaced font, while using different size fonts than Navigator and Internet Explorer. The only way to be sure how a particular tag is going to make text look in a particular browser is to check it out in that browser.

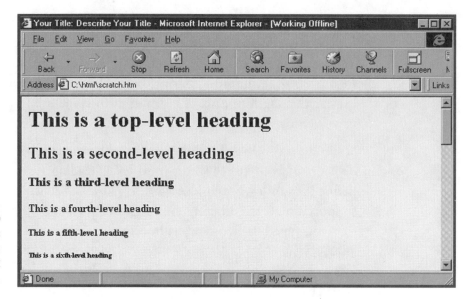

Figure 2.2

Web browsers
display heading
levels in different
font sizes.

NOTE   Don't forget to periodically save your HTML file in Notepad, and then press Alt+Tab to hop over to your browser to check out the results of your work. You only need to load your HTML file the first time you hop over to your browser. After that, just press Ctrl+R to reload the page. After checking out your HTML file in your browser, press Alt+Tab again to hop back over to Notepad. Remember, you don't really know whether you're doing it right until you can actually see it in your Web browser.

Creating Paragraphs and Line Breaks

The P (Paragraph) and BR (Line Break) tags let you insert paragraphs and lines of text on your page.

The P (Paragraph) tag

You can't just type text into an HTML document. Always tag any plain text (text not included in some other element, such as a heading, list,

block quote, and so on) that you want to include with the P tag. You shouldn't have any untagged text in an HTML document.

The P tag is a container element, but with an implied ending. You don't have to include the </P> end tag. The end of the tag is implied by any following start tag that defines a new block element (a heading, a list, another paragraph, and so on). So when you use the P tag, just insert the <P> start tag at the beginning of a paragraph but leave off the </P> at the end. Any paragraph that you tag with the P tag should show up in a browser with at least one blank line after it.

Enter the following paragraph, using just the P start tag (<P>):

```
<P>This is paragraph text. This is paragraph text. This
is paragraph text. This is paragraph text. This is
paragraph text. This is paragraph text.
```

The problem is that even though this is spelled out in specifications for HTML 2.0, some browsers still won't interpret a paragraph properly in every case without the </P> at the end. A list following a paragraph should be separated by extra space. Internet Explorer 2.0 doesn't insert the extra space unless you include the </P> end tag at the end of a paragraph preceding a list. Other earlier browser versions may also have the same problem, but current Web browsers should be able to handle this properly.

Part of the confusion surrounding how to use this tag element properly goes back to HTML 1.0, where the P tag was defined as a stand-alone element functioning as a separator. HTML 2.0, however, specifically defined this element as a container, but with an implied ending. HTML 3.2 and 4.0 reconfirm the HTML 2.0 definition.

Since it's hardly nonstandard, you should feel free to leave off the </P> end tag. Browsers that don't handle this right clearly deserve to be spanked. If you want to be conservative, feel free to include the </P> end tag at the end of your paragraphs. Figure 2.3 shows how a Web browser ought to display a paragraph without the end tag when the next element is a list.

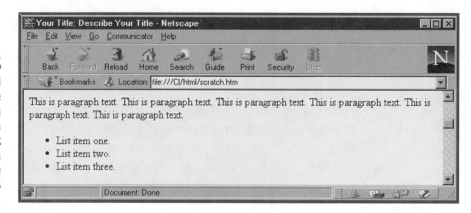

Figure 2.3

A browser should
insert extra space
between a
paragraph and a
following block
element, such as a
list, even if the
</P> end tag is
left off.

NOTE

I checked out how leaving off the </P> end tag is treated in three other browsers. Sun's pre-beta release of their HotJava Web browser adds the extra space between the end of a paragraph and a following list. I-View and AOLpress do not. Since leaving off the implied </P> end tag is part of the standard for HTML (both 2.0 and 3.2), I expect these nonconforming browsers to ultimately conform to the standard.

TIP

A Web browser automatically wraps text in an HTML file to fit inside its window. Therefore, you don't have to insert returns at the ends of your lines to get them to fit inside a browser window. It wouldn't work anyway, because Web browsers completely ignore hard returns. If you let Notepad wrap your text (turn on Word Wrap), this is purely for your convenience, and will have no effect on where the text will break in your Web browser.

Nesting Paragraphs

Generally, your paragraphs are nested in the BODY tag. You can also nest paragraphs in block quotes (BLOCKQUOTE), glossary definitions (DD), list items (LI), and address blocks (ADDRESS). A paragraph can

contain plain text, highlighting (B, I, EM, STRONG, and so on), special characters (like accented characters or the copyright symbol), line breaks (BR), hypertext links (A), and inline images (IMG). You can learn about these codes later in this session.

Don't Use Multiple P Tags to Add Blank Lines

Generally, a P tag that contains no text has no effect. None of the big browsers let you add blank lines by adding P tags. To illustrate this point, following the text paragraph you just typed, type three <P> tags (leave off the </P> end tags), followed by another text paragraph:

```
<P>This is paragraph text. This is paragraph text. This
is paragraph text. This is paragraph text. This is
paragraph text. This is paragraph text.

<P>

<P>

<P>

<P>This is paragraph text.
```

Hop over to your Web browser to see what this looks like. Multiple P tags, with or without their end tags, will probably have no effect. Most browsers completely ignore them, as shown in Figure 2.4. Even if a browser does display them, you wouldn't want to write exclusively for it anyway.

Figure 2.4

The multiple P tags inserted between two paragraphs will probably be completely ignored by a Web browser, as shown here.

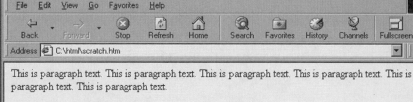

The BR (Line Break) Tag

The BR (Line Break) tag is an empty, or stand-alone, tag that inserts a line break. Type three text lines separated by BR tags:

```
<P>These lines are separated by BR (Line Break) tags.<BR>
These lines are separated by BR (Line Break) tags.<BR>
These lines are separated by BR (Line Break) tags.
```

As Figure 2.5 shows, only a single line break separates these lines when a browser displays them. (Paragraphs, you may remember, are separated by a line break and an extra blank line.)

NOTE You can use the BR tag almost anywhere you have text, not just inside of P (Paragraph) tags. You can put them inside an H1 or H2 tag to force a heading to show up on two lines.

Using Multiple BR Tags to Add Blank Lines

You might think you could use multiple BR tags to add blank lines to your page. To see what happens when you try this, type a line of text followed by four BR tags:

```
<P>Four BR (Line Break) tags follow this line.<BR>
<BR>
<BR>
<BR>
Four BR (Line Break) tags precede this line.
```

You're not supposed to get away with such a maneuver (according to the official HTML specs, that is). Netscape Navigator, however, has always let you get away with it, and the latest versions of Internet Explorer also let you get away with it, as shown in Figure 2.6.

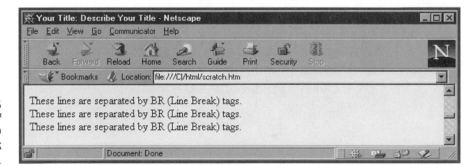

Figure 2.5

Use the BR tag to insert a line break at the end of a line.

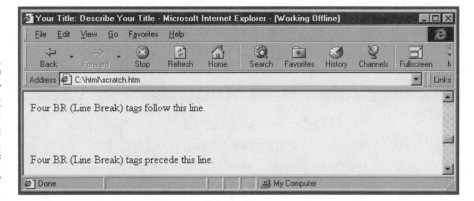

Figure 2.6

Both Navigator and Internet Explorer will display multiple BR tags, but in contravention of the standards for HTML.

Both Navigator and Internet Explorer treat multiple BR tags in a *nonstandard* fashion. To quote from the draft specification for HTML 4.0, "a sequence of contiguous white space characters such as spaces, horizontal tabs, form feeds and line breaks should be replaced by a single word space."

So should you or shouldn't you use BR tags for blank lines? Even though Netscape Navigator, Internet Explorer (versions 3.0 and 4.0), and any number of other Web browsers let you use multiple BR tags, it still doesn't constitute standard HTML. The best bet is to avoid nonstandard HTML, even if your favorite Web browser allows you to get away with using it. Besides, you can get the same result in a perfectly legal way.

The trick for inserting blank lines into a Web page works for all browsers. To insert blank lines into your HTML file, enclose regular hard returns inside the PRE (Preformatted Text) tag:

```
<P>Inserting a PRE tag containing hard returns will add
    extra space between paragraphs.
<PRE>


</PRE>
<P>This line should be three lines down.
```

For more information on the PRE tag, see "Using Preformatted Text," later in this chapter.

Spacing, Tabs, and Returns: For Your Eyes Only

In HTML, the tags do all your page's formatting. A browser ignores more than one space inserted into text (two, five, or ten spaces all appear as if they are a single space), as well as all tabs and hard returns (unless they're inside a PRE tag). Any formatting of your HTML file using extra spaces or tabs and returns is for your eyes only. So feel free to use all the extra spaces, tabs, and returns you want to make your raw HTML files more readable as you work on them.

Other than inserting a totally transparent image, the only way to insert multiple horizontal spaces in your HTML file is to use nonbreakable space characters. You insert these into an HTML file as either   or . To simulate a paragraph tab, for example, you would insert   three times at the start of a paragraph:

This will work in any Web browser, although there are a couple X-Windows Web browsers that won't display nonbreakable spaces at all, displaying them as zero-width characters. But if you want space in a line of text, other than using tables, this is the only way to do it.

Adding Comments

You can also add comments to annotate your HTML files. The comment tag is a stand-alone tag that enables you to include messages that will not be displayed in a Web browser in your HTML files, for future reference. What is a little confusing about this tag, however, is that no "name" is included in the tag. Instead, a comment always begins with a <!– and ends with a –>.

Any text inserted between these is comment text that a browser completely ignores. Here's an example of the form in which you would enter a comment into an HTML file:

```
<!—Put your comment here—>
```

Now, go ahead and type a comment between two lines of text, like this:

```
<P>This line is followed by a comment.
<!—Comments are not displayed by a browser.—>
<P>This line follows a comment.
```

The above two paragraph lines appear in a Web browser without any additional vertical space between them. The browser ignores any text inside the Comment tag.

Highlighting Your Text

Just as in a normal book or report, an HTML document can use text highlighting to clarify the text's meaning. You can easily make text in an HTML file boldfaced or italicized as well.

Using Italic and Bold Highlighting

HTML has two ways to include italic or bold text on your Web page. The first way involves using "literal" tags: the I (Italic) and B (Bold) tags. The second way is to use "logical" tags: the EM (Emphasis) and STRONG (Strong Emphasis) tags. Most browsers should display the I (Italic) and EM (Emphasis) tags identically, just as they should display the B (Bold) and STRONG (Strong Emphasis) tags identically.

So what's the difference? The basic philosophy behind HTML is to logically represent the elements of a page rather than literally describe them. The browser can freely interpret the logical elements of an HTML page and display them as it sees fit. Thus, the philosophically correct method is to always use logical tags and to avoid using literal tags. So if you want to be more true to the basic spirit of HTML, use the EM (Emphasis) tag rather than the I (Italic) tag and the STRONG (Strong Emphasis) tag rather than the B (Bold) tag. You can also do it the other way around, as you get the same result.

As an example of using the I, B, EM, and STRONG tags for text highlighting, type the following lines of text using these tags, as shown here:

```
<P><I>This is italic text.</I>
<P><B>This is bold text.</B>
<P><EM>This is emphasized text.</EM>
<P><STRONG>This is strongly emphasized text</STRONG>.
```

Figure 2.7 shows how these tags appear in Netscape Navigator.

You can use two other tags, CITE (Citation) and VAR (Variable), to highlight text—but Web browsers interpret them exactly like the I (Italic) or EM (Emphasis) tags.

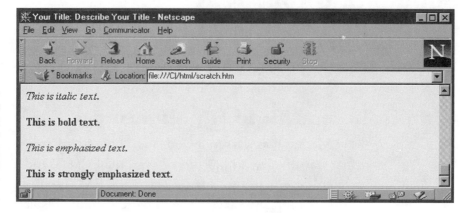

Figure 2.7

You can use literal tags (I and B) or logical tags (EM and STRONG) to italicize or bold text.

TIP

You can combine the I and B tags or the EM and STRONG tags to get text that is both italicized and bolded. To do this, just combine the tags, like this:

```
<P><I><B>This text is both italicized and bolded.</B></I>
<P><EM><STRONG>This text is also both italicized (empha-
sized) and bolded (strongly emphasized).</STRONG></EM>
```

Be sure to nest these tags rather than overlap them.

Embedding Monospace Text

You may want to embed monospace text within a paragraph, such as to request keyboard input or to represent screen output. A *monospace font,* also called a fixed-pitch font, is a font in which all the characters occupy the same amount of space on a line (in a *proportional font,* on the other hand, each character occupies a unique amount of space on a line). For example, the following line uses a monospaced font:

```
This line uses a monospace font.
```

The most widely used tag for embedding monospace text is the TT (Tele-type) tag. It appears as a monospace font in all Web browsers. You can think of it as a general-purpose monospace text tag that you can use when-ever you want to embed monospace text within a paragraph. Two other tags, the CODE and SAMP tags, produce the same results as the TT tag.

The only other useful tag is the KBD (Keyboard) tag. Unfortunately, how a Web browser displays this tag is unpredictable. Navigator displays it the same as the TT tag. Earlier versions of Internet Explorer display it in a boldface monospace font, although the latest version of Internet Explorer follows Navigator's example. NCSA Mosaic displays this tag as an itali-cized proportional font.

Type the following as an example of using the TT and KBD tags:

```
<P>This is regular text. <TT>This is an example of the
TT (Teletype or Typewriter Text) tag.</TT> This is
regular text. <KBD>This is an example of the KBD (Key-
board) tag.</KBD>
```

Figure 2.8

The tendency among current Web browsers is to display text marked with the TT and KBD tags identically.

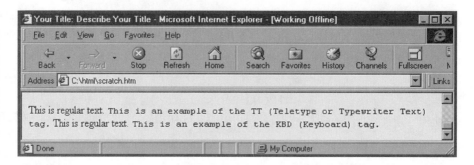

The KBD tag is useful because it allows you to distinguish between screen output (the TT tag) and keyboard input (the KBD tag). Since both Navigator and Internet Explorer treat these tags identically, as shown in Figure 2.8, you should probably just stick to using the TT tag and ignore the KBD tag.

NOTE To insert monospace text as a separate text block rather than embedding it inside a paragraph, see "The PRE (Preformatted Text) Tag" section, later in this session.

Inserting Reserved and Special Characters

You may need to enter a special code for a character into your HTML file under two different circumstances: If you want to insert a reserved character that is used to parse (interpret and display) an HTML file, and if you want to enter a special, or extended, character that isn't part of the regular keyboard character set.

You insert both of these characters into an HTML file in the form of a numerical entity code or a named entity code. Numerical entity codes are inserted in the following form, where *number* is a three-digit decimal number between 000 and 255:

&#*number*;

Named entity codes are inserted in the following form, where *name* is the name of a character as listed in the HTML specs:

&*name*;

Reserved Characters

HTML uses the <, >, &, and " characters to parse, or interpret, an HTML document for display. Except for angle brackets, you rarely need to automatically replace these characters with their entity codes:

- **Angle brackets (< and >)** should always be replaced by their corresponding entity codes if you want them to display properly in an HTML file. Use them only to signal the beginning or the end of an HTML tag.

- **Double quotes (")** only need to be replaced if they're part of an HTML tag that you want to appear as is rather than as interpreted by a browser.

- **Ampersands (&)** signal the beginning of an entity code, but only need to be replaced if they're part of an HTML entity code that you want to appear as is rather than as interpreted by a browser. You never need to replace stand-alone ampersands.

◆ ◆

If you use a word processor to create HTML files, be sure to turn off the "smart quotes" feature. When creating HTML files, you always want to use regular "keyboard" quotes. In other words, each quotation mark should be straight up and down, not curled to the left or right.

◆ ◆

You can use character entities exclusively to insert any of these characters into an HTML file when you want an HTML tag to appear on your Web page as is rather than as interpreted by the browser. To have a browser show "<EM>" onscreen instead of interpreting it as a formatting code, you would enter it like this:

```
&lt;EM&gt;
```

All Web browsers recognize the named entity codes for these characters, so you don't have to use the numerical entity codes here. For an easy reference, Table 2.1 shows the named entity codes for inserting HTML reserved characters.

TABLE 2.1 HTML RESERVED CHARACTER ENTITY CODES

Character	Entity	Code
Less Than	<	&lt;
Greater Than	>	&gt;
Ampersand	&	&amp;
Double Quote	"	&quot;

Special Characters

Suppose you want to post a page devoted to an article you've written, and you want to protect it by showing your copyright. Since the copyright symbol (©) isn't available on the keyboard, you can't just type it into your HTML document as you would a normal keyboard character. Instead, you must use a special code that tells the browser to insert the character where you want it.

In HTML, there are two ways to enter such characters: as numerical entity codes or named entity codes. You can insert the copyright symbol, for example, by using its numerical entity code (©) or its named entity code (©).

HTML uses the ISO 8859-1 character set, which is an 8-bit character set that provides 256 positions (0-255). Of these, however, 000 through 032 and 127 correspond to control characters, while 128 through 159 are designated as undisplayable. Thus, only the last 95 codes (160 through 255) represent all the special characters that, according to the ISO 8859-1 standard, should be legally used on a Web page. These include many special symbols (cent, copyright, degree, and so on), plus many accented characters (like a capital A with an acute accent) that are commonly used in many foreign languages.

NOTE There is one exception to the general rule that codes outside of 160 through 255 should not be used: the trademark symbol. The numerical code (™) will display the trademark symbol on Windows, Macintosh, and Unix computers, which is pretty darn close to universal support—but that is only because the native character sets of all those platforms include it. You should avoid using the named entity code (™)—Internet Explorer, NCSA Mosaic, and many other Web browsers will recognize it, but Navigator won't. One workaround is to insert (TM) inside SMALL and SUP (Superscript) tags (see "HTML 3.2 Text Highlighting Tags" in the Intermediate HTML Tutorial for how to use these tags).

Numerical character entities use the actual decimal numeration of the character in the ISO-8859-1 character set. For instance, you could insert a copyright symbol into a Web page by using its numerical character entity like this:

©

Named entity codes have been designated to correspond to many of these special characters. To insert a copyright symbol using its named character entity, you would type this:

©

Whether a Web browser will display a named character entity is another matter. Other than the uppercase and lowercase accented characters (A-grave, a-acute, and so on) that many foreign languages require, only the copyright and registration signs have anything close to universal support. Feel free to use the named entity codes for the copyright or registration symbol and for any of the accented characters, but otherwise stick to the numerical character entities.

CAUTION

◆◆◆

Although the ISO-8859-1 character set is used to designate special characters to insert in a Web page, it is not the universal native character set for all computer operating systems. It is the native character set for both Unix and Windows, but not for the Macintosh or DOS. On a Macintosh, certain characters in the ISO-8859-1 character set aren't available, so if you try to display one of these characters in a Web page on a Macintosh, you'll see a different character than the one that you intend. The solution is to avoid using these characters on a Web page. Table 2.2 shows these characters and what you want to appear onscreen versus what the Macintosh substitutes.

◆◆◆

TABLE 2.2 CHARACTERS THAT WON'T DISPLAY ON A MACINTOSH

Numerical Entity	Named Entity	Character	Macintosh Displays
&#166;	&brvbar;	¦ (broken bar)	|
&#178;	&sup2;	^{2} (superscript 2)	2
&#179;	&sup3;	^{3} (superscript 3)	3
&#185;	&sup1;	^{1} (superscript 1)	1
&#188;	&frac14;	¼ (one quarter)	π
&#189;	&frac12;	½ (one half)	∏
&#190;	&frac34;	¾ (three quarters)	≤
&#215;	&times;	x (multiplication)	x
&#221;	&Yacute;	Ý (Y-acute)	Y
&#253;	&yacute;	ý (y-acute)	y

Of these, you might possibly use only the broken bar (¦) and the multiplication sign (×), because Macintosh substitutes a straight vertical bar (|) for the broken bar and a lowercase x for the multiplication sign. For the others, you can see that Macintosh uses entirely different characters.

Table 2.3 shows some of the most commonly used special characters, their numerical and named entity codes, and support by browsers (universal support for named entities cannot be guaranteed).

TABLE 2.3 SPECIAL CHARACTERS			
Character	**Number**	**Name**	**Name Support**
Trademark	&#153;	&trade;	Not Navigator (all versions)
Cent	&#162;	&cent;	Only latest 4.0+ browsers*
Copyright	&#169;	&copy;	All browsers
Registered	&#174;	&reg;	All browsers
Multiply	&#215;	&times;	Only latest 4.0+ browsers*
Divide	&#247;	&divide;	Only latest 4.0+ browsers*

*Netscape Navigator 4.0+ or Microsoft Internet Explorer 4.0+

Table 2.3 is just a partial list of special characters you can insert into an HTML file. For a full listing of all the special characters you can use, see Appendix D, "Special Characters."

CAUTION   Named entity codes such as © or ® are case-sensitive. You should type them exactly as they are listed. À and à, for instance, stand for two separate accented characters: an uppercase "A" with a grave accent and a lowercase "a" with a grave accent, respectively.

Enter the following example of using the numerical entity code for the copyright symbol and the named entity code for the registered symbol:

```
<H2>&#169; Copyright 1997.</H2>
<H2>Crumbies&reg;</H2>
```

See Figure 2.9 for how these display in a Web browser.

Using Block Quotes

The BLOCKQUOTE (Block Quote) tag double-indents a block of text from both margins. You usually use it to display quotations, as the name of the tag implies. You can use it to double-indent any block of text, but you aren't limited to using it on quotations. According to the specification for the tag, you aren't supposed to put raw text inside a block quote—you are only supposed to put other text elements, such as paragraphs (P tag elements), inside a block quote, and then put the text in those other elements. If you want to play it safe, put the P tags in; otherwise, don't worry about it.

Type a paragraph of text, followed by a paragraph of text inside a BLOCKQUOTE tag:

```
<P>In <EM>Notes From Underground</EM> Dostoevsky plumbs
the depths of human psychology, revealing the complexity
and contradictions underlying even the most normal and
decent of human beings:

<BLOCKQUOTE>

<P>Every man has some reminiscenses which he would not
tell to everyone, but only to his friends. He has others
which he would not reveal even to his friends, but only
to himself, and that in secret. But finally there are
still others which a man is even afraid to tell himself,
and every decent man has a considerable number of such
things in his mind.

</BLOCKQUOTE>
```

Figure 2.9

You can insert
special characters
such as the
copyright and
registered symbols
using numerical
or named
entity codes.

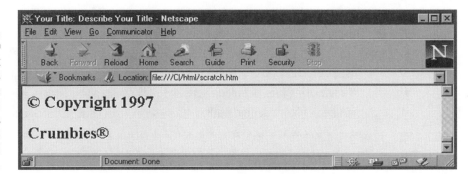

The latest versions of Navigator and Internet Explorer display the
BLOCKQUOTE tag the same way: double-indented and in a normal,
proportional font (see Figure 2.10). Internet Explorer 2.0, however, displays it in a bold italic font. NCSA Mosaic 2.0 displays it in a bold font.
Although using the BLOCKQUOTE tag as a formatting device has
become very common on the Web, you might want to think twice before
using BLOCKQUOTE simply as a formatting device to indent text.
Generally, if you use BLOCKQUOTE to display indented quotations,
some browsers might italicize them, but it's no big deal.

Figure 2.10

The BLOCKQUOTE
tag is used to
double-indent text
from the margins.

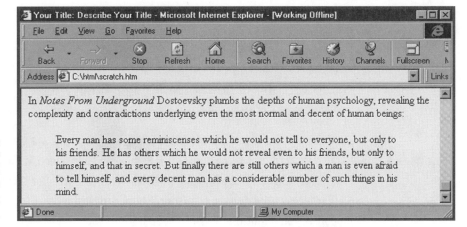

Using the P tag to nest text inside a BLOCKQUOTE tag enables you to include multiple paragraphs within a block quote. Besides paragraph text, you can also include headings, lists, definition lists, preformatted text, and other block quotes inside a block quote. (I cover using lists, definition lists, and preformatted text later in this tutorial.) Everything will be double-indented until it reaches the </BLOCKQUOTE> end tag.

Using BR (Line Break) Tags in a Block Quote

You can use BR (Line Break) tags in a block quote to display stanzas of poetry, the verses of a song, or other indented text for which you don't want the lines to wrap. Type a paragraph of text, followed by a paragraph of text using BR tags inserted inside a BLOCKQUOTE tag.

```
<P>In <EM>Porgy and Bess</EM>, in the song "Summertime,"
George Gershwin evokes the hazy, lazy days of a Southern
summer:
<BLOCKQUOTE>
<P>Summertime and the living is easy,<BR>
Fish are jumping and the cotton is high.<BR>
Oh your Daddy's rich and your Ma is good looking,<BR>
So hush little baby, don't you cry.
</BLOCKQUOTE>
```

Figure 2.11 shows how a block quote using BR tags appears in a Web browser.

NOTE

HTML 4.0 specifies a new attribute, CITE, that can be included in the BLOCKQUOTE tag. You would use it to specify the URL where the source for a quote can be found (CITE="http://www.dummy.com/source.html", for instance). Even though no browsers support it, you might use it just to keep track of your online sources for quotes.

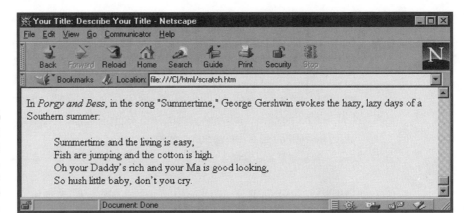

Figure 2.11

By combining BR
tags with the
BLOCKQUOTE tag,
you can create
indented stanzas
for a poem or song.

Using Preformatted Text

You would use the PRE (Preformatted Text) tag to display text in a mono-space, fixed-pitch font. As its name implies, you use the PRE tag to display text as is, including all spaces and hard returns. The primary use for this tag is to display text in a tabular or columnar format in which you want to make sure that columns are properly aligned.

TIP

Always use spaces, not tabs, to align columns when using the PRE tag, because different browsers display tabs in PRE tagged text differently.

Actually, the PRE tag is the original "tables" tag for HTML. Unlike the TABLE tag (part of HTML 3.2 but not HTML 2.0), all Web browsers support it, which is a real advantage. It can be particularly handy for displaying worksheets or reports. Another common usage is for displaying program code or output.

CAUTION

◆ ◆

When typing tabular or columnar text with a PRE tag, make sure that you have a monospace, fixed-pitch font such as Courier turned on in your editor or word processor. Notepad automatically displays all text in a monospace font. Word processors, however, normally use a proportional font as the default. Most HTML editors display PRE tagged text in a monospace font, but a prominent exception is HTML NotePad (Version 1.9 displays everything in a proportional font).

◆ ◆

For an example of using the PRE tag, type a table using rows and columns:

```
<PRE>
            Sales Figures for First Quarter of 1996
 _ _ _ _ _ _ _ _ _ _ _ _ _ _ _ _ _ _ _ _ _ _ _ _ _ _ _ _ _ _

            January      February        March       Totals
Anderson   $ 10,200    $  20,015     $  14,685    $  44,900
Baker        30,500       25,885        50,225      106,610
Peterson     15,900       20,115        18,890       54,905
Wilson       40,100       35,000        29,000      104,100

          _ _ _ _      _ _ _ _        _ _ _ _      _ _ _ _
Totals    $ 96,700    $ 101,015     $ 112,800    $ 310,515
</PRE>
```

Figure 2.12 shows this table as it appears in a Web browser.

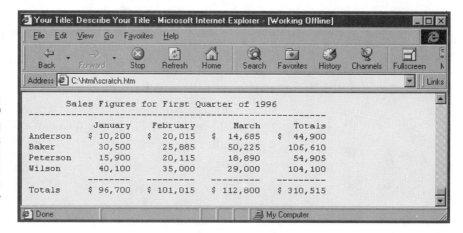

Figure 2.12

The PRE tag displays text blocks in a monospaced font, preserving all spaces and line breaks in columnar and tabular text.

To double-indent preformatted text in both Netscape Navigator and NCSA Mosaic, put it inside a BLOCKQUOTE tag. Enclose the PRE tag text you just typed inside a BLOCKQUOTE tag, as follows:

```
<PRE>

<BLOCKQUOTE>
        Sales Figures for First Quarter of 1996
_ _ _ _ _ _ _ _ _ _ _ _ _ _ _ _ _ _ _ _ _ _ _ _ _

          January    February      March     Totals
Anderson  $ 10,200  $  20,015  $  14,685  $  44,900
Baker       30,500     25,885     50,225    106,610
Peterson    15,900     20,115     18,890     54,905
Wilson      40,100     35,000     29,000    104,100

          _ _ _ _    _ _ _ _    _ _ _ _    _ _ _ _

Totals    $ 96,700  $ 101,015  $ 112,800  $ 310,515
</BLOCKQUOTE>
</PRE>
```

This doesn't work in Internet Explorer Version 2.0, which will still display the table flushed left. Also, you might think that you could reverse the nesting order here, placing the PRE tags inside the BLOCKQUOTE tags, but a bug in Internet Explorer 4.0 will still cause it to be displayed flush to the left margin. This has been fixed in versions 4.01 and later of Internet Explorer, but there are plenty of people still using version 4.0, so you'd better just stick to putting the BLOCKQUOTE tags inside the PRE tags.

Take a Break

This seems like a good place to chill for a bit. Get up and stretch those arms and legs. Pour another cup of coffee. Or take the dog for a walk. I'll see you back in five or ten minutes for the remainder of this session.

Creating Lists

Only headings and paragraph text elements are used more commonly than lists. Many Web pages are nothing but lists of hypertext links. You, like anyone else surfing the Web, have been on that merry-go-round a few times—going from one page of lists to another page of lists to another. If you're going to create Web pages, you need to know how to make lists! There are two types of lists: ordered and unordered. An ordered list is simply a numbered list and an unordered list is a bulleted list.

TIP
You don't have to physically type the numbers for the items in an ordered list or insert bullet characters for an unordered list. A Web browser automatically numbers any list items included in an OL (Ordered List) tag. When a Web browser encounters the UL (Unordered List) tag, it inserts the bullet characters for you.

The OL (Ordered List) Tag

The OL (Ordered List) tag defines a sequentially numbered list of items. Therefore, the OL tag must surround the entire list. The LI (List Item) tag is nested inside the OL tag and defines each individual item within the list.

Create an ordered list to see how these tags work together:

```
<P>When visiting Florence, one should be sure to visit:
<OL>
<LI>The Church of Santa Maria Novella
<LI>The Medici Chapels
<LI>The Church of San Lorenzo
<LI>The Baptistry of St. John
</OL>
```

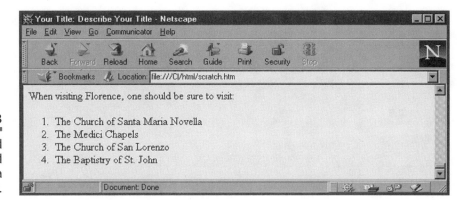

Figure 2.13

The OL (Ordered List) tag is used to create a numbered list.

> The LI tags do not have end tags in this example because the end tag (</LI>), like the end tag for the P tag, is implied. It's another case of a container tag masquerading as an empty tag. You should be aware that HTML 4.0 treats this a bit differently than earlier versions of HTML, specifying that extra space should be added between list items if the end tag (</LI>) is present (no browsers support this).

Figure 2.13 shows how an ordered or numbered list is displayed in a Web browser.

The UL (Unordered List) Tag

The UL (Unordered List) tag defines a bulleted list of items. Once again, the LI (List Item) tag is nested inside the UL tag and defines each item within the list.

Create a bulleted list:

```
<P>In this course we will be studying the philosophical
thought of the Milesians:
<UL>
<LI>Thales
<LI>Anaximander
<LI>Anaximenes
</UL>
```

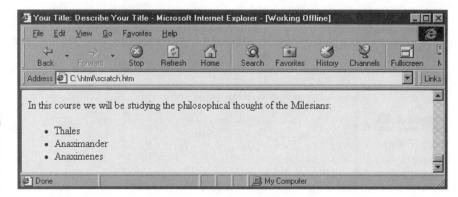

Figure 2.14

The UL (Unordered List) tag is used to create a bulleted list.

In this course we will be studying the philosophical thought of the Milesians:

- Thales
- Anaximander
- Anaximenes

Done   My Computer

Figure 2.14 shows how an unordered, or bulleted, list is displayed in a Web browser.

NOTE So how do you create all those fancy 3-D bullets that you see all over the Web? Well, they don't use OL or UL tags. Those fancy bullets are actually inline graphic images that the Web author has inserted into the page. The separate lines are paragraphs broken up by line breaks (BR tags). I cover how to insert inline images using the IMG tag later in this tutorial. In the Intermediate HTML Tutorial, you'll learn how to create *indented* link lists with fancy 3-D bullet icons. I'll also be showing you another way to do this using tables in the Tables Tutorial this evening.

Nesting Lists

You can nest a list inside another list. The browser automatically indents nested list levels. You can nest the same or different kinds of lists.

The following list examples use spaces to indent the different nested levels of the list. You also could use tabs. The only purpose of this spacing is to make the raw text here more readable during editing, as a Web browser will completely ignore them. Feel free to insert tabs or spaces to approximate the layout shown:

```
<UL>
<LI>Some Pre-Socratic Philosophers
   <UL>
   <LI>The Milesians
     <UL>
     <LI>Thales
     <LI>Anaximander
     <LI>Anaximenes
     </UL>
   <LI>The Eleatics
     <UL>
     <LI>Parmenides
     <LI>Anaxagoras
     </UL>
   </UL>
</UL>
```

Most Web browsers should display the top-level bullets quite similarly,
but they may differ in how they display the lower-level bullets, as shown
in Figures 2.15 and 2.16.

Figure 2.15

Internet Explorer
displays a
multilevel bulleted
list like this.

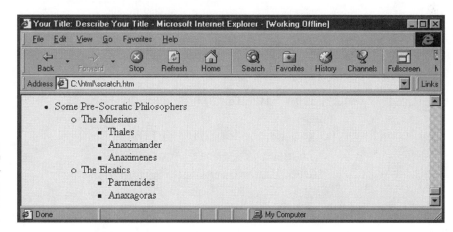

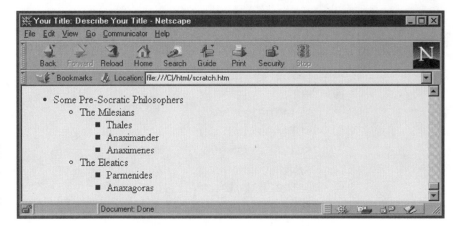

Figure 2.16

Navigator displays
a multilevel
bulleted list
differently.

Mixing Lists

You can nest an ordered list within an unordered list (or the other way around):

```
<UL>
<LI>King-Side Openings
   <OL>
   <LI>Ruy Lopez
   <LI>King Bishop's Opening
   <LI>King's Gambit
   </OL>
<LI>Queen-Side Openings
   <OL>
   <LI>Queen's Gambit Declined
   <LI>Queen's Gambit Accepted
   <LI>English Opening
   </OL>
</UL>
```

Figure 2.17 shows ordered, or numbered, lists nested inside an unordered, or bulleted, list.

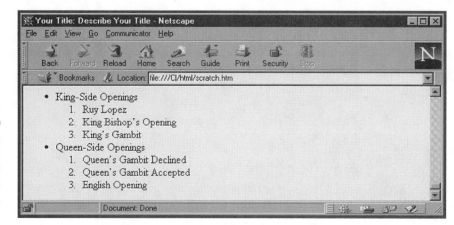

Figure 2.17

You can nest a numbered (ordered) list inside a bulleted (unordered) list, and vice versa.

There are two other list tags: the DIR and MENU tags. The DIR tag was intended for displaying multicolumn directory lists, and the MENU tag was intended for displaying single-column menu lists. In practice, all versions of Navigator and Internet Explorer display these tags exactly the same as the UL (Unordered List) tag. The only browser that displays these tags any differently than the UL tag is NCSA Mosaic 2.0. The HTML 4.0 specification also recommends that the UL tag be used instead.

Creating Definition Lists

The DL (Definition List) tag allows you to create glossaries, or lists of terms and definitions. A glossary actually consists of three tag elements that all work together: the DL (Definition List) tag to define the list, the DT (Definition Term) tag to define the terms, and the DD (Definition Data) tag to define the definitions. Set up a short glossary now:

```
<DL>
<DT>Appeal
<DD>A proceeding by which the decision of a lower court
may be appealed to a higher court.
<DT>Arrest
<DD>The legal apprehension and restraint of someone
charged with a crime so that they might be brought
before a court to stand trial.
```

```
<DT>Bail
<DD>A security offered to a court in exchange for a
person's release and as assurance of their appearance in
court when required.
</DL>
```

Figure 2.18 shows the preceding glossary list code as it appears in a Web browser.

As you've probably noticed, the end tags for the DT (Definition Term) and DD (Definition Data) tags are implied, as is the LI (List Item) tag in a regular list. The only difference is that a glossary, or definition list, has a two-part item (both a term and a definition), rather than a one-part item. As long as you keep this in mind, you should have no trouble creating glossaries.

By itself, a glossary list is a bit bland. You can dress it up by adding emphasis or tagging the definition terms with a heading tag. Here is an example of adding bold italic emphasis to a definition term:

```
<DT><I><B>Appeal</B></I>
```

Here is an example of tagging a definition term using an H3 heading tag:

```
<DT><H3>Appeal</H3>
```

DD (Definition Data)

DT (Definition Term)

Figure 2.18

A glossary is created using three tags: the DL (Definition List), DT (Definition Term), and DD (Definition Data) tags.

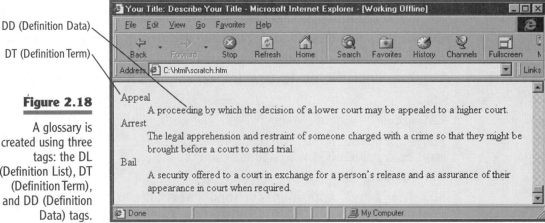

TIP You can include multiple DD (Definition Data) elements following a DT (Definition Term) element. If you want space to be inserted between multiple DD elements, you should insert a P tag following the second and any following DD tags: <DD><P> *Your definition item text,* for instance.

Creating Hypertext Links

One of the main reasons to create a Web page is to create links to other pages, right? To do that, you need to know how to use the A (Anchor) tag.

If you've surfed the Web at all, you should be quite familiar with hypertext links. You've probably used hypertext links not only to jump to and view another Web page, or jump to a specific place in either the same or another Web page, but to read a Gopher file, display an image, download a program, send an e-mail message, play an audio or video clip, run a script, access a database, telnet to a server, and so on. You can use hypertext links to jump to anything that has an address on the Internet (not just on the Web), as long as you don't need a password. Of course, what happens after you make the jump depends on where you go.

In a sense, the Web is a kind of giant "What's behind door #3?" game, although this perhaps helps explain much of its basic appeal. It's all quite easy and transparent: just click and go. However, explaining how to make this happen on your Web page isn't nearly as easy or transparent. This section will make the A (Anchor) tag as clear as possible. The three basic kinds of hypertext links are as follows:

✪ **Links to other HTML documents or data objects.** These are by far the most commonly used links on the Web. They allow you to jump from one Web page to another, as well as to anything else that has an address on the Net (not just the Web), such as Gopher files, FTP archives, images, and so on.

✪ **Link to other places in the same HTML document.** These links allow you to jump from one place in a Web page to another point on the same Web page. Many Web pages have directories or "tables of contents" at the beginning of the page, allowing you to decide which part of the page you would like to view and then click on the link to jump to that section of the page or document.

✪ **Links to places in other HTML documents.** These links are quite similar to links to places in the same document, except you can jump to certain sections on other pages. If you've clicked on a hypertext link and then jumped to some point halfway down another Web page, you've used this type of link.

You use the A (Anchor) tag to anchor one or both ends of a hypertext link. The first kind of link, where you link to another Web page or data object, requires only one anchor. The second and third kinds of links, where you link to another place in the same or another Web page, require both ends of the link—that is, both a launch pad and a landing spot. This other end of a hypertext link, where you link to a specific place in the same or another Web page, is often called a target anchor.

 NOTE You can include a "target" anchor inside a Gopher text file, which is just a plain text file, and then have a hypertext link jump to that specific place in that file, even though it isn't an HTML file. You don't see this often, but you can do it.

Anatomy of the A (Anchor) Tag

Think of a hypertext link as being composed of the following three elements:

✪ Start and end tags that enclose the whole link
✪ The link target
✪ The link text

Figure 2.19 illustrates the three parts of a hypertext link.

Figure 2.19

A hypertext link has three parts: the start and end tags, the link target, and the link text.

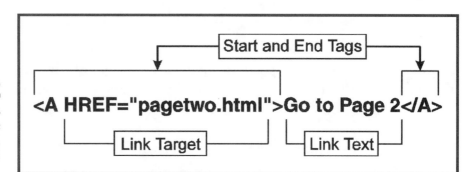

In Figure 2.19, the HREF (Hypertext Reference) attribute specifies the URL or address of the object of the link, which here is simply another Web page. Note that the full address (URL) is not given, just the file name. This means that the object of the link, most commonly another Web page, is located in the same folder as the Web page from which the link is being made. If you wanted to make a link with a Web page somewhere else on the Web, you'd have to include the full URL (http://www.somewhere.com/somepage.html, or something like that), rather than just the file name (somepage.html).

When using the A (Anchor) tag, you must include either an HREF attribute or a NAME attribute. If you are linking to another Web page or other data object, you only need to use *one* anchor tag with an HREF attribute, and if you are linking to a location in the same or another Web page, you need to use *two* anchor tags, the first with an HREF attribute defining the take-off location and the second with the NAME attribute defining the target location.

If you find this a bit confusing, don't worry—it is confusing! The following sections provide some hands-on examples of creating the three kinds of links and using both the HREF and NAME attributes. Learning by doing should go a long way toward dissipating your confusion.

Linking to a File or Data Object

You can form an HTML link to anything on the Web that has an address. To create a hypertext link that jumps to a file that is somewhere on the Web (as opposed to a folder on your own server), include the whole URL of the file to which you want to jump. For instance:

```
<P>Click here to jump to <A HREF="http://www.somewhere.com/
else.html">somewhere else</A>.
```

TIP

Notice that the A tag falls inside a P tag. You should always nest the A tag inside a document element, not simply within the BODY tag. You can nest an A tag inside a P tag, a heading (such as H1 or H2), or an ADDRESS, PRE, LI, DT, or DD tag.

If a "www.somewhere.com" actually existed somewhere with a file in its root directory called "else.html," you could link to it by putting the above A tag in your own HTML file. Substitute an actual URL for the dummy URL when you want to link to a real site somewhere. Do that now by creating a hypertext link that jumps to a real document on an actual Web site:

```
<P>You can find out more about the WWW at the home page
of the <A HREF="http://www.w3.org/">W3 Consortium</A>.
```

Figure 2.20 shows how this appears in a Web browser.

When you click on the hypertext link shown in Figure 2.20, a hypertext "jump" takes you to the target address, displaying the page shown in Figure 2.21. (You must actually go online if you want to check this out on your browser.)

Figure 2.20

The underlining flags a hypertext link to the home page of the W3 Consortium.

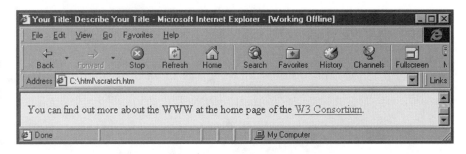

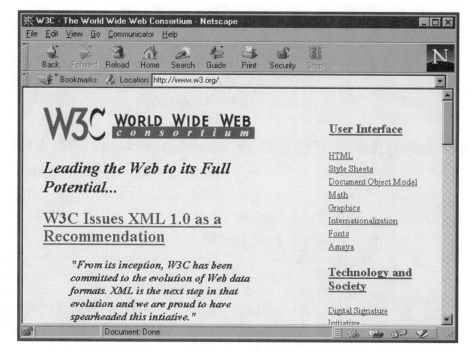

Figure 2.21

The home page of the W3C appears when you click on the link shown in Figure 2.20.

NOTE

Netscape Navigator and Internet Explorer display a hypertext link in a blue, underlined font. NCSA Mosaic displays a hypertext link in a blue font, leaving off the underlining. Your browser may display links that you have already visited in a different color. Also, Web page authors can specify the color in which a regular link, a previously visited link, and an active link will be displayed—I'll show you how to do that in this afternoon's Intermediate HTML Tutorial. Style sheets can also be used to exert even further control over how a hypertext link will appear on a Web page.

Linking to Non-WWW Files

Your browser should be able to directly display any text file or GIF or JPG graphic on a Web, FTP, or Gopher server. Other kinds of files may require viewers or players, such as sound, animation, or video files.

RealAudio and Shockwave allow audio and animation clips to be streamed (played while being downloaded) rather than downloaded first and then played. (For pointers on where to find information on audio and video players, plug-ins, and RealAudio and Shockwave, see Appendix B, "The Web Tools Directory.")

Linking to a Place in the Same HTML File

To link to another place in the same HTML file requires both an HREF anchor and a NAME anchor. An HREF anchor that links to a NAME anchor has a special form:

```
<A HREF="#anchorname">anchortext</A>
```

Notice the # sign. In an HREF anchor, the # sign is the only thing that identifies the HREF attribute as the name of a NAME anchor rather than an address or file name. (The # sign combined with the following anchorname is sometimes called a "fragment identifier.")

Some of the more common uses for linking HREF and NAME anchors on the same page are to create a directory or table of contents that links to the major headings of a page, make cross references between different points in the same Web page, and form links to footnotes or endnotes.

The following is an example of creating a menu or table of contents for the top of a Web page to link to subheading sections located lower on the same Web page (feel free to cut and paste to create the paragraph text for the sections):

```
<H2>Table of Contents</H2>
<P><A HREF="#one">Section One</A><BR>
<A HREF="#two">Section Two</A><BR>
<A HREF="#three">Section Three</A>
<H3><A NAME="one">Section One</A></H2>
```

```
<P>This is the text following the first subheading. This
is the text following the first subheading. This is the
text following the first subheading. This is the text
following the first subheading. This is the text follow-
ing the first subheading. This is the text following the
first subheading.
<H3><A NAME="two">Section Two</A></H2>
<P>This is the text following the second subheading. This
is the text following the second subheading. This is the
text following the second subheading. This is the text
following the second subheading. This is the text follow-
ing the second subheading. This is the text following
the second subheading.
<H3><A NAME="three">Section Three</A></H2>
<P>This is the text following the third subheading. This
is the text following the third subheading. This is the
text following the third subheading. This is the text
following the third subheading. This is the text follow-
ing the third subheading. This is the text following the
third subheading.
```

Figure 2.22 shows how this looks in a Web browser.

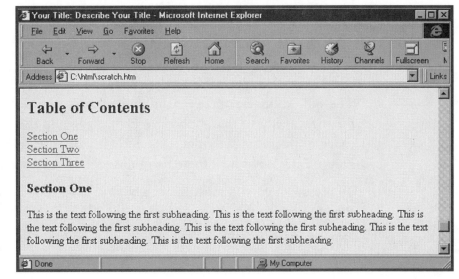

Figure 2.22

You can create a table of contents using hypertext links that will jump to subheadings within your document.

Since only the first subheading and subsection is shown in the previous figure, you should save your file and hop over to your browser to check out what this whole example looks like.

Linking to a Place in Another HTML File

Just as you can make a hypertext link with a place in the same HTML file, you can also make a link with a place in another HTML file. Both work the same way, except in the second instance the NAME anchor (your landing spot) is placed in an entirely different file from the one in which the link is being made. The form for an HREF anchor that links to a place in another HTML file is:

```
<A HREF="address#anchorname">anchortext</A>
```

This actually combines the forms for linking to another page and linking to a place on a page. First, the link is made to the *address,* which is either a URL or a file name of an HTML file, then following the # sign, the link is made to the *place in that file* that is marked by the NAME anchor corresponding to the anchorname. Create a hypertext link that jumps to a place in another (hypothetical) HTML file:

```
<P>Go to <A HREF="links.htm#parttwo">Part Two</A> of the
<A HREF="links.htm">How to Use Links</A> web page.
```

The preceding HTML includes links both to Part Two of the "How to Use Links" Web page and to the whole "How to Use Links" Web page. The only difference between linking to a location in a Web page and linking directly to that Web page is that you add the target name (also called a "fragment identifier"), here #parttwo, to the HREF string value. Figure 2.23 shows how these two links look in a Web browser.

To use this link, you must create a second HTML file, "links.htm," with the heading for Part Two marked with a NAME anchor, as shown here:

```
<H2><A NAME="parttwo">Part Two</A></H2>
```

Figure 2.23

The first link jumps to a place in the "How to Use Links" Web page, and the second link jumps to the Web page itself.

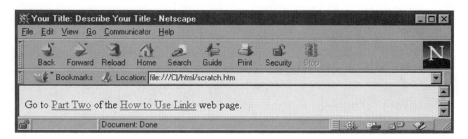

When you activate the first link in the other Web page, you jump first to LINKS.HTM and then to the place in that Web page where the preceding target anchor has been placed.

Creating Link Lists

So far, the discussion has focused on creating lists and creating links, but hasn't explained creating link lists. A link list is a list of hypertext links, usually bulleted but sometimes numbered. Because link lists are so ubiquitous, everybody should know how to create them. To create a link list, you need to combine an unordered list and some hypertext links.

Creating a Simple Link List

The text of each link forms the entire list item. Often the link text is the title of a Web page being linked, and sometimes a little editing is necessary to make it more informative. In this example, no other explanatory or descriptive text is included (outside the link, but on the list item line). Set up a simple list of actual yo-yo links using the titles of the linked Web pages as the link text:

```
<H2>Yo Yo Links</H2>
<UL>
<LI><A HREF="http://www.li.net/~autorent/yo-yo.htm">Jon's Yo-Yo Kingdom</A>
```

```
<LI><A HREF="http://pages.nyu.edu/~tqm3413/yoyo/index.htm">
Tomer's Page of Exotic Yo-Yo</A>

<LI><A HREF="http://www.socool.com/socool/yo-yo.html">
Just Say YO-YO</A>

<LI><A HREF="http://www.pd.net/yoyo/">American Yo-Yo
Association</A>

<LI><A HREF="http://www.socool.com/socool/yo_hist.html">
The History of the Yo-Yo</A>

</UL>
```

NOTE When you enter Web addresses (URLs), you should always type them exactly as they appear. Unix commands are case-sensitive, and most Web servers run Unix.

Figure 2.24 shows how the preceding link list example appears in a Web browser.

Creating a Link List with Descriptions

A list of links can prove somewhat empty. It would be nice to add more information so visitors would have a clearer idea of what awaits at the other end of the link. One option is to edit the link text to include more information than the title affords. It is best to try to keep the actual link text as concise as possible so that a visitor can scan it at a glance. The solution is to add explanatory text following the hypertext link. In the list of links you just typed, add some explanatory text for each link:

```
<H2>Yo Yo Links</H2>

<UL>

<LI><A HREF="http://www.li.net/~autorent/yo-yo.htm">Jon's
Yo-Yo Kingdom</A> Claims to have the largest Yo-Yo link
list on the Web.

<LI><A HREF="http://pages.nyu.edu/~tqm3413/yoyo/index.htm">
Tomer's Page of Exotic Yo-Yo</A> Dedicated to the
"little-known, original, unusual, difficult, or otherwise
interesting tricks."
```

```
<LI><A HREF="http://www.socool.com/socool/yo-yo.html">Just
Say YO-YO</A> Features the Web's first Yo-Yo animation.
<LI><A HREF="http://www.pd.net/yoyo/">American Yo-Yo
Association</A> Read past issues of the AYYA Newsletter.
<LI><A HREF="http://www.socool.com/socool/yo_hist.html">
The History of the Yo-Yo</A> All you want to know about
Yo-Yo history.
</UL>
```

Figure 2.25 shows the newly expanded list.

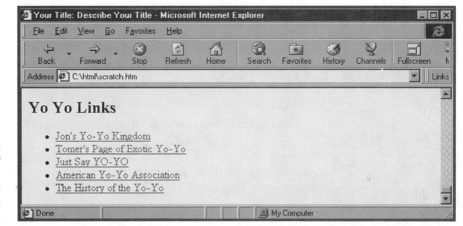

Figure 2.24

In a simple link list, the link text and the link items are the same.

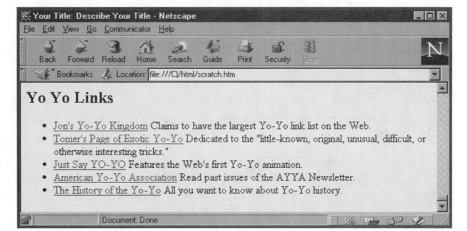

Figure 2.25

Sometimes a short list of links with explanations is better than a long one without.

Other Ways to Create Link Lists

The preceding examples illustrate the most simple and direct ways to create link lists. A variation you might want to try is using a definition list in which the hypertext links are inserted in the DT tags, with the descriptions inserted in the DD tags. You could also tag the definition terms with a heading tag to display the links more prominently. Using a definition list for a list of links can be particularly handy if you want to provide more than just a sentence or two of explanatory or descriptive text. Later, in the Intermediate HTML Tutorial and the Tables Tutorial, I'll show you some ways to create indented link lists using 3-D bullet icons.

Using Inline Images

The IMG (Image) tag allows you to display inline images on your Web page. The term *inline* here means that an image is inserted at a particular location in a line within a Web page.

The most commonly used formats for inline images are GIF and JPG. All current graphic Web browsers display GIF and JPG files as inline images. These two graphic formats tend to serve different purposes. GIF images are limited to 256 colors but can have a color set to transparent. They can also be interlaced, allowing the image to be progressively displayed while its file is still being downloaded to the browser. GIF images can also be animated. JPG images can select from a palette of up to 16.7 million colors, but can't be transparent or animated. A rule of thumb is to use JPG images when you want to include a photographic image, or a graphic using a gradient fill effect, where reducing the number of colors to 256 or less will negatively affect image quality (for example, by producing a banding effect). When you want to include a nonphotographic image, in most cases you should stick to using GIFs, because they're much less likely to require more than 256 colors to display effectively.

A relatively new image format that is rapidly gaining support on the Web is the PNG graphic format. Like GIF images, PNG images can have a color set to transparent and be progressively displayed while still being downloaded. Additionally, the PNG format supports up to 48-bit true color images (the JPG format supports up to 24-bit true color images). PNG, at first glance, offers the best of both GIF and JPG. The latest versions of Navigator and Internet Explorer support PNG graphics. Paint Shop Pro, available on the CD-ROM, can open, edit, and save PNG images. The only holdup is that there are still a lot of older browsers in use. The best advice, unless you want to create a Web site aimed only at the latest browsers, is to stick with GIF and JPG.

The IMG (Image) tag is an empty, or stand-alone, element. Its form is:

```
<IMG SRC="imagefile">
```

The SRC (Source) attribute is a required attribute that identifies the full or partial address (URL) or the name of the file to display. Now, insert an inline graphic into your HTML file:

```
<P>The inline graphic, SAMPLE.GIF, is displayed here:</P>
<P><IMG SRC="sample.gif">
```

Notice that the IMG tag follows a P (Paragraph) tag. That's because the IMG tag inserts an *inline* image—so if you want an image to be displayed on its own line, you need to precede it by a P or other block element tag.

■ ■

 TIP If the graphics file you want to display as an inline graphic resides in the same folder as its HTML file, you only need to refer to the name of the graphics file, "sample.gif," for instance, rather than its whole address. Any of the sample graphic files you've copied from the CD-ROM to C:\HTML can be included in any HTML file you save in the same folder, just by including its file name in the IMG tag.

■ ■

Figure 2.26 shows SAMPLE.GIF as an inline image in a Web browser.

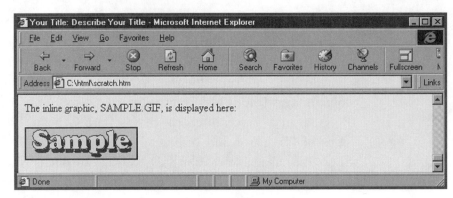

Figure 2.26

All graphical Web browsers can display inline graphic images.

You can link to a graphics file anywhere on the Web and display it on your own Web page by using the IMG (Image) tag. For instance, you might do something like this:

```
<IMG SRC="http://www.anywhere.com/some.gif">
```

Doing so is generally frowned upon on the Web. Not only might you be violating somebody's copyright, you most certainly would be generating traffic on his server so you can display a particular inline image on your Web page. Also, he can tell you are doing it, and trace it back to you. It may not be against the law, but he could complain to whoever is running your server and maybe get you kicked off your server. Bottom line: it's not the way to make friends on the Web.

It's perfectly okay to link to others' Web pages, though. That's how you make friends on the Web. Just don't claim their Web stuff as your own. And if they give you permission to use any of their graphics, you can download them to your server and include them on your own Web page. But don't just go around downloading and using other people's graphics. Plenty of repositories of public domain graphics exist on the Web. See Appendix A, "The Web Resources Directory," for references to where you can find public domain graphics on the Web.

Using the ALT Attribute

The ALT attribute can be included in the IMG tag to help identify an image. In the newer browsers, for instance, if you pass the cursor over an image, the contents of any included ALT attribute will be displayed. Also, since surfing the Web can often be like wading through hip-deep molasses, there are a lot of people who surf the Web with the display of images turned off in order to help speed things up. And there are still a lot of people using text-based browsers that don't display images at all. Using the ALT attribute will cue these surfers in on what an image is.

Here's an example of how to use the ALT attribute with your IMG tags:

```
<IMG SRC="sample.gif" ALT="">
```

The above example viewed in Lynx would show nothing. On a Web browser that has image loading turned off, the ALT="" attribute value has no effect.

To have a message replace [Image] in Lynx or display along with the dummy graphic in a graphical browser with the graphics turned off, enter the following:

```
<IMG SRC="sample.gif" ALT="A sample graphic">
```

This example, when viewed in Lynx, displays the message "A sample graphic" rather than just "[Image]." For a graphical Web browser with image-loading turned off, the message "A sample graphic" would appear alongside the dummy graphic, as shown in Figure 2.27.

Figure 2.27

SAMPLE.GIF is shown here, first without the ALT attribute and then with the ALT attribute, as displayed in Navigator with the display of images turned off.

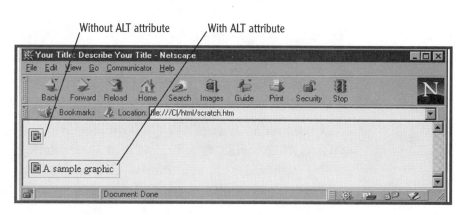

NOTE

If an image is decorative and serves no informational purpose, use the ALT attribute with a blank attribute value (ALT=""). That way, you don't clutter up a Web page in a text-only browser with [Image] references. If your graphic has informational import, you should always include an ALT attribute text string (ALT="Georgy-Porgy's Home Page" or ALT="Diagram of the X-27P Circuit Board" or something like that). This is especially important where an image is being used by itself to perform a function, such as displaying the title of a Web page in a banner graphic (where no corresponding H1 element is included), or functioning as a navigational icon or image link where no text is included on the Web page to describe what the link is. Including an ALT attribute will allow somebody using a text-only browser or a graphical Web browser with graphics turned off to see what is going on.

Using the ALIGN Attribute in Inline Graphics

The ALIGN attribute allows you to position an inline image relative to the line of text that it is on. All current graphical Web browsers should recognize these values: "top," "middle," and "bottom."

Insert an inline graphic using the "top" ALIGN value:

```
<P>The image on this line <IMG ALIGN="top" SRC="top.gif">
is top-aligned.
```

Here's an example of the "middle" ALIGN value:

```
<P>The image on this line <IMG ALIGN="middle"
SRC="middle.gif"> is middle-aligned.
```

Insert an inline graphic using the "bottom" ALIGN value:

```
<P>The image on this line <IMG ALIGN="bottom"
SRC="bottom.gif"> is bottom-aligned.
```

Figure 2.28 shows these examples as they appear in a Web browser.

There are two additional ALIGN attributes that can be included in the IMG tag, "left" and "right," that I'll show you how to use in this afternoon's Intermediate HTML Tutorial. These are HTML 3.2 attributes that

are used to wrap text around an image, rather than align an image horizontally on a page. To center-align or right-align an image on a page, you need to use another method, which I'll also show you in this afternoon's tutorial.

Using Relative URLs

When creating a hypertext link or inserting an inline image, you don't always need to specify a full, or absolute, URL or Web address. If a Web page or file to which you are linking, or a graphic file you are inserting into your Web page, is in the same folder or on the same server (in the same domain), you can leave off those parts of the URL that are common to both. A URL that provides only those parts of a Web address that are not common to both the linking and the linked file is often called a partial URL. One of the advantages of using this type of URL, apart from being shorter, is that you can move a Web page and its locally linked files from one directory to another, and even from one server to another, without having to redo the links.

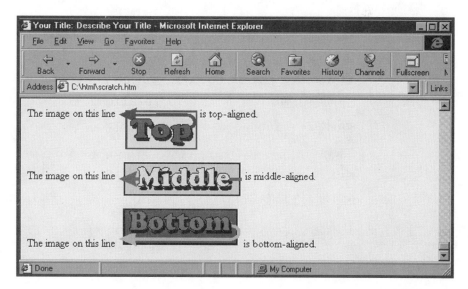

Figure 2.28

Inline images can be aligned relative to the baseline of the line they are on.

You have already used some partial URLs. For instance, <IMG SRC="sample.gif"> uses a partial URL. The full, or absolute, URL would be `file:///C|/html/sample.gif`, which is what the full URL for a local file on your own hard drive looks like. If you used the full URL here, you wouldn't be able to put your Web page, along with any included inline images, up onto the Web without having to redo all your links. You want to create and test your Web pages on your computer and FTP them up to your Web site (when you get one) on your server without having to redo any of the links.

Linking to a File in a Subdirectory of the Linking Page's Directory

If C:\HTML is the directory where you currently store your HTML files, you might want to store your graphic files in C:\HTML\IMAGES. You could then use a relative or partial URL (rather than an absolute or full URL) to display the graphic, like this:

```
<IMG SRC="images/sample.gif">
```

If you plan to create a Web site that uses multiple subpages, you might want to store your subpages in a separate directory from your home page. For example, if your home page is in the \HTML directory and the subpage (SUBPAGE.HTM) to which you want to link is in the \PAGE\SUBPAGES directory, a hypertext link between the two might look like this:

```
<A HREF="subpages/subpage.htm">
```

The two previous examples would indicate a directory structure something like this:

```
\HTML - | - \IMAGES
        |
        | - \SUBPAGES
```

Linking to a File in a Subdirectory of a Directory in Which Your HTML File Is a Subdirectory

Suppose your HTML files are stored in /PUB/HTML, but your graphic files are stored in /PUB/IMAGES. To display an inline image, FLOWER.GIF, stored in /PUB/IMAGES, you would use this partial URL in your Web page:

```
<IMG SRC="../images/sample.gif">
```

Or, suppose you want to insert a hypertext link in the same Web page mentioned earlier, /PUB/HTML, to another Web page, PRICES.HTM, stored in a parallel directory, /PUB/SALES. For this, the hypertext link between the two would look like this:

```
<A HREF="../sales/prices.htm">
```

The two previous examples would then indicate a directory structure like this:

```
\PUB-|-\HTML
     |
     |-\IMAGES
     |
     |-\SALES
```

Using Horizontal Rules

The HR (Horizontal Rule) tag is a stand-alone, or empty, document element that allows you to add horizontal rules to your Web pages. Set up a text paragraph followed by an HR tag:

```
<P>A horizontal rule is displayed below this line.
<HR>
```

Figure 2.29 shows a horizontal rule displayed in Netscape Navigator.

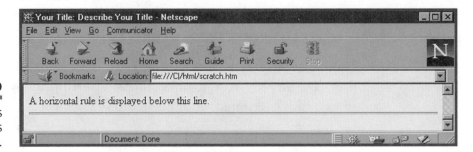

Figure 2.29

Navigator displays
a horizontal rule as
a shaded line.

You can use certain additional attribute values to alter the appearance of horizontal rules. You probably have noticed on the Web horizontal rules of different colors, shades, and effects. These are actually graphic files inserted as inline graphics. The Intermediate HTML Tutorial covers how to assign attribute values to HR tags and how to include multicolor graphic lines in your Web pages.

Signing Your Work

You generally use the ADDRESS tag to define a signature block for your Web page. It might contain your name, title, organizational or business affiliation, and information on how to contact you. A horizontal rule usually separates an address from the rest of a Web page.

Following the HR tag you created in the last example, type some address text separated into individual lines by BR tags:

```
<HR>
<ADDRESS>
Ricardo De Caro<BR>
Fantastic Creations, Inc.<BR>
(800) 569-8432<BR>
</ADDRESS>
</HTML>
```

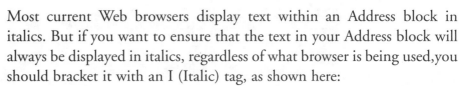
Most current Web browsers display text within an Address block in italics. But if you want to ensure that the text in your Address block will always be displayed in italics, regardless of what browser is being used, you should bracket it with an I (Italic) tag, as shown here:

```
<HR>
<ADDRESS>
<I>
Ricardo De Caro<BR>
Fantastic Creations, Inc.<BR>
(800) 569-8432<BR>
</I>
</ADDRESS>
```

TIP Substitute your own name, company name, phone number, or whatever.

Adding a Mailto Link to Your Address

You can also add a Mailto link, which is a hypertext link, to your e-mail address. When a user clicks on a Mailto link, the browser pops up a form that allows the reader to send a message to the e-mail address in the link. See Figure 2.30 for an example of a Mailto pop-up window in Netscape Navigator.

Not all browsers support Mailto links. Internet Explorer 3.0 requires that Internet Mail be installed. Internet Explorer 4.0 requires that you have Outlook Express installed. Even if your browser supports Mailto links, it has to be configured properly. Therefore, no matter which way you cut it, you are going to have viewers who can't use a Mailto link.

Does that mean you should avoid Mailto links? Absolutely not! The solution is to make sure that your full e-mail address is the link text for your Mailto link. This means you need to enter your e-mail address twice for a Mailto link, as shown in the following example. That way, if someone

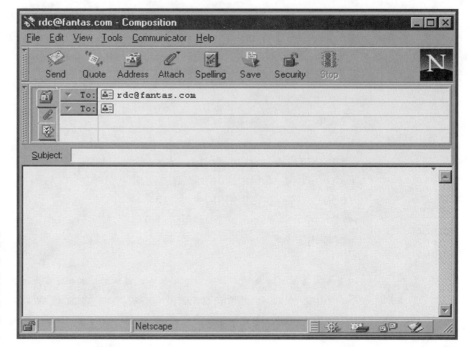

Figure 2.30

When you click on a Mailto link, you can send an e-mail message to the address included in the link.

can't use your Mailto link, he or she can always click and drag to copy your e-mail address or just write it down and then send you a message using his or her regular e-mail client. Go ahead and add the following Mailto link to your Address block:

```
<HR>
<ADDRESS>
<I>
Ricardo De Caro<BR>
Fantastic Creations, Inc.<BR>
(800) 569-8432<BR>
<A HREF="mailto:rdc@fantas.com">rdc@fantas.com</A><BR>
</I>
</ADDRESS>
```

TIP Feel free to substitute your own e-mail address in this example in place of the sample e-mail address.

Adding Your URL to Your Address

If your home page is different from the page you are currently creating, you might want to add a hypertext link to it. Of course, since you haven't actually created any Web pages yet, you don't have a home page. After you create your first Web page, you will undoubtedly want to create others. Your home page might then serve as an index to the rest of your pages. You could then include that URL in the Address block of each of your other Web pages, as follows:

```
<HR>
<ADDRESS>
<I>
Ricardo De Caro<BR>
Fantastic Creations, Inc.<BR>
(800) 569-8432<BR>
E-Mail: <A HREF="mailto:rdc@fantas.com">rdc@fantas.com</A><BR>
URL: <A HREF="http://www.fantas.com">http://www.fantas.com</A>
</I>
</ADDRESS>
```

Figure 2.31 shows how the final address section appears in a Web browser.

Save the HTML file you just created. You can use it later as a reference. When you first saved it, you named it SCRATCH.HTM. If more than one person is going to be doing this tutorial and you want to make sure that this file doesn't get overwritten, you might want to give it a new name, such as using your first initial and last name for the file name (JMILLER.HTM, for instance, if your name is John Miller).

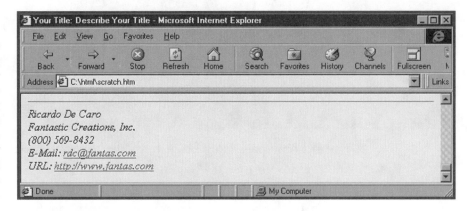

Figure 2.31

An Address block might contain your name, company name, street address, phone numbers, and a Mailto link to your e-mail address and a hypertext link to your home page.

What's Next?

You should now have a working knowledge of basic HTML. Don't worry if you don't remember or fully understand everything that you've done in this tutorial; the best way to learn is by doing. You've also saved your scratch pad file, either as SCRATCH.HTM or with another name you've given it, so you can come back and use it as a reference later. Feel free to load it into your text editor and view it in your Web browser to refamiliarize yourself with how a particular tag works.

The Basic HTML Tutorial has covered everything you need to know to be able to plan and create your first Web page. If doing the Basic HTML Tutorial has taken you most or all of the day, or you just feel you have reached the point of information overload for today, feel free to skip the following sessions. The Intermediate HTML Tutorial and the Tables Tutorial are both optional to do tomorrow's work. I'll see you tomorrow morning for the Sunday Morning session, "Planning Your First Web Page."

If you still have time and energy left over after doing the Basic HTML Tutorial and are ready for more, take a break, get up and stretch those muscles, and get a bite to eat. I'll see you back in a bit for the Intermediate HTML Tutorial.

The Intermediate HTML Tutorial

- ✪ Working with Text
- ✪ Working with Images
- ✪ Working with Lists
- ✪ Working with Rules

This tutorial is optional. The Basic HTML Tutorial covers everything you need to know for tomorrow, and you should finish it before attempting to do this afternoon's tutorial. After doing both tutorials, you'll have that much more to put into practice when you create your first Web page.

The Intermediate HTML Tutorial covers:

✪ Some HTML 2.0 features not covered in the Basic HTML Tutorial, including creating banner graphics and image links

✪ Most of HTML 3.2, including wrapping text around images, creating indented icon link lists, and making font size, color, and face changes

✪ A few of the new HTML 4.0 features, including marking insertions and deletions, and an example of applying styles to a span of text

This tutorial does not cover the more advanced features of HTML such as forms, scripts or applets, embedded objects, style sheets, or frames. Tables, although not covered in this tutorial, are covered in a separate bonus tutorial that you can do this evening if you have the time and energy. In Appendix A, "The Web Resources Directory," you'll also find many links to where you can find out about using these more advanced HTML features. Another good reference is Prima's *Learn HTML In a Weekend*, which includes software tutorials for creating frames, forms, image maps, and GIF animations.

NOTE   You should have already installed the example graphic files for this tutorial at the start of the Basic HTML Tutorial. If you haven't installed these files, please return to "Loading the Example Files" in the Saturday Morning session before doing this tutorial.

Running Your Web Browser and Text Editor

Run your Web browser, preferably offline, so you'll be able to check the results of your work in your browser while doing this tutorial. You can easily hop back and forth between Notepad and your Web browser, dynamically updating your work as you go.

To deal with this tutorial, you need a Web browser that is HTML 3.2-compliant. You should use Netscape Navigator 2.0 or greater or Microsoft Internet Explorer 3.0 or greater to do this tutorial. If you don't currently have either of these browsers installed, I've included Opera, an excellent HTML 3.2-compliant Web browser, on the CD-ROM.

If you want to be able to do the HTML 4.0 sections of this tutorial, you should use the latest version of Netscape Navigator or Microsoft Internet Explorer. I've tested this tutorial with the release versions of Navigator 4.04 and Internet Explorer 4.01. If you are using an earlier browser than these, feel free to skip the few HTML 4.0 sections I've included—you can do them later, after you've downloaded one of these latest versions (hey, those are *big* downloads, after all, and time's a wasting).

Run the text editor you want to use to edit HTML files. As mentioned earlier, I recommend using Notepad until you master the fundamentals of HTML. In Windows 3.1, you can usually find Notepad in the Accessories window in Program Manager. In Windows 95, you can find it on the Start Menu, under Programs and Accessories.

 TIP
When you first open Notepad, Word Wrap is not turned on. To turn on Word Wrap, select Edit, then Word Wrap (so that it is checked).

Loading Your Starting Template

Load the starting template you saved this morning, C:\HTML\START.HTM. It should look like the following listing (if you didn't save the template, just retype it now):

```
<HTML>
<HEAD>
<TITLE>Your Title: Describe Your Title</TITLE>
</HEAD>
<BODY>
</BODY>
</HTML>
```

 NOTE
If you substituted a Title element of your own for "Your Title: Describe Your Title," don't worry if your version of START.HTM differs in this regard. Otherwise, your START.HTM should look like my example.

Save your "scratch pad" file that you'll be using in this afternoon's tutorial. In Notepad, select File, Save As. Change the folder where you are going to save your file to C:\HTML, then save your file as SCRATCH2.HTM.

Working with Text

This section covers some nifty things that you can do when working with text, including using additional HTML 3.2 text highlighting tags, using

HTML 4.0 text highlighting tags, and right-aligning and center-aligning paragraphs, headings, and other document sections.

HTML 3.2 Text Highlighting Tags

HTML 3.2 recognizes a number of character rendering tags, including the SUP (Superscript), SUB (Subscript), U (Underline), and STRIKE (Strikethrough) tags.

SUP, SUB, and U are HTML 3.0 tags that have been implemented widely in current browsers. The STRIKE tag was a proposed HTML 2.0 tag that never made it to the final cut, but nonetheless gained wide acceptance from browsers anyway. An S tag for strikethrough was proposed for HTML 3.0, but was dropped in favor of STRIKE in HTML 3.2.

The SUP and SUB tags are highly useful tags that you should use wherever you need superscripts or subscripts. The STRIKE command comes in handy mainly when you're using the Web in workgroup document preparation processes, rather than for displaying final renditions. Most current Web browsers support these tags.

The U tag is supported by Navigator 3.0 and greater. Internet Explorer and a number of other browsers support the U tag. Because there are still quite a few people using Navigator 2.0, it may be a good idea to avoid the U tag. If you want to emphasize text, you may want to consider using the EM tag.

To check out how these tags look in your browser, enter the following:

```
<P>This is regular text. <SUP>Use SUP for super-
scripts.</SUP> This is regular text. <SUB>Use SUB for
subscripts.</SUB> This is regular text. <U>Use U for
underlining.</U> This is regular text. <STRIKE>Use STRIKE
for strikethrough.</STRIKE>
```

Figure 3.1 shows how this appears in an HTML 3.2–compliant Web browser.

Figure 3.1

In HTML 3.2, you can add superscripting, subscripting, underlining, and strikethrough to text.

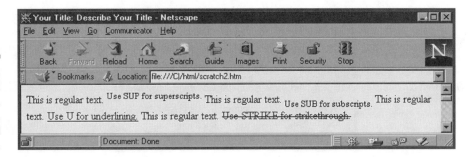

 TIP

■ ■

Many browsers don't display superscripts or subscripts. To account for these browsers, enclose superscripts or subscripts within parentheses to set them apart from preceding or following text. For instance, to include a superscripted trademark symbol, you might type:

```
Xerox<SUP>(TM)</SUP>
```

That way, it appears in Lynx as "Xerox(TM)" rather than as "XeroxTM." In a browser that supports superscripting, you're stuck with the parentheses—but who ever said it was a perfect world?

■ ■

HTML 4.0 Text Highlighting Tags

A number of new text highlighting tags have been incorporated in HTML 4.0. These include the DEL (Delete), INS (Insert), S (Strikethrough), Q (Quote), and SPAN tags. The DEL and INS tags are only supported by the 4.0 version of Internet Explorer. The 4.0 version of Navigator does not support either of these tags. Neither browser supports the Q tag, but both support the S tag. The SPAN tag is supported by the 4.0 versions of both Navigator and Internet Explorer.

The DEL and INS tags allow you to mark deletions and insertions in an HTML file. Enter the following for an example of using these tags:

```
<P><DEL>This text is marked for deletion.</DEL> This is
regular text. <INS>This text is marked for insertion.</INS>
```

Figure 3.2 shows how this appears in Internet Explorer 4.01.

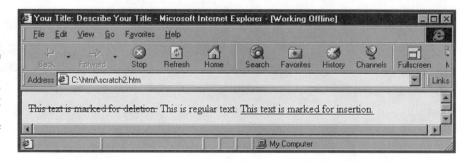

Figure 3.2

In HTML 4.0, you
can mark deletions
and insertions, but
this only works in
the latest version of
Internet Explorer.

NOTE There are two attributes, CITE and DATETIME, that can be used with the DEL and INS tags. The CITE attribute is used to reference a URL where information about the reviser can be referenced. The DATETIME attribute can be used to include the date and time of the revision (DATETIME="19980213", for instance, to reference February 13, 1998 as the revision date). However, the values included with these attributes are not displayed in Internet Explorer 4.01, the only browser that supports these tags. Pretty pointless, unless you are using a third-party software tool to automate workgroup HTML document revision. If you are into hand-coding your HTML, don't bother.

The S (Strikethrough) tag works exactly the same as the STRIKE or DEL tags. Even though it is supported by the latest versions of both Navigator and Internet Explorer, it is hardly worth bothering with because earlier versions of Navigator don't support it. The Q (Quote) tag, on the other hand, could be quite useful. It is supposed to be a "smart" container tag that will automatically detect if quotation marks are already present and, if absent, add the quotes that are appropriate to the language type that has been specified for the page. Unfortunately, no browser supports this tag.

The SPAN tag is a kind of general-purpose text highlighting element. By itself, it does absolutely nothing, but in a style sheet, it comes to life. For an example of how the SPAN tag works with a style sheet, enter the following:

```
<P>Regular text. <SPAN>Unspanned text.</SPAN> Regular text.
```

Next, nest the following inside the HEAD element, right after the TITLE element:

```
<TITLE>Your Title: Describe Your Title</TITLE>
<STYLE type="text/css">
<!--
SPAN {font-family: sans-serif; font-style: italic; font-size: 125%; color: #FF8000}
-->
</STYLE>
</HEAD>
```

NOTE

You'll notice the comment tags (<!-- and -->) in the previous example. The STYLE tag can actually be placed anywhere in an HTML file, not just in the HEAD element. A Web browser that is savvy to styles will ignore the comment tags, while one that isn't will read the contents of the Style tag as a comment and not display any of it. So, why use the comment tags in the HEAD element? If you don't include the comment tags, search engine robots are liable to index and display your STYLE tag, rather than the first sentences or paragraph of your page.

Figure 3.3 shows how this appears in a Web browser that supports using Cascading Style Sheets.

Figure 3.3

In HTML 4.0, you can use the SPAN tag to apply a style to a "span" of text.

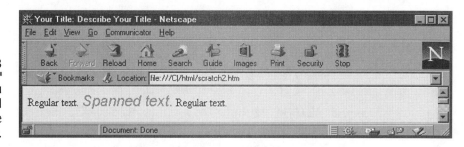

Aligning Paragraphs, Headings, and Divisions

You can align paragraphs, headings, or other document divisions in a number of ways in HTML 3.2. You can use the ALIGN attribute with paragraphs or headings to center-align, right-align, or left-align these elements. The DIV tag can also use the ALIGN attribute. Additionally, you can use the CENTER tag to center-align any of the divisions noted here, plus many other document elements. The following sections look at each of these individually.

Aligning Headings and Paragraphs

In HTML 3.2, you can use the ALIGN attribute to center-align or right-align headings and paragraphs by using an attribute value of either "center" or "right" ("left" is the default). For instance, to center-align a level-two heading, you would tag your heading like this:

```
<H2 ALIGN="center">Your Heading Here</H2>
```

You would right-align a level-two heading like this:

```
<H2 ALIGN="right">Your Heading Here</H2>
```

You would center-align or right-align paragraph text in exactly the same way as you would with headings. For instance, to center-align a text paragraph, you would tag your paragraph like this:

```
<P ALIGN="center">Your paragraph text here.
```

You would right-align a text paragraph like this:

```
<P ALIGN="right">Your paragraph text here.
```

To see what this looks like in your browser, enter the following, save your file, and hop over to your browser to check it out:

```
<H3 ALIGN="right">This is a Right-Aligned Level-Three
Heading</H3>
<P ALIGN="right">This is a right-aligned text paragraph.
This is a right-aligned text paragraph. This is a right-
aligned text paragraph. This is a right-aligned text
paragraph.
```

```
<H3 ALIGN="center">This is a Center-Aligned Level-Three
Heading</H3>
```

```
<P ALIGN="center">This is a center-aligned text para-
graph. This is a center-aligned text paragraph. This is
a center-aligned text paragraph. This is a center-aligned
text paragraph.
```

Figure 3.4 shows how this appears in a Web browser that supports horizontal-alignment of headings and paragraphs.

Aligning Document Divisions

The DIV tag defines a division within a document. Within it you can nest and align headings, paragraphs, unordered and ordered lists, definition lists, preformatted text, address blocks, tables, and even images.

The DIV tag is an HTML 3.2 element that was previously an HTML 3.0 proposed tag. It allows you to block tag a whole section (a division) of a document as center or right-aligned.

Enter the following for an example of using the DIV tag to apply center-alignment to a document division that includes a level-two heading, a paragraph, and a bullet list:

```
<DIV ALIGN="center">
<H2>Level-Two Heading</H2>
<P>This paragraph, and the level-two heading above it, is
centered using the DIV tag's ALIGN attribute.
<UL>
<LI>First list item.
<LI>Second list item.
</UL>
</DIV>
```

Figure 3.5 shows how this appears in a Web browser.

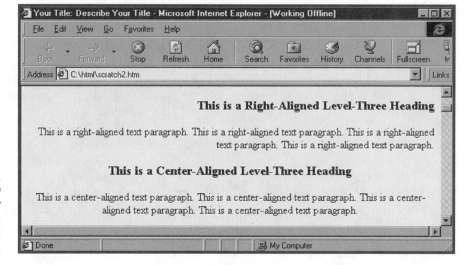

Figure 3.4

Figure 3.4

You can right- or center-align headings and paragraphs.

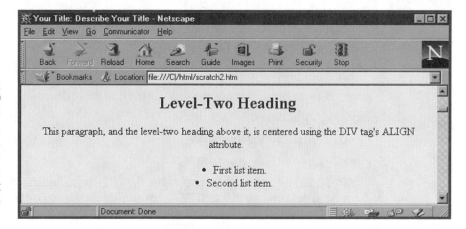

Figure 3.5

You can center- or right-align a document division, here including a heading, paragraph text, and a bullet list, using the DIV tag.

The DIV tag also works well for aligning images. For an example of using the DIV tag to align inline images, see "Working with Images" later in this session.

Style sheets, which are part of HTML 4.0, make this tag even more useful, allowing users to apply different formatting or display characteristics to different sections of a document, such as a table of contents, an

index, or a glossary. For links to where you can find more information on using style sheets, see Appendix A, "The Web Resources Directory."

ON THE

CD

A shareware software program, CoffeeCup StyleSheet Maker++, can help automate creating HTML style sheets for your Web pages. For even more tools for creating style sheets, see Appendix B, "The Web Tools Directory."

Using the CENTER Tag

The CENTER tag is a Netscape extension that is included in HTML 3.2, where it represents a shortcut for <DIV ALIGN="center">. Anything that can be nested inside a DIV element can also be nested in a CENTER element. All three major browsers support use of the CENTER tag.

For an example of using the CENTER element to center-align text and other document elements, copy and paste the text you just entered as an example of using the DIV tag, then edit it, replacing <DIV ALIGN="center"> and </DIV> with <CENTER> and </CENTER>, so it looks like this:

```
<CENTER>
<H2>Level-Two Heading</H2>
<P>This paragraph, and the level-two heading above it,
is centered-aligned using the CENTER tag.
<UL>
<LI>First list item.
<LI>Second list item.
</UL>
</CENTER>
```

The end result in your browser should look the same as using the DIV tag with center-alignment set, as shown previously in Figure 3.5.

■■■■■■■■■■■■■■■■■■■■■■■■■■■■■■■■■■■■■■■

TIP   Some older browsers support the CENTER tag (Navigator 2.0, for instance), but not the DIV tag. Some other browsers may support the DIV tag but ignore the CENTER tag. To cover all bases, just combine both at the same time:

```
<CENTER><DIV ALIGN="center">The text to be
centered.</DIV></CENTER>
```

■■■■■■■■■■■■■■■■■■■■■■■■■■■■■■■■■■■■■■■

Working with Images

The Basic HTML Tutorial covered adding inline images to your Web page, as well as top-aligning, middle-aligning, and bottom-aligning an inline image relative to a line of text. It also covered using the ALT attribute with inline images to make life easier for users of text-only browsers or graphical browsers with the graphics turned off. This section of the Intermediate HTML Tutorial covers several additional things you can do with inline images: using a banner graphic, right-aligning or center-aligning graphics, wrapping text around a graphic, and creating image links.

Adding a Banner Graphic

A banner graphic is an inline image that runs along the top of your Web page. It might be your company name or logo, or a piece of art to add some graphic appeal and pizazz to your page. You don't have to create a banner graphic right now—the following example uses a sample banner graphic I've created.

If you want to create your own banner graphic, use a graphic editor like Paint Shop Pro to create a GIF file. You want to keep your graphic to less than 600×150 pixels (my sample is 595×134 pixels).

To add a banner graphic to your Web page, go to the top of your Web page and add the following:

```
<BODY>
<P ALIGN="center"><IMG SRC="banner.gif">
<H1 ALIGN="center">The Intermediate HTML Tutorial</H1>
```

Even if your banner graphic takes up most or all of the screen, it is a good idea to place it on a center-aligned paragraph. That way, it will always be centered, regardless of the screen resolution. I also included a centered level-one heading, since it is fairly common for a banner graphic to be followed by the main heading for the page.

Also, in this example, the SRC attribute uses a relative URL, the file name of the banner graphic file. As long as an image is in the same folder as the Web page in which you want to display it, you only need to use the file name as the SRC attribute value. (For more information on absolute versus relative URLs, see "Using Relative URLs," in the Saturday Morning session.) Figure 3.6 shows how your page should look after you add the banner graphic.

Reducing Image Size

Graphic images take up major disk space and can take a long time for the reader to download. For this reason, smart Web publishers do everything they can to reduce the size of the images they use on their Web pages.

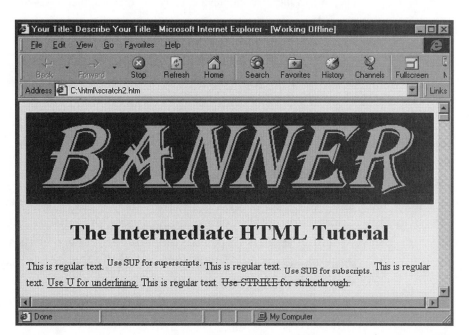

Figure 3.6

A banner graphic runs across the top of a Web page.

One way to manipulate the size of an image is to change its format. Although all the sample graphics used in this book are GIF-format graphics, most current Web browsers allow you to display both GIF and JPG graphics as inline images. GIF graphics are limited to 256 colors, while JPG graphics can have up to 16.7 million colors. JPG graphics also use a compression scheme that can make a continuous-tone color or grayscale photograph smaller than a corresponding GIF image. With images other than photos, a GIF file is almost always smaller than a JPG file. So, if you want to include continuous-tone photographic images, JPG is the best format to use. For other images, stick to GIFs.

NOTE JPG files use what is called "lossy" compression, which achieves file size reductions by selectively subtracting pixels from the image. If the compression ratio is set too high, it can have a deleterious effect on image quality. Finding the right compression ratio for a JPG image usually takes a bit of experimenting—you need to save an image, check out the results, and adjust the compression level until you find the best mix to keep your image sizes down (very important on the Web!). You also need to be aware that if you open a JPG file that you have already compressed, then resave it, the file will be compressed all over again (applying a 50% compression ratio, for instance, to an image that has already been compressed at a 50% ratio). So, you should only apply a compression ratio to a JPG file the first time you save it, making sure you turn off compression if you reload and resave the same file.

Another way to reduce the size of your graphics file is to reduce its color depth. Many graphic editors and photo-paint programs, such as Paint Shop Pro or LView Pro, allow this.

You can switch the color palette of the image to one that supports fewer colors (from 256 colors to 16 colors, for instance). However, while switching to a color palette that supports fewer or different colors than those in the original image will shrink the file size, it may also result in a significant loss of image quality. One solution is to create an "adaptive palette" that matches the actual colors in the graphic. For instance, you

might have a palette of 16 colors, but an image that has only eight colors in it—by creating an adaptive palette that has only those specific eight colors in it, you could significantly reduce the size of the file with no loss in image quality.

Setting Image Height and Width

HTML 3.2 allows you to specify the height and width of an inline graphic. Normally, a Web browser has to download an image before it can allocate space for it on a Web page. This means that if you have a relatively large graphic, everything else has to wait until the image downloads. A banner graphic, usually the largest graphic on your page, can be especially guilty of this.

However, if you set the dimensions of the graphic using the HEIGHT and WIDTH attributes of the IMG tag, Netscape Navigator and Internet Explorer can allocate space for the graphic and then display the remainder of the page without waiting for the banner graphic to download completely. So if you want to use a banner graphic that takes longer to load than it takes ice to melt, be gracious and set the height and width of the image. To add WIDTH and HEIGHT attributes to your banner graphic:

```
<P ALIGN="center"><IMG SRC="banner.gif" WIDTH="595"
HEIGHT="134">
```

The dimensions set here are the actual dimensions of the graphic. Using dimensions other than the actual ones provides no immediate advantage in this case. You could increase the dimensions of a smaller graphic to fit, but image quality would probably suffer. Likewise, you could reduce the dimensions of a larger graphic to fit, but that would be a waste of bandwidth—better that you reduce it to fit in your graphic editor, rather than on your Web page.

Many Web gurus will tell you to set the WIDTH and HEIGHT attributes for all images you want to include in a Web page. I don't bother doing this for small graphics such as icon bullets, but I do include them in any other images. I also don't bother to include these attributes in the other sample images that are used in this tutorial, since the scratch pad file you are creating will only be viewed by you locally. If you were to put the tutorial up on the Web as a regular Web page (*not* something I recommend!), you would probably want to add WIDTH and HEIGHT attributes to any images other than really small ones.

Using Width Percentages

You can also specify a percentage for the WIDTH attribute in the IMG tag. For instance, you could set WIDTH to 75%, like this:

```
<P ALIGN="center"><IMG SRC="banner.gif" WIDTH="75%">
```

This will automatically resize the graphic so it will fill 75% of the browser window, regardless of the screen resolution or the width of the browser window. The height of the graphic will be resized relative to the height. Setting the HEIGHT attribute to a percentage should be avoided. Also, realize that older browsers that don't support WIDTH percentages will display the image at its actual size.

Using Interlaced and Transparent GIF Graphics

An interlaced GIF will load progressively over several passes, generating what has been called a venetian blind effect. It allows the reader to see what the image is going to be before it comes through. A transparent GIF is a GIF graphic that has one of its colors set to transparent, allowing any background color or background image to show through the graphic. This can be handy if you want your graphic to look like it's floating on top of the background.

I cover creating interlaced and transparent GIF graphics in the Graphics Tutorial that is scheduled as a bonus session for Sunday evening. See also Appendix A, "The Web Resources Directory," for links to additional resources on creating transparent and interlaced GIFs that are available on the Web.

Aligning Images

The default alignment of an image is flush with the left margin. Contrary to what you might think, you can't use ALIGN attributes in the IMG tag to center- or right-align an image. The best way to horizontally align an image on your Web page is to place it in a center- or right-aligned paragraph. (You could also place it in a center- or right-aligned DIV tag, or inside a CENTER tag.) Go to the end of your file, just before the </BODY> and </HTML> end tags, and enter the following to right-align an image using paragraph alignment:

```
<P ALIGN="right"><IMG SRC="right.gif">
```

Figure 3.7 shows how a right-aligned graphic looks in a Web browser that supports paragraph alignment.

To center-align an image using paragraph alignment, do this:

```
<P ALIGN="center"><IMG SRC="center.gif">
```

Figure 3.8 shows how this appears in a Web browser that supports paragraph alignment.

Aligning Images Horizontally

You can also use the DIV or the CENTER tag to align an image. The CENTER tag is the more widely supported, but the DIV tag allows you to right-align an image as well.

If you choose to use the DIV tag to right-align an image, this is how you should do it:

```
<DIV ALIGN="right"><IMG SRC="right.gif"></DIV>
```

If you choose to use the DIV tag to center-align an image, this is how you should do it:

```
<DIV ALIGN="center"><IMG SRC="center.gif"></DIV>
```

You can also center-align an image using the CENTER tag. If you choose to do so, this is how you should do it:

```
<CENTER><IMG SRC="center.gif"></CENTER>
```

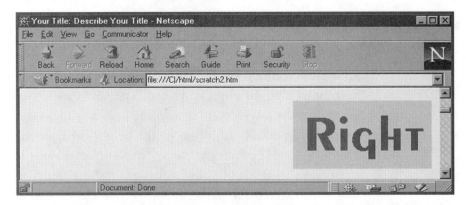

Figure 3.7

You can right-align an image in an HTML 3.2–compliant Web browser by placing it inside a right-aligned paragraph.

Figure 3.8

You can center-align an image in an HTML 3.2–compliant Web browser by placing it inside a center-aligned paragraph.

Wrapping Text around Images

In the Basic HTML Tutorial, you learned how to align an image relative to a line of text using the ALIGN attribute values of "top," "bottom," and "middle." In addition to these attribute values, HTML 3.2 allows you to set two additional ALIGN attribute values: "left" and "right." You might think that the purpose of these attributes is to align an image at either the left or right margin, but that's not so. Rather, these attributes are used to wrap text around the right side or left side of an image.

Wrapping Text around a Left-Aligned Image

Enter the following as an example of wrapping text around a left-aligned image:

```
<P><IMG ALIGN="left" SRC="left.gif">If you set left-
alignment in an inline image, the text will wrap around
the right side of the graphic. If you set left-alignment
in an inline image, the text will wrap around the right
side of the graphic. If you set left-alignment in an
inline image, the text will wrap around the right side
of the graphic.<BR CLEAR="left">
```

NOTE You're probably wondering what the <BR CLEAR="left"> code is doing at the end of the paragraph. You'll notice similar BR tags using the CLEAR attribute in some of the following examples. Their purpose is to *stop* the text from wrapping—otherwise, the following image is liable to wrap as well. Later, in "Using the BR Tag's CLEAR Attribute," I'll tell you more about using this attribute.

Wrapping Text around a Right-Aligned Image

Enter the following as an example of wrapping text around a right-aligned image:

```
<P><IMG ALIGN="right" SRC="right.gif">If you set right-
alignment in an inline image, the text will wrap around
the left side of the graphic. If you set right-alignment
in an inline image, the text will wrap around the left
side of the graphic. If you set right-alignment in an
inline image, the text will wrap around the left side of
the graphic.<BR CLEAR="right">
```

Figure 3.9 shows text wrapped around both a left-aligned and a right-aligned image in Netscape Navigator.

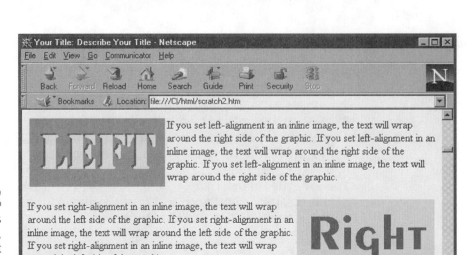

Figure 3.9

Using the IMG tag's ALIGN attribute, you can wrap text around the left or right side of an image.

You aren't limited to just wrapping text around an image. All other elements, including headings, lists, and other images, will wrap around an image with either left- or right-alignment set. (You don't have to do anything to make this happen, other than use a left- or right-aligned image. The trick is stopping it from happening. For that, see "Using the BR Tag's CLEAR Attribute," later in this tutorial.)

Adding Spacing between an Image and Wrapping Text

When you hopped over to take a look at the last few examples in your browser, you may have noticed that text wrapping around an image, especially around a left-aligned image, is not separated from the image by much space. To add spacing between wrapping text and a left- or right-aligned image, you can insert an HSPACE (Horizontal Space) attribute in the IMG tag. Edit the example you created for wrapping text around a left-aligned image and add the following to insert 10 pixels on either side of the image:

```
<P><IMG ALIGN="left" SRC="left.gif" HSPACE="10">If you
set left-alignment in an inline image, the text will
wrap around the right side of the graphic. If you set
left-alignment in an inline image, the text will wrap
around the right side of the graphic. If you set left-
alignment in an inline image, the text will wrap around
the right side of the graphic.<BR CLEAR="left">
```

Figure 3.10 shows what this looks like in a Web browser.

Flowing Text between Images

You can not only wrap text around the right or left side of an image, but flow text between two images. For example, enter the following:

```
<P><IMG ALIGN="left" SRC="left.gif"><IMG ALIGN="right"
SRC="right.gif">Text will flow between a left-aligned and
a right-aligned image. Text will flow between a left-
aligned and a right-aligned image.<BR CLEAR="all">
```

Figure 3.11 shows what this looks like in a Web browser.

Flowing an Image between Two Other Images

You can even flow a non-aligned image between a left-aligned image and a right-aligned one. To make this even slicker, stick the whole thing in a center-aligned paragraph, so the flowing, non-aligned image is centered between the two aligned images. This is a bit of a parlor trick, but both Navigator and Internet Explorer handle it fine. I've seen other browsers (including Opera, on this book's CD-ROM) flub it by not aligning the middle image evenly with the other images.

For an example of how to do this, enter the following:

```
<P><IMG ALIGN="left" SRC="one.gif"><IMG ALIGN="right"
SRC="three.gif"><P ALIGN="center"><IMG SRC="two.gif">
<BR CLEAR="all">
```

Notice above that two P (Paragraph) tags are used, the first at the start of the line and the second to center-align the image (TWO.GIF) you want to flow and center between the two other images (ONE.GIF and THREE.GIF).

See Figure 3.12 for what this should look like in a Web browser.

Figure 3.10

Using the IMG tag's
HSPACE attribute,
which adds space
to the left and right
of an image, you
can add space
between an image
and wrapping text.

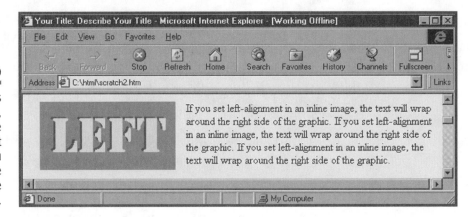

Figure 3.11

You can flow text
between a left-
aligned and a
right-aligned
image in an HTML
3.2–compliant
Web browser.

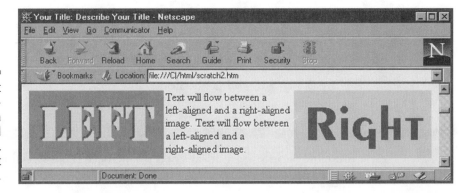

Figure 3.12

You can also flow
an image between
a left-aligned
and a right-
aligned image.

Using the BR Tag's CLEAR Attribute

The BR tag's CLEAR attribute, as its name indicates, is used to cause whatever follows to *clear* a left-aligned image, a right-aligned image, or both. In the previous examples, it was used to ensure that each following example cleared the previous one. If the BR tag's CLEAR attribute is set to "left," it causes whatever follows to clear and move down below a left-aligned image. A "right" attribute value causes whatever follows to clear a right-aligned image. An "all" attribute value causes whatever follows to clear a left-aligned or a right-aligned image, or both.

Clearing a Left-Aligned Image

To see how this works with a left-aligned graphic, insert the following into the example you just created for wrapping text around a left-aligned image (you can copy and paste it if you want):

```
<P><IMG ALIGN="left" SRC="left.gif">If you set left-
alignment in an inline image, the text will wrap around
the right side of the graphic.
<BR CLEAR="left">
If you set left-alignment in an inline image, the text
will wrap around the right side of the graphic. If you
set left-alignment in an inline image, the text will wrap
around the right side of the graphic.<BR CLEAR="left">
```

As Figure 3.13 shows, the CLEAR="left" attribute has the effect of moving all following text past a left-aligned graphic to a position where the left margin is clear.

Clearing a Right-Aligned Image

To see how this works with a right-aligned graphic, insert the following as indicated into the example you created for wrapping text around a right-aligned image (you can copy and paste it if you want):

```
<P><IMG ALIGN="right" SRC="right.gif">If you set right-
alignment in an inline image, the text will wrap around
the left side of the graphic.
```

```
<BR CLEAR="right">
```

```
If you set right-alignment in an inline image, the text
will wrap around the left side of the graphic. If you
set right-alignment in an inline image, the text will
wrap around the left side of the graphic.<BR
CLEAR="right">
```

As you can see in Figure 3.14, the CLEAR="right" attribute has the effect of moving all following text past a right-aligned graphic to a position where the right margin is clear.

Figure 3.13

A BR tag with CLEAR="left" set will cause following text to break past a left-aligned image.

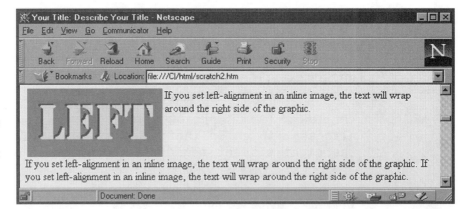

Figure 3.14

A BR tag with CLEAR="right" set will cause following text to break past a right-aligned image.

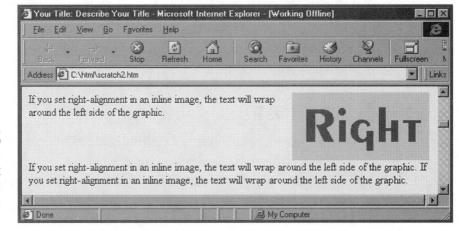

Clearing Both Left-Aligned and Right-Aligned Images

Finally, to see how this works when flowing text between both a left-aligned and a right-aligned graphic, insert the following into the example you created for flowing text between a left-aligned and a right-aligned image (you can copy and move it if you want):

```
<P><IMG ALIGN="left" SRC="left.gif"><IMG ALIGN="right"
SRC="right.gif">Text will flow between a left-aligned
and a right-aligned image.
<BR CLEAR="all">
Text will flow between a left-aligned and a right-aligned
image.<BR CLEAR="all">
```

As Figure 3.15 shows, the CLEAR="all" attribute has the effect of moving all following text past a left-aligned or a right-aligned graphic to a position where both margins are clear.

Working with Image Links

In the Basic HTML Tutorial, you learned how to place inline images on your page, and you also learned how to create hypertext links. What you haven't learned yet is how to create an inline image that functions as a hypertext link, where clicking on the image will activate the link. Hey, if you want to brag about knowing HTML, you've got to know how to create image links!

Figure 3.15

A BR tag with CLEAR="all" set will cause following text to break past both a left-aligned image and a right-aligned image.

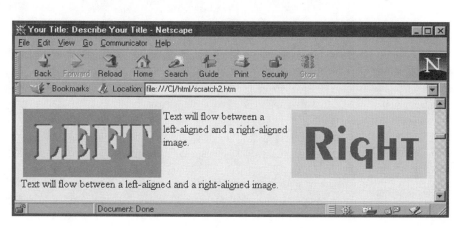

Including an Image in a Link

To activate an image as a hypertext link, you have nest it inside an A (Anchor) tag, like this:

```
<P><A HREF="link.htm">
<IMG SRC="link.gif">This is the text.</A>
```

TIP You'll be using this text in later examples. If you copy the example you just created to the Clipboard now (highlight it with the cursor and press Ctrl+C), you won't have to retype it later.

The file name in the previous example, "link.htm," is a dummy file name. In an actual link, you would need to insert the file name (if it's in the same directory) or the URL of an actual Web page. Figure 3.16 shows that when an image is placed inside a hypertext link, the image itself becomes a hot link.

NOTE If you include the ALIGN="right" attribute value in the IMG tag in the previous example, the image will be displayed flush to the right margin while still being included in the link.

Figure 3.16

The image, displayed with a blue border, and the link text, underlined with a blue line, are both part of the same hypertext link.

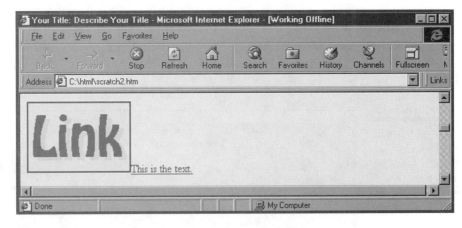

Using an Image Link by Itself

In the previous example, the link included both the image and the text, meaning that clicking on either one would activate the link. You can also specify the image as the link, but not the text. To do this in the example, you would move the </A> end tag so only the image is enclosed within the A (Anchor) start and end tags, like this:

```
<P><A HREF="link.htm">
<IMG SRC="link.gif"></A>This is the text.
```

Figure 3.17 shows how this looks in a Web browser.

Creating Navigational Icons

A navigational icon is often used when only a picture is enough to convey the action that will occur when the user activates the link. For instance, a left-hand arrow at the top or bottom of a page indicates returning to the previous page, a right-hand arrow indicates going to the next page, and a house indicates returning to the home page. You create a navigational icon by nesting only an image inside the A (Anchor) tag, without any accompanying text inside or outside the link.

To take care of text-only browsers or graphical browsers with graphics turned off, you should always include ALT text in a navigational icon's IMG tag, indicating that it's a link and describing what it links to. Here's an example of including ALT text in an image link:

```
<P><A HREF="prev.htm">
<IMG SRC="back.gif" ALT="Go to Previous Page"></A>
```

Figure 3.18 shows the navigational icon as it appears in a Web browser with the display of graphics turned on. Figure 3.19 shows this same image with the display of graphics turned off.

Figure 3.17

When you place the image inside the hypertext link, the image will function as the link.

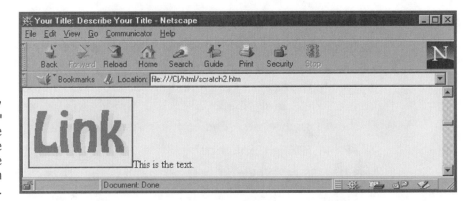

Figure 3.18

Navigation icons are usually displayed by themselves, without any accompanying text.

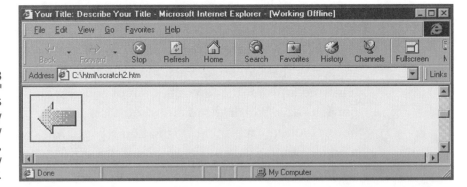

Figure 3.19

Including ALT text in the IMG tag for a navigation icon will clue in users who have turned the graphics display off or use a text-only browser.

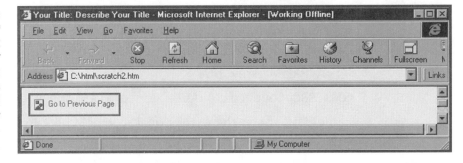

You'll have to exit and rerun Navigator before turning the display of graphics off will have an effect. If you are using Navigator, feel free to skip this right now if you wish. In Explorer, click on the Refresh button after

turning the graphics display off to cause the setting to take effect immediately. In case you want to try this, I've included the steps for Navigator 4.0 and Internet Explorer 4.0 to turn display of images off.

In Netscape Navigator 4.0 or greater:

1. Select Edit, Preferences, and select Advanced in the Categories menu.
2. Click on the "Automatically load images" check box so that it is unchecked. Click on OK.
3. Exit, then rerun Navigator.

In Internet Explorer 4.0 or greater:

1. Select View, Options (or Internet Options in Internet Explorer 4.1), and select the Advanced tab.
2. Under Multimedia, click on the "Show pictures" check box so that it is unchecked. Click on OK.
3. Click on the Refresh button (or press Ctrl+R).

Controlling the Border around an Image Link

The default width of the border around an image link is 2 pixels in Netscape Navigator. The IMG tag's BORDER attribute allows you to specify a custom width for the border. For instance, to increase the width of the border around the image link to 10 pixels, you would do the following:

TIP If you earlier copied the example text preceding Figure 3.16 to the Clipboard, you can paste it for each of the following examples, and edit it as shown.

```
<P><A HREF="link.htm">

<IMG SRC="link.gif" BORDER="10">This is the text.</A>
```

As shown in Figure 3.20, when you increase the border width to 10 pixels, you really increase it.

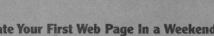

Figure 3.20

Using the
BORDER attribute
in the IMG tag,
you can increase
the width of the
border around an
image link.

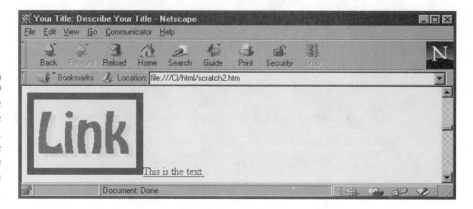

Turning the Image Link Border Off

Navigational icons often have their borders turned off. You may want to turn the border of an image link off in other situations. Edit the previous example to turn off the image link border:

```
<P><A HREF="link.htm">

<IMG SRC="link.gif" BORDER="0">This is the text.</A>
```

Figure 3.21 shows how this should look in a Web browser.

Positioning Link Text Relative to an Image Link

All the examples so far have lined the text up at the bottom and to the right of the image link. It might be nice to align the link text with the middle of the image. Just insert an ALIGN="middle" attribute value inside the IMG tag. For the example, copy and paste the first image link example that you used in "Including an Image in a Link" and then insert ALIGN="middle" in the IMG tag (or you can retype the whole example):

```
<P><A HREF="link.htm">

<IMG SRC="link.gif" ALIGN="middle">This is the
text.</A>
```

See Figure 3.22 for how this should look in a Web browser.

Figure 3.21

Sometimes you want an image without a border to be a link.

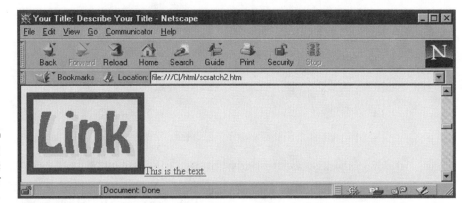

Figure 3.22

You can middle-align an image link relative to the link text.

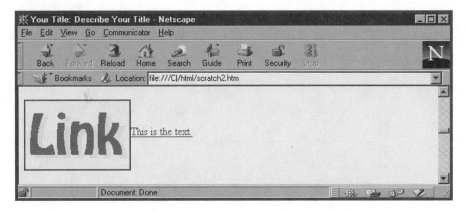

To align the link text with the top of the image link, just insert ALIGN="top" as the attribute value (ALIGN="bottom" is the default).

NOTE You can position only a single line of text relative to an image using ALIGN="top"—any additional lines will wrap below the image.

Horizontally Aligning an Image Link

You can also align an image link relative to the Web page by using an ALIGN attribute in the P (Paragraph) tag that contains the link. For

example, to center the link text and image link relative to the page, add the following:

```
<P ALIGN="center"><A HREF="link.htm">

<IMG SRC="link.gif" ALIGN="middle">This is the
text.</A>
```

Figure 3.23 shows the centered image and text.

Using a right-aligned paragraph in the HTML code for Figure 3.23 rather than a center-aligned one would cause the link text and image link to be right-aligned. Left-alignment, on the other hand, is the default.

Displaying the Link Text Underneath the Image Link

You can also center the link text under the image link by inserting a BR tag in front of the link text, as shown here:

```
<P ALIGN="center"><A HREF="link.htm">

<IMG SRC="link.gif" ALIGN="middle"><BR>This is the
text.</A>
```

Figure 3.24 shows how this looks in a Web browser.

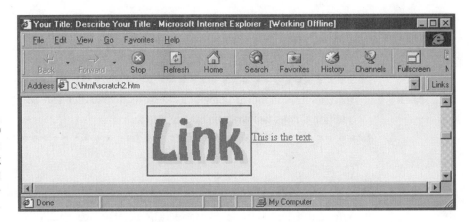

Figure 3.23

You can center an image link and link text by placing them in a center-aligned paragraph.

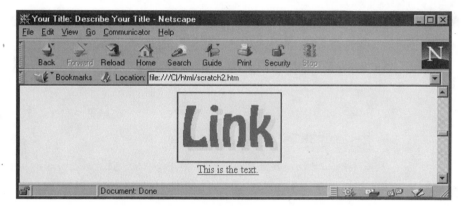

Figure 3.24

By inserting a BR tag, you can position link text beneath an image link.

Reversing the Position of the Image Link and Link Text

You can reverse the relative position of an image link and its associated link text by placing the image link after the link text. As an example, enter the following (paragraph alignment is set to "center"):

```
<P ALIGN="center"><A HREF="link.htm">This is the text.
<IMG SRC="link.gif"></A>
```

Figure 3.25 shows the positions of the link image and link text reversed.

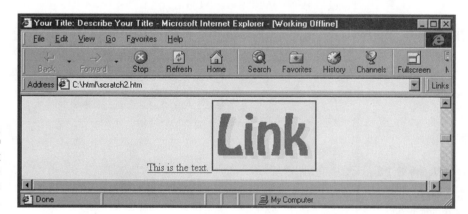

Figure 3.25

You can also put the link text to the left of the image link.

Displaying the Link Text above the Image Link

You can also display link text above the image link if you put the link text ahead of the image. Then all you need to do is put a BR tag at the end of the link text, as shown here:

```
<P ALIGN="center"><A HREF="link.htm">This is the text.<BR>
<IMG SRC="link.gif"></A>
```

In your browser, the link text is centered directly above the image link, as shown in Figure 3.26.

CAUTION

You should add the </P> end tag at the end of the paragraph text when you immediately follow a P (Paragraph) tag that has the ALIGN="center" attribute value with an OL (Ordered List) or a UL (Unordered List) tag. Microsoft Internet Explorer 3.02 does not recognize that a list should be a new block element—if the </P> end tag does not precede the list, it will center-align the list as well. The same thing applies if the paragraph text is right-aligned.

Since the following examples deal with creating lists, add the </P> end tag at the end of the previous example, like this:

```
<P ALIGN="center"><A HREF="link.htm">This is the
text.<BR><IMG SRC="link.gif"></A></P>
```

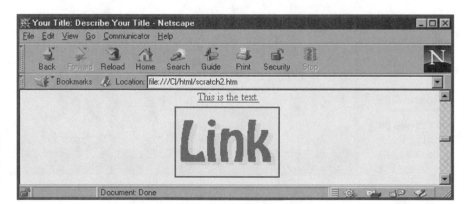

Figure 3.26

You can center link text directly above an image link.

Working with Images and Links

The examples given so far are only some of the things you can do when working with images and links in HTML. The section "Creating Icon Link Lists," presented later in this tutorial, covers how to create indented icon link lists using colorful icon bullet graphics instead of the simple black and white bullets that you get when you use an unordered list. You'll also find a section in the Tables Tutorial scheduled for Saturday evening that covers using tables to create indented icon link lists.

Working with Lists

The Basic HTML Tutorial covered creating ordered (numbered) lists and unordered (bulleted) lists. It also covered nesting, mixing, and matching lists. This section of the Intermediate HTML Tutorial covers some additional ways you can control the display of ordered and unordered lists.

Specifying the Number Type

Netscape provides an extension to HTML 2.0, the TYPE attribute, that allows you to specify the number type for an ordered (OL) list. This attribute value has been incorporated into HTML 3.2. Besides making it possible for you to specify a number type for a numbered list, this attribute also allows you to create multilevel outlines.

You can use the TYPE attribute to specify the number type for an ordered (OL) list. The values that you can use with the TYPE attribute are "A," "a," "I," "i," and "1," for specifying uppercase letters, lowercase letters, uppercase roman numerals, lowercase roman numerals, or Arabic numbers, respectively.

Enter the following for an example of specifying uppercase roman numerals for an ordered list:

```
<OL TYPE="I">
<LI>This is item one.
```

```
<LI>This is item two.
<LI>This is item three.
<LI>This is item four.
</OL>
```

Figure 3.27 shows how this looks in a Web browser that supports the TYPE attribute for ordered (numbered) lists.

Creating a Multilevel Outline

You might expect Web browsers to vary the number types of nested ordered (numbered) lists automatically. After all, they usually vary the bullet types of nested unordered (bulleted) lists, as you saw in the Basic HTML Tutorial this morning. But no current Web browser automatically varies the number type in nested ordered lists.

To vary the number types of nested ordered lists, you need to use the TYPE attribute of the OL tag. This was originally a Netscape Extension that is now part of HTML 3.2. As mentioned in the previous section, you use the values "A," "a," "I," "i," and "1," for specifying uppercase letters, lowercase letters, uppercase roman numerals, lowercase roman numerals, or Arabic numbers, respectively. This allows you to create a multilevel outline.

Figure 3.27

The TYPE="I" attribute causes an ordered list to be displayed with roman numerals.

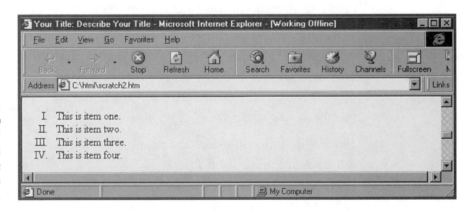

CAUTION

◆ ◆

This can look awful in a Web browser that doesn't support the TYPE attribute for ordered lists, so if you use this feature, you might want to label your page "HTML 3.2 or greater only."

◆ ◆

Enter the following as an example of creating a multilevel outline using TYPE attributes:

TIP

■ ■

Tab or space to create the indents, but realize that this is for your eyes only and it will have no effect when displayed in a browser. Your browser will automatically indent nested ordered lists. Also, be careful that you "nest" instead of "overlap" the different nested outline levels.

■ ■

```
<OL TYPE="I">
<LI>Level-one outline level.
  <OL TYPE="A">
  <LI>Level-two outline level.
    <OL TYPE="1">
    <LI>Level-three outline level.
      <OL TYPE="a">
      <LI>Level-four outline level.
      <LI>Level-four outline level.
      </OL>
    <LI>Level-three outline level.
    </OL>
  <LI>Level-two outline level.
  </OL>
<LI>Level-one outline level.
</OL>
```

Figure 3.28 shows how this appears in an HTML 3.2–compliant Web browser. Remember—the indenting you see in the figure (or in your browser) comes from nesting the OL tags; it has nothing to do with any spaces or tabs you may have added here.

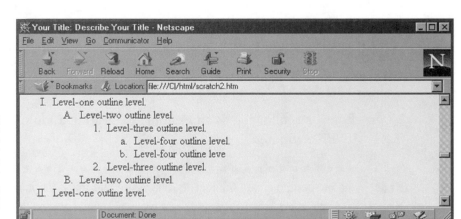

Figure 3.28

By using the TYPE attribute to assign different number types, you can create a multilevel outline.

You can dress up your outline by bolding or italicizing different levels. You can also apply any of the heading-level tags to have your different outline levels appear in fonts of varying sizes. Later in this tutorial, you'll learn how to use the FONT tag to specify font sizes and colors, which you can also use to further emphasize your outline levels. When you use any of these tags to vary the size or color of an outline level, always nest the OL start and end tags inside the tags you want to use to visually differentiate your outline levels.

Including Paragraphs in a Multilevel Outline

You can insert paragraphs inside a multilevel outline by inserting a paragraph following a list item. The paragraph will automatically line up vertically with the text of the preceding list item. For instance, insert the following:

NOTE

Feel free to use tabs or spaces to indent the paragraph text so it's flush with the preceding list item. This is for your eyes only—any tabs or extra spaces you enter will have no effect in a browser.

```
<OL TYPE="I">

<LI>Level-one outline level.

<P>Paragraph text following a list item will automati-
cally be indented flush with the list item text.</P>

   <OL TYPE="A">

   <LI>Level-two outline level.

   <P>Paragraph text following a list item will automati-
   cally be indented flush with the list item text.</P>

      <OL TYPE="1">

      <LI>Level-three outline level.

      <P>Paragraph text following a list item will automat-
      ically be indented flush with the list item text.</P>

         <OL TYPE="a">

         <LI>Level-four outline level.

         <LI>Level-four outline leve

         </OL>

      <LI>Level-three outline level.

      </OL>

   <LI>Level-two outline level.

   </OL>

<LI>Level-one outline level.

</OL>
```

NOTE

You'll notice in the previous example that the paragraph elements end with a </P> end tag. This is another case where you need to add the </P> end tag if you want a paragraph to be displayed properly. That's because Navigator and Internet Explorer don't add extra space between the paragraph and the following list items without it.

Figure 3.29 shows how this looks in a Web browser.

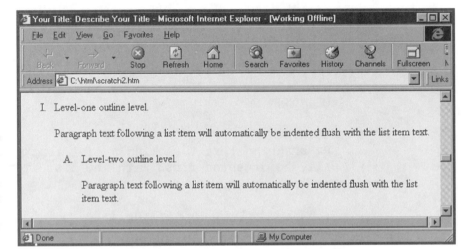

Figure 3.29

Paragraphs
included in a
multilevel outline
automatically line
up vertically with
the preceding
list item.

Using START and VALUE Attributes in an Ordered List

The START and VALUE attributes were Netscape extensions that were incorporated into HTML 3.2. You can use the START attribute in an OL start tag to start the numbering sequence at a particular number. You can use the VALUE attribute in an LI tag to restart the numbering sequence at a particular number. For an example of first starting the numbering sequence at 3, then restarting it at 8, enter the following:

```
<OL START="3">
<LI>This should be numbered as 3
<LI>This should be numbered as 4.
<LI VALUE="8">This should be numbered as 8.
<LI>This should be numbered as 9.
</OL>
```

Figure 3.30 shows how this appears in an HTML 3.2–compliant Web browser.

Figure 3.30

You can use the OL tag's START attribute and the LI tag's VALUE attribute to start or restart the numbering of an ordered list.

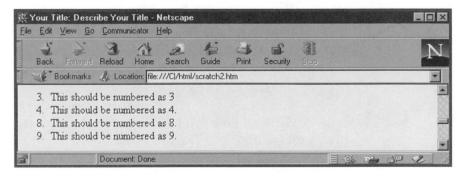

The numbering sequence will be started or restarted using the current TYPE attribute value. For instance, if TYPE="A" is used in the OL tag, then START="3" in an OL tag or VALUE="3" in an LI tag would start or restart the numbering at "C."

Specifying Bullet Types in Unordered Lists

You can also use the TYPE attribute with unordered (bulleted) lists to specify the type of bullet to display. Originally a Netscape extension, this has also become part of HTML 3.2. Navigator 2.0 or greater and Internet Explorer 4.0 or greater support this attribute.

The values that you can use with the UL tag's TYPE attribute are "disc," "circle," and "square." Navigator and Internet Explorer (4.0 or greater) by default display nested bullet lists with the progression of a disc for the first level, a circle for the second level, and a square for the third level.

Enter the following for an example of specifying a bullet-type sequence other than the default for a bullet list three levels deep:

```
<UL TYPE="square">
<LI>First-level bullet.
<LI>First-level bullet.
  <UL TYPE="disc">
  <LI>Second-level bullet.
  <LI>Second-level bullet.
    <UL TYPE="circle">
```

```
        <LI>Third-level bullet.
        <LI>Third-level bullet.
        </UL>
    </UL>
</UL>
```

Figure 3.31 shows how this looks in a Web browser that supports the UL tag's TYPE attribute.

TIP   Just as you can include automatically indented paragraphs in an outline, you can do the same in a nested bulleted list. Just insert paragraphs following a list item but inside the list, and they will automatically line up to match the list item's indentation.

Take a Break

Ready for a breather? Coming up next, you'll learn how to create those fancy 3-D icon bullet link lists I've been telling you about, so you might want to take the chance now to get up and get some of the kinks out. Do some deep breathing. Unglue your eyes from the screen and stare at the horizon. Grab a snack or a soda. I'll see you back in 5 to 10 minutes.

Figure 3.31

Using the TYPE attribute, you can assign nondefault bullet types to nested unordered lists (UL).

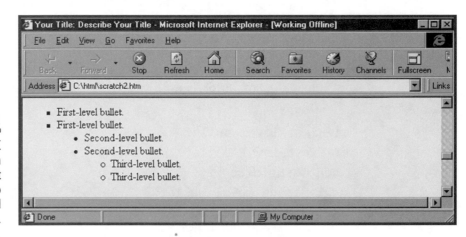

Creating Icon Link Lists

An *icon link list* is a list of hypertext links that uses colorful 3-D graphical icon bullets (inline images) rather than plain, black-and-white bullets like those you get when you create an unordered list by using the UL tag. This is a good way to add some pizazz to your Web page.

There are a number of ways you can set up an icon link list. I'll be showing you three different ways here. The first method uses left-aligned bullet icons and BR tags. This allows you to create an indented icon link list. The second method uses the COMPACT attribute of the DL (Definition List) tag to create an indented icon link list. The third method uses a regular glossary list

All the examples use the same set of links. Rather than retype them each time, type the links first and then copy them twice, so that you have a list of links for each example.

TIP These are the same links and descriptions you created in the Basic HTML Tutorial. You can cut and paste these links from SCRATCH.HTM and then edit them to match what is shown here.

```
<A HREF="http://www.li.net/~autorent/yoyo.htm">Jon's YoYo
Kingdom</A> Claims to have the largest YoYo link list on
the Web.
```

```
<A HREF="http://pages.nyu.edu/~tqm3413/yoyo/index.htm">
Tomer's Page of Exotic YoYo</A> Dedicated to the "little-
known, original, unusual, difficult, or otherwise inter-
esting tricks."
```

Make two copies so you have three copies in all, and use one copy for each example of creating an icon link list in the following sections.

Using Left-Aligned Bullet Icons

This method for creating an icon link list uses left-aligned bullet icons and BR tags to create the list. Edit your first copy of the list of links as shown here:

```
<P><IMG SRC="redball.gif" ALIGN="left" HSPACE=5 VSPACE=5>
```

```
<A HREF="http://www.li.net/~autorent/yoyo.htm">Jon's
YoYo Kingdom</A> Claims to have the largest YoYo link
list on the Web.<BR CLEAR="left">
```

```
<IMG SRC="redball.gif" ALIGN="left" HSPACE=5 VSPACE=5>
```

```
<A HREF="http://pages.nyu.edu/~tqm3413/yoyo/index.htm">
Tomer's Page of Exotic YoYo</A> Dedicated to the
"little-known, original, unusual, difficult, or other-
wise interesting tricks."<BR CLEAR="left">
```

Figure 3.32 shows what this looks like in a Web browser that supports wrapping text around left-aligned images.

Notice that this is really one paragraph with BR (Line Break) tags used to separate the lines. ALIGN="left" causes the text to wrap around the bullet icon—otherwise, the second line would jump down below the bullet. The CLEAR attribute in the BR tags ensures that each icon bullet is flush to the left margin and isn't part of the previous bullet's wrap (in case you have a bullet item with only a single line of text).

Besides requiring a browser that supports wrapping text around images before the indents will show, this method has one other limitation: it can indent only two lines of text. A third line runs flush to the left margin.

Figure 3.32

An indented icon bullet list can be created by using left-aligned bullet images and BR tags with the CLEAR attribute.

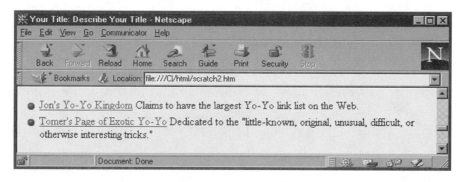

The VSPACE amount allows you only two lines of indented text. Any additional lines will wrap to the left margin. Unfortunately, VSPACE adds space above and below the bullet, so you can't increase the VSPACE amount without moving the icon bullet down so it is no longer even with the following text.

TIP Someone using a text-only browser or a graphical Web browser with graphics turned off might not realize that the graphics are icon bullets. To clue them in, you might want to edit the IMG tags for the icon bullets above, adding ALT="*", so they look like this:

```
<IMG SRC="redball.gif" ALIGN="top" HSPACE=5 VSPACE=5 ALT="*">
```

If you're wondering where to get more graphic icons to spice up your Web pages, you can find a collection of public domain graphic icons and other Web art on the CD-ROM. Appendix A, "The Web Resources Directory," also lists pointers to tons of Web art that you can download from the Web. The Web site for this book (`http://www.callihan.com/create2/`) also offers lists of updated and current resources, including links to graphics and Web art sources.

Using a Compact Definition List

This method uses the COMPACT attribute of the DL (Definition List) tag to create an indented icon link list. The COMPACT attribute should cause the DT (Definition Term) and DD (Definition Data) elements to show up on the same line, as with a regular definition list.

This might actually be the preferred method for creating an icon link list (it can indent an unlimited number of lines) if it weren't for a couple of potentially serious drawbacks:

1. Although Navigator has always supported the COMPACT attribute in the DL tag, Internet Explorer has only started supporting it with the 4.0 version. Support for this attribute among other browsers is spotty.

2. If a browser does not support the COMPACT attribute, the result
    can be ugly—with all text, including both the link and any descrip-
    tive text, displayed below the icon bullet.

With the first method, if a browser does not support the ALIGN="left"
attribute value, the only negative result will be that the text following the
bullet will not be indented. For that reason, if you are concerned with
compatibility with the widest range of browsers, the first method is better
than the second. Use the second method if you only care about the latest
versions of Navigator or Internet Explorer, and be sure to warn visitors to
your page that other browser versions may not be up to snuff.

Edit your second copy of the sample links to create the following:

```
<DL COMPACT>

<DT><IMG SRC="redball.gif" ALIGN="top" HSPACE="10"
VSPACE="3">

<DD><A HREF="http://www.li.net/~autorent/yo-yo.htm">
Jon's Yo-Yo Kingdom</A> Claims to have the largest Yo-
Yo link list on the Web. This text further explains
the link above. This text further explains the link
above. This text further explains the link above.

<DT><IMG SRC="redball.gif" ALIGN="top" HSPACE="10"
VSPACE="3">

<DD><A HREF="http://pages.nyu.edu/~tqm3413/yoyo/index.htm">
Tomer's Page of Exotic Yo-Yo</A> Dedicated to the
"little-known, original, unusual, difficult, or other-
wise interesting tricks." This text further explains
the link above. This text further explains the link
above. This text further explains the link above.

</DL>
```

Figure 3.33 shows what this looks like in a Web browser that supports the
COMPACT attribute of the DL (Definition List) tag.

You'll notice in the previous example that the HSPACE attribute has been
set to 10 pixels to move the icon bullet a bit closer to the following text.

Figure 3.33

Using the DL tag's
COMPACT attribute,
as many description
lines as you want
can be indented,
but pre-HTML 3.2
browsers may trip
over this.

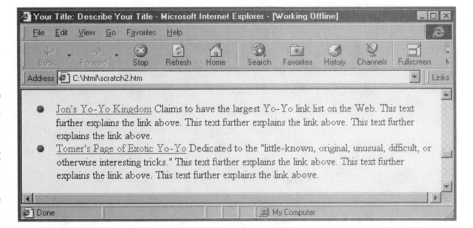

While Internet Explorer 4.0 will allow you to set this to as many as 12 pixels without bumping the DD (Definition Data) text down a line, Navigator won't let you set this value to more than 10 pixels without getting the same unwelcome effect.

Other Ways to Create Icon Link Lists

There are other ways to create icon link lists. One way is to dispense with trying to indent the text following the icon bullet. Leave out the ALIGN="left" attribute value that you used in the first method. You should also get rid of the VSPACE attribute as well. Whenever I see an unindented icon link list, I grit my teeth.

Another interesting alternative is to use a regular definition list, without the COMPACT attribute, including the link with the bullet image in the DT (Definition Term) tag, while leaving any text describing or commenting on the link in the DD (Definition Data) tag.

Last but not least, check out the bonus session, the Tables Tutorial scheduled for tonight. You'll learn how to create indented icon bullet lists using tables and make them compatible with browsers that don't support tables.

Working with Rules

You learned how to use the HR (Horizontal Rule) tag in the Basic HTML Tutorial. In the following section, I'll show you how to create custom horizontal rules by changing the height, width, alignment, and shading of a horizontal rule. I'll also show you how to use inline images as graphic rules, which lets you include fancy and colorful horizontal rules in your Web pages.

Creating Custom Horizontal Rules

The default horizontal rule looks rather bland. True, it does have some shading to give it a bit of a 3-D look—although it is entirely washed out in Internet Explorer if you've set your browser's background to white. So this section covers some things you can do to dress up your horizontal rules, including changing their height, width, and alignment. You'll also learn how to use 3-D graphic rules you may have seen on the Web.

The attributes used here in the HR tag were all originally Netscape Navigator extensions. HTML 3.2 includes them, so they can now qualify as "official HTML." Most current Web browsers support these attributes.

Changing the Height of a Horizontal Rule

To change the height of a horizontal rule, set the SIZE attribute value in the HR tag. The value you set is the rule's height, or thickness, in pixels. Enter the following for an example of creating a horizontal rule that has a thickness of 10 pixels and another one that has a thickness of 15 pixels (along with a regular rule so you can see the difference):

```
<P>This is the default horizontal rule:
<HR>
<P>This is a 10-pixel horizontal rule:
<HR SIZE="10">
<P>This is a 15-pixel horizontal rule:
<HR SIZE="15">
```

Figure 3.34 shows how this will look in Netscape Navigator.

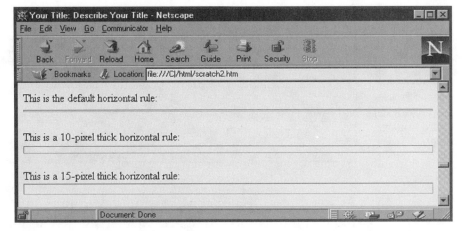

Figure 3.34

You can vary the thickness of a horizontal rule.

Changing between Shaded and Unshaded Horizontal Rules

The default setting for a horizontal rule is "shaded." To set an unshaded horizontal rule, just add the NOSHADE attribute to the HR tag, as shown here:

```
<P>This is an unshaded 15-pixel horizontal rule:
<HR SIZE="15" NOSHADE>
```

The following figures, Figure 3.35 and Figure 3.36, show how this looks in Netscape Navigator and Internet Explorer, which take somewhat different approaches to displaying unshaded horizontal rules.

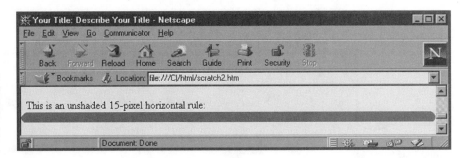

Figure 3.35

Navigator rounds off the corners of an unshaded horizontal rule.

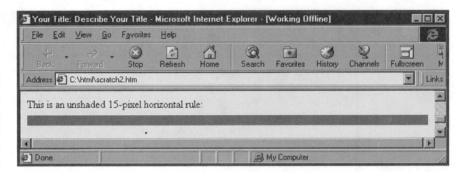

As you can see, Navigator fills an unshaded rule with a gray shade and rounds off its corners. Internet Explorer also fills an unshaded rule with a gray shade, but displays it with square corners. Other browsers may display unshaded rules in other ways—NCSA Mosaic 2.0, for instance, fills an unshaded rule with black, while displaying it with square corners.

Changing the Width of a Horizontal Rule

You also can change the width of a horizontal rule, either by setting the width in pixels or by specifying a percentage of the total width of the browser window. By default, horizontal rules are centered in the browser window. Enter the following for an example of creating a 15-pixel horizontal rule with a width that is 75 percent of a browser's window:

```
<P>This is a 75% wide unshaded 15-pixel horizontal rule:
<HR WIDTH="75%" SIZE="15" NOSHADE>
```

Figure 3.37 shows the resulting rule in Netscape Navigator.

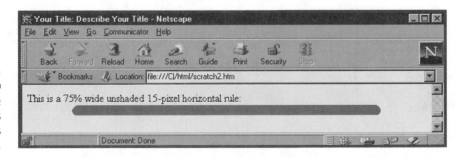

◆◆

CAUTION You might be tempted to stack up horizontal rules of different widths, to generate an effect similar to this:

―――――――――――――――――――――――――――

―――――――――――――――――――――

―――――――――――

Be advised that in a Web browser that doesn't support setting the WIDTH attribute for the HR tag, it will turn out something like this:

―――――――――――――――――――――――――――――――――――――――

―――――――――――――――――――――――――――――――――――――――

―――――――――――――――――――――――――――――――――――――――

This is a good example of a situation in which both Navigator and Internet Explorer support doing something, but you probably still shouldn't do it. The general rule is not to do tricks specific to only a few browsers if they're going to mess up other browsers. One way around this is to provide alternative pages, or at least label your page as "Netscape Navigator Only," "Microsoft Internet Explorer Only," or "HTML 3.2 Only." Both Netscape and Navigator have icon buttons you can use to link directly to their sites.

◆◆

Setting the Alignment of a Horizontal Rule

HTML 3.2 allows the use of the ALIGN attribute in the HR tag to left-align or right-align a horizontal rule (center-alignment is the default). Enter the following for an example of doing this:

```
<P>This is a left-aligned, 75% wide unshaded 15-pixel
horizontal rule:

<HR ALIGN="left" WIDTH="75%" SIZE="15" NOSHADE>
```

Both Netscape Navigator and Internet Explorer support left- or right-aligning a horizontal rule. Figure 3.38 shows how this looks in Internet Explorer.

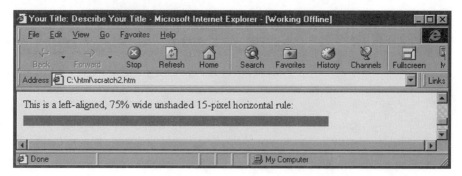

Figure 3.38

You can either left- or right-align a horizontal rule.

Setting the background of Internet Explorer to its default color of gray shows how Internet Explorer displays rule shading. (With the background set to white, Internet Explorer washes out the shading entirely.)

Using Graphic Rules

Instead of the HR tag, you can use a graphic rule, which is simply a graphic of a rule that you can insert on your page as an inline image. Enter the following as an example of inserting a graphic rule on your Web page:

```
<P>This is a graphic rule:
<P><IMG SRC="rain_lin.gif">
```

Figure 3.39 shows what this looks like in any graphical Web browser.

Centering a Graphic Rule

You can center a graphic rule like any inline image by placing it in a center-aligned paragraph. Edit the example you just created to center it, like this:

```
<P ALIGN="center"><IMG SRC="rain_lin.gif">
```

Now, as shown in Figure 3.40, the graphic rule appears centered in a Web browser.

Figure 3.39

Instead of a plain horizontal rule, you can use a fancy graphical horizontal rule.

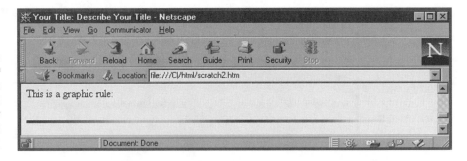

Figure 3.40

You can center a graphic rule by placing it on a center-aligned paragraph.

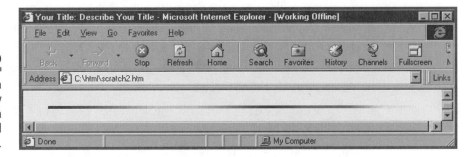

Setting the Width and Height of a Graphic Rule

You can also get your graphic rule to extend across more (or less) of the screen by setting the width of the image. And, while you're at it, you may as well enhance your graphic rule by increasing its height. Reedit the example you just created so it looks like this:

```
<P ALIGN="center"><IMG SRC="rain_lin.gif" HEIGHT="10"
WIDTH="595">
```

As Figure 3.41 shows, the graphic rule now extends across more of the screen. The impact has been further enhanced by increasing the graphic rule's height.

Figure 3.41

The width of the graphic rule has been increased to 595 pixels, while the height has been increased to 10 pixels.

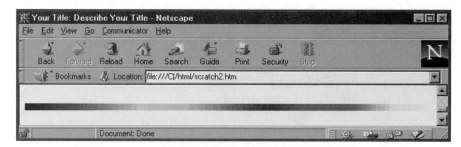

 TIP

To create graphic rules in your graphics editor that are much smaller, byte-wise, than a normal graphic rule, create a small graphic (10 by 10 pixels) using the color of your choice as the background color and save it to C:\HTML as a GIF file. Next, insert the graphic into your Web page as an inline image and then set the height and width attributes to 10 pixels and 595 pixels. For instance:

```
<P ALIGN="center"><IMG SRC="yourfile.gif" WIDTH="10"
HEIGHT="595">
```

If the color of your 10×10 graphic was red, then a red graphic rule, 10 pixels high and 595 pixels wide, would appear onscreen. Also, notice the use of a center-aligned paragraph—those browsers that don't support setting the height and width of an inline image will center your 10x10 graphic onscreen (if they support paragraph center-alignment).

You can also set the width as a percentage of the total width of the browser window: just insert WIDTH="75%", for instance. You need to remember not to set a height percentage when you set a width percentage, although you can set a fixed pixel height.

Experiment with different colors and combinations of colors. Some graphic editors allow you to add textures or patterns to an image—experiment with those if they are available.

Working with Fonts

The FONT tag allows you to change font sizes, colors, and faces. In the following sections, I'll show you how to apply the FONT tag's SIZE, COLOR, and FACE attributes.

• •

The FONT tag, which had only been recently included in standard HTML with HTML 3.2 (after a long career as a Netscape Extension), has been deprecated in HTML 4.0 in favor of using style sheets to achieve the same results. That a tag has been deprecated is supposed to serve as a warning that it may be made obsolete in a future version of HTML, and thus its use is to be discouraged. This doesn't mean that it will be dropped from HTML. The FONT tag is easier and more straightforward than are style sheets for a novice HTML user to learn and apply, and so many pages have already been created using this tag that future versions of HTML will have no choice but to continue to support it to maintain backward compatibility with those pages. For those reasons, you shouldn't worry that the FONT tag will ever be obsoleted.

• •

Changing Font Sizes

The FONT tag allows you to specify the size and color of a section of text. The FONT tag uses the SIZE attribute to change the size of a font. You can set font sizes using absolute or relative size values.

There are seven *absolute* (or fixed) sizes, numbered from "1" to "7," that you can set using the SIZE attribute of the FONT tag. The default is "3," which is the same as regular paragraph text. "1" is the smallest and "7" is the largest, which means you can set two absolute font sizes that are smaller than normal paragraph text and four sizes that are larger. Each Web browser determines the sizes of these fonts. To see what these different font sizes look like in your Web browser, enter the following and then hop over to your browser:

```
<P><FONT SIZE="1">Font Size 1.</FONT><BR>
<FONT SIZE="2">Font Size 2.</FONT><BR>
<FONT SIZE="3">Font Size 3 (the default).</FONT><BR>
<FONT SIZE="4">Font Size 4.</FONT><BR>
<FONT SIZE="5">Font Size 5.</FONT><BR>
<FONT SIZE="6">Font Size 6.</FONT><BR>
<FONT SIZE="7">Font Size 7.</FONT>
```

As you can see in Figure 3.42 (or in your browser if you're using Netscape Navigator or Internet Explorer), the font sizes you can set range from very small to quite large.

TIP   You can also nest font tags inside each other, so you could do something like this to switch back to the default font size in the middle of a larger set font size:

```
<FONT SIZE="4">This is Font Size 4. <FONT SIZE="3">This
is the default size font.</FONT> This is Font Size 4
again.</FONT>.
```

Setting Relative Font Size Changes

You can also set relative font sizes. Relative font size changes are indicated by either a plus (+) or minus (–) sign preceding the font size number. For instance, FONT SIZE="+1" indicates a font size that is one size larger than the base font. Since the default base font is the same as a Size 3 absolute font size, a Size +1 relative font would be the same as a Size 4 absolute font (3 + 1 = 4). For instance, enter the following for an example of using relative font size changes to indicate the seven possible font sizes:

```
<P><FONT SIZE="-2">Font Size -2.</FONT><BR>
<FONT SIZE="-1">Font Size -1.</FONT><BR>
Default Font Size.<BR>
<FONT SIZE="+1">Font Size +1.</FONT><BR>
<FONT SIZE="+2">Font Size +2.</FONT><BR>
<FONT SIZE="+3">Font Size +3.</FONT><BR>
<FONT SIZE="+4">Font Size +4.</FONT>
```

Figure 3.43 illustrates the seven font sizes, specified in relative terms.

You'll notice that a relative –2 is the same as an absolute 1, –1 is the same as 2, +1 is the same as 4, and so on. The default font size, which requires no font size change, is the same as 3.

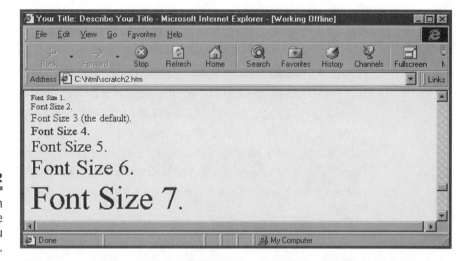

Figure 3.42

There are seven different absolute font sizes that you can set.

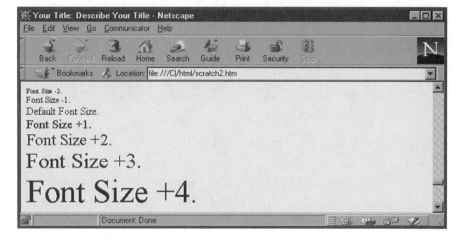

Figure 3.43

There are seven different relative font sizes that you can set.

Now, you may be asking, "If relative fonts are just another way to specify the same fonts as absolute fonts, why bother?" The next section, "Setting the Base Font," provides the answer to that question.

Setting the Base Font

The BASEFONT tag allows you to change the size of the *base font*—the font used in paragraph text. You can set it to any of the absolute font sizes, 1 through 7 (3 is the default). It's a stand-alone (or empty) tag. You set the base font size the same way you set an absolute font size.

NOTE

• •

The BASEFONT tag was a Netscape extension that never made it into HTML 3.2, but was included in HTML 4.0—and then deprecated, along with the FONT tag. But it is still a very handy means for doing what it does, and there are undoubtedly loads of pages that use the BASEFONT tag. It's great for bumping the default base font size up a notch, for instance. You should feel free to continue to use it. You are limited, however, to seven fixed font-sizes, and cannot assign any colors. If you want more versatility, you may want to check out using style sheets (see Appendix A, "The Web Resources Directory," for links to where you can find out more about style sheets).

• •

To increase the base font size one notch ("3" is the default base font size), set the base font to an absolute font size of "4":

```
<BASEFONT SIZE="4">
```

When you change the base font size using the BASEFONT tag, all following relative font sizes will change relative to the new base font. For instance, if you change the base font size to "4" as above, then a relative font size of "+1" would then be the same as an absolute font size of "5" (4 + 1 = 5).

You can insert the BASEFONT tag at any point within a Web page to set the base font to any of the absolute font sizes. It stays in effect until another BASEFONT tag changes the base font size. It not only affects relative font sizes, but also any SMALL and BIG font changes (described later in the session), as well as the size of all paragraph text, character rendering (italic, bold, and so on), list elements, definition lists, block quotes, predefined text, and address blocks that follow it. Headings and text set with absolute font size tags are not affected, however.

Other Ways to Change Font Sizes

The SMALL and BIG tags are Netscape extensions that were incorporated into HTML 3.2. They are container tags that specify a font size that is one size smaller and one size bigger than the current base font size. The tags can be nested to get even smaller and larger font sizes. These tags

have been deprecated in HTML 4.0, and (unlike the other deprecated tags) they don't perform any function that cannot be done just as easily by other means—especially the more versatile FONT tag. The BIG and SMALL tags have also been less widely used than the FONT tag, and thus are more likely to actually be obsoleted in a future version of HTML. Since these tags don't provide any functionality not offered by the FONT tag, I recommend that you avoid using these tags.

Changing Font Colors

The FONT tag uses the COLOR attribute to change the color of a font. To specify a font color, you can either use one of 16 color names that match the Windows 16-color palette, or you can use RGB hex codes—which is more difficult but gives you access to a much wider range of colors.

The 16 Windows color names are black, white, aqua, blue, fuchsia, gray, green, lime, maroon, navy, olive, purple, red, silver, teal, and yellow. Enter the following for an example of specifying font colors using color names (this example omits "black" and "white"):

```
<P><FONT SIZE=7>

<FONT COLOR="aqua">Aqua </FONT><FONT COLOR="blue">Blue
</FONT>

<FONT COLOR="fuchsia">Fuchsia </FONT><FONT COLOR="gray">Gray
</FONT>

<FONT COLOR="green">Green </FONT><FONT COLOR="lime">Lime
</FONT>

<FONT COLOR="maroon">Maroon </FONT><FONT COLOR="navy">Navy
</FONT>

<FONT COLOR="olive">Olive </FONT><FONT COLOR="purple">Purple
</FONT>

<FONT COLOR="red">Red </FONT><FONT COLOR="silver">Silver
</FONT>

<FONT COLOR="teal">Teal </FONT><FONT COLOR="yellow">Yellow
</FONT>

</FONT>
```

The illustration in Figure 3.44, shown here in monochrome, gives only a rough idea of what this looks like in a browser. Be sure to hop over to your browser to see what the colors really look like.

Setting the font color using RGB hex codes is a much more difficult way to set font colors than using color names, but it gives you the choice of a very large range of colors. Essentially, it lets you specify values from 0 to 255 for the red, green, and blue components of a color, providing you with a grand total of 16.7 million different colors from which to choose.

Finding the perfect color when you use this method is somewhat akin to finding a needle in a haystack. Also, many of the possible color specifications may not obtain the effect you want on a monitor that can display only 256 colors. You have to specify the RGB values in hexadecimal rather than decimal number format. (One of the reasons hexadecimal is used for this type of thing is that every number between 0 and 255 can be represented with only two characters. For instance, 159 in hex is 9F.)

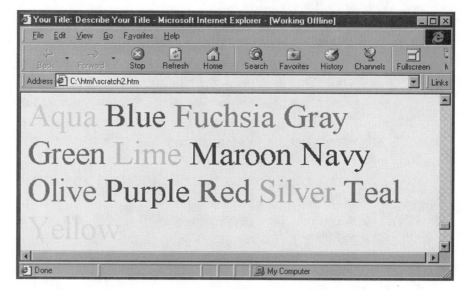

Figure 3.44

There are 16 color names, including black and white (not shown here), that you can use to set font colors.

You set the RGB hex code for a color in the FONT tag in this general form, where rr is the hex value for red, gg the hex value for green, and bb the hex value for blue:

```
<FONT COLOR="#rrggbb">This is the text to be colored.
</FONT>
```

For instance, a red color here could be specified as FF0000, a green color as 00FF00, and a blue color as 0000FF. (FF is the highest hexadecimal number, equaling 255, while 00 is the lowest, equaling 0.) Enter the following as an example of assigning font colors using RGB hex codes (the example also sets the font size so it will be more visible in your browser):

```
<FONT SIZE="6"><FONT COLOR="#FF0000">Red (FF0000) </FONT>
<FONT COLOR="#00FF00">Green (00FF00) </FONT><FONT
COLOR="#0000FF">Blue (0000FF)</FONT></FONT>
```

Since this is shown in Figure 3.45 only in monochrome, you'll have to hop over to your browser if you want to check out what it really looks like.

Showing you how to count in hexadecimal or how an RGB color scheme works is beyond the scope of this book. Unless you already know hex and RGB color theory, the only practical way is to use some kind of color chart, wheel, or cube that allows you to select the color you want and get the corresponding hex code. Many charts, tables, and utilities are available on the Web for getting the hex codes for colors. You'll find links to some of these in Appendix A, "The Web Resources Directory."

Figure 3.45

These are just a few of the wide range of colors you can set using hex codes.

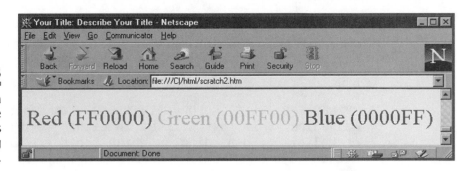

Many HTML editors also have built-in color charts and utilities that let you choose a color and then insert the hex code into your Web page. This is a department in which an HTML editor can be far superior to a mere text editor like Notepad. Figure 3.46 shows HTML Notepad's built-in color picker.

Changing Font Faces

The FACE attribute for the FONT tag was a Microsoft extension, but it is now part of HTML 4.0. It allows you to specify a font, or list of fonts, in which you would like to have text displayed. A browser that supports this attribute will check to see if any of the fonts specified are present on a local computer and then display the text in that font if it is available. If not, it will display the text in the default font.

One of the tricks to using this attribute is to specify a list of fonts that will snag as many computers as possible. You should realize that just because a font is available on your system doesn't mean that it will be available on someone else's system. If most systems aren't liable to have a particular font, there really isn't much point in specifying it. For that reason, I don't think trying to specify one particular font is the way to go, and you certainly shouldn't base the design of your Web page on having any one particular font available. Even if you stick with fonts that are included with Windows 95 or Windows 3.1, you should realize that those fonts may not be available on a Macintosh or a Unix system.

A good way to use this attribute is to specify a list of fonts that fit into the same category, such as serif, sans serif, or monospaced fonts. For instance, to maximize the chances that the following example will be displayed in a sans serif font, enter the following:

```
<P><FONT SIZE="6" COLOR="blue" FACE="Verdana, Arial,
Helvetica">This text will be in either Verdana, Arial,
or Helvetica, depending on which fonts are installed on
a local system.</FONT>
```

Figure 3.47 shows what this looks like in a browser that supports the FONT tag's FACE attribute, on a system that has the Verdana font available.

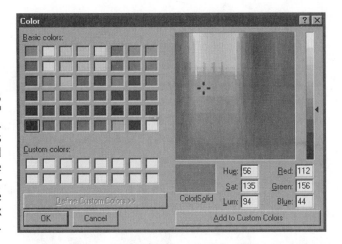

Figure 3.46

Many HTML editors, such as HTML Notepad (shown here), have built-in color pickers that make inserting color hex codes a snap.

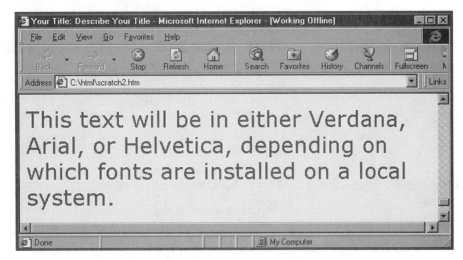

Figure 3.47

The FONT tag's FACE attribute is an HTML 4.0 feature (formerly a Microsoft extension) that can be used to display text in a font face, here Verdana, different from the default font.

Alternatively, you could specify a monospaced font for a different effect:

```
<P><FONT SIZE="6" COLOR="blue" FACE="Courier New,
Courier, Monospaced, Memorandum,">This text will be in
either Courier New, Courier, Monospaced, or Memorandum,
depending on which fonts are installed on a local
system.</FONT>
```

Figure 3.48 shows what this looks like in a browser that supports the FONT tag's FACE attribute, on a system that has the Courier New font available.

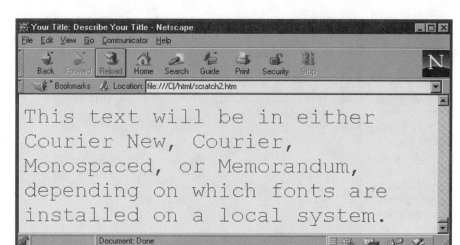

Figure 3.48

Here, the FACE attribute specifies a monospaced font face, Courier New.

Using Background Colors and Images

Using a background color or image is a great way to dress up the appearance of your Web page. In the following sections, I'll be showing you how to set a background color (as well as matching text and link colors) and how to use a background image with your Web page.

Using a Background Color

Using the right background color is a simple and easy way to make your Web page look really great. (Or really horrible, depending on the color you choose!) In this section, I'll be showing you how to set a background color and matching text and link colors.

You can set the colors for the background, text, and links by using these attributes of the BODY tag: BGCOLOR sets the background color, TEXT the text (or foreground) color, LINK the color of hypertext links, VLINK the color of visited links, and ALINK the color of activated links (where you hold down the mouse button on a link, but haven't released it). These were originally Netscape extensions, but have since been included in HTML 3.2. As with the FONT tag's COLOR attribute, you can set

these attributes using any of the 16 color names (black, white, aqua, blue, fuchsia, gray, green, lime, maroon, navy, olive, purple, red, silver, teal, and yellow) or by using RGB hexadecimal codes.

The general form for entering these attributes as color names is shown here, where colorname is one of the 16 color names given:

```
<BODY BGCOLOR="colorname" TEXT="colorname" LINK="color-
name" VLINK="colorname" ALINK="colorname"
```

The general form for entering these attributes as RGB hexadecimal codes is shown here, where *rrggbb* is three hexadecimal numbers forming the RGB code for setting the red, green, and blue components of an RGB color:

```
<BODY BGCOLOR="#rrggbb" TEXT="#rrggbb" LINK="#rrggbb"
VLINK="#rrggbb" ALINK="#rrggbb"
```

The following example sets the colors for the background, the text (or foreground), and the three varieties of links—regular links, visited links, and activated links. Go to the top of the Web page and then add the following to the BODY tag as an example of setting these attributes:

```
<BODY BGCOLOR="#336699" TEXT="#FFFF00" LINK="#FFCC00"
VLINK="#ff6666" ALINK="#FF0000">
```

This sets the background color to slate blue, the text to yellow, the links to orange gold, visited links to a salmon peach (or something like that), and activated links to bright red.

TIP If you stick to hexadecimal codes 00, 33, 66, 99, CC, and FF when inserting RGB hex codes, you can reduce the total number of colors from which you must select to 216. The background, text, and link colors set in the example are all combinations of these codes. This will verify that your colors will display as anticipated on a 256-color system.

Since the illustrations in this book are not printed in color, Figure 3.49 can only show you the contrast and tone of the colors you set in the example. You need to hop over to your Web browser to see what it really looks like.

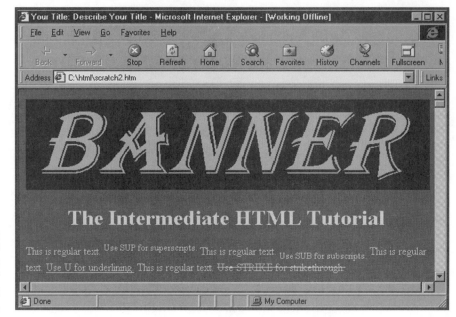

Figure 3.49

You can set a
background color
and matching text
and link colors.

◆ ◆

If you decide to set colors (and nothing says you have to), you should try to avoid color combinations that render your text font less readable. Some color combinations on the Web render Web pages entirely unusable. The important thing is to develop and organize your content and hone the appearance of your Web page. Setting the colors for a badly conceived and poorly organized Web page can only make it worse.

◆ ◆

Using a Background Image

The BACKGROUND attribute of the BODY tag allows you to specify a background image. Originally a Netscape extension, it is now part of HTML 3.2. All current graphical Web browsers should support this attribute. The background image can be a GIF, JPG, or PNG file. The general format for entering this attribute is shown as follows, where *filename* is a graphic file that is in the same directory as the Web page and

URL is a relative or absolute address of a graphic file that is in another directory than the Web page:

```
<BODY BACKGROUND="filename or URL">
```

A key consideration when using background images is to avoid busy or high-contrast images. If you're going to use a dark background image, you should set the color of your text and links to a lighter color. Go to the top of the Web page, and, as shown in the following example, comment out the previous BODY start tag, then add a new BODY start tag using the BACKGROUND attribute to assign BACKGRND.GIF as the background image:

```
<!--<BODY BGCOLOR="#336699" TEXT="#66CC66"
LINK="#FFCC00" VLINK="#ff6666" ALINK="#FF0000">-->
```

```
<BODY BACKGROUND="backgrnd.gif">
```

Figure 3.50 shows a Web page that has BACKGRND.GIF tiled in the background. To see what this really looks like, you need to hop over to your browser.

Figure 3.50

One of the more effective ways to add visual appeal to your Web page is to use a background image.

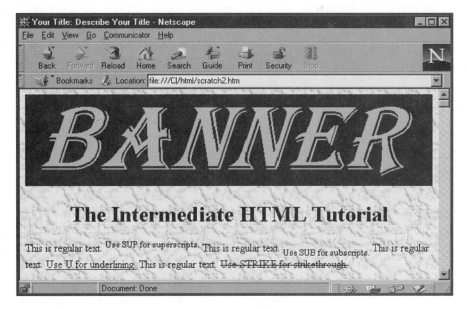

You should keep your background images small to minimize the time it takes them to load. Background images that are smaller than the window are tiled to fill it. Keep your background images to 100×100 pixels or smaller. You can also use a photo-paint program to reduce the contrast and increase or decrease the brightness of a background image, change the hue or saturation, diffuse the image, and so on. Also, you may have to play around with some images, using the spray paint or the smudger to prevent the edges of the graphic from showing when you tile it. Many photo-paint programs also have patterns you can use to create background images. Use the same background image for all Web pages in a related group—that way the image must load only once.

TIP If you use a GIF image as a background image, you can set one of its colors to transparent. This allows you to use both a background image and a background color at the same time. You might create a series of pages with the same background image but different background colors, or the same background color but different background images.

Save the HTML file you just created. You can use it later as a reference. When you first saved it, you named it SCRATCH2.HTM. If more than one person will be doing this tutorial and you want to make sure that this file doesn't get overwritten, you might want to give it a new name, such as using your first initial and last name for the file name (JMILLER2.HTM, for instance, if your name is John Miller).

What's Next?

If you've made it this far, you're doing well. As I mentioned at the start of this session, you didn't need to complete this tutorial to plan and create your first Web page tomorrow. So, if you've been able to complete all or part of this tutorial, congrats!

If you are not completely exhausted and want to learn even *more* HTML, I've included a Tables Tutorial as a bonus session scheduled for tonight. If your eyes are ready to fall out of their sockets, however, feel free to come back and do the Tables Tutorial at a later date. As with the Intermediate HTML Tutorial, you don't need to do it to be able to plan and create your first Web page tomorrow.

You may also want to start thinking about what kind of Web page you want to create. To start out, think primarily in terms of aims, purposes, and relevant content. Conceptualize it first, then design it to fit the concept. Get some text typed if you want. To start out, keep it as simple as you can. A simple structure for a Web page might be a banner graphic, a level-one heading, an introductory paragraph, a link list, and an address block. You'd be surprised how many Web pages fit that profile. Stick to the basics. I'll be giving you some more in-depth pointers tomorrow morning on how to go about planning your first Web page.

I provide sample banner graphics that you can use tomorrow when you create your first Web page, but if you want to experiment tonight with creating a banner graphic for yourself, that's okay too. You don't need to get fancy—just create something to personalize your page, not more than 595 pixels wide. Any graphics program capable of creating a GIF or JPG graphic will do just fine (Paint Shop Pro is on the CD-ROM). Also, for Sunday evening after you've created your first Web page, I've got a Graphics Tutorial scheduled as a bonus session that'll show you how to create interlaced and transparent GIF images, as well as how to create graphics including shadow, fill, and button effects. So don't feel you have to become a graphics whiz right now—but if you want to get your feet wet, go ahead.

These are things you can do if you have the time and energy, but don't burn the midnight oil. You're going to need a good night's sleep, because I've got lots more scheduled for you tomorrow.

SATURDAY EVENING

The Tables Tutorial

(BONUS SESSION)

- ✿ Working with the TABLE Tag
- ✿ Inserting an Image
- ✿ Assigning Background Colors
- ✿ Creating Icon Bullet Link Lists

Although tables are included in the HTML 3.2 specification, the Intermediate HTML Tutorial wasn't the place to deal with them. Tables are a significant feature, and they aren't that difficult to implement in your Web pages.

This tutorial should take less time to complete than the Basic or Intermediate HTML Tutorials. You should be able to complete it in one to two hours. If you run short on time, feel free to leave any unfinished portion of the tutorial until another day.

 NOTE

• •

If you have not yet completed the Intermediate HTML Tutorial that was scheduled for Saturday afternoon, you should complete that tutorial before attempting to do the tables tutorial.

• •

The Tables Tutorial shows you everything you need to know about tables to be able to effectively and easily implement them in your Web pages:

- ✿ Defining rows and columns
- ✿ Adding and controlling borders
- ✿ Setting spacing and padding
- ✿ Defining column headings
- ✿ Adding a caption

- ✿ Setting table width and height
- ✿ Setting cell alignment and column widths
- ✿ Inserting an image
- ✿ Spanning columns and rows
- ✿ Defining head, body, and foot sections
- ✿ Creating icon bullet link lists using tables

This tutorial uses two example graphics files that have already been used in previous tutorials. No other example files are required. If the example graphics files have worked properly in the Basic and Intermediate HTML Tutorials, you need do nothing further to make available the two example graphics used in this tutorial.

If you haven't yet copied and unzipped the example files, please return to "Loading the Example Files" at the start of the Saturday Morning session and do so now before doing this tutorial.

Running Your Web Browser and Text Editor

Run your Web browser, preferably offline, so you'll be able to check the results of your work in your browser while doing this tutorial. Hop back and forth between Notepad and your Web browser, dynamically updating your work as you go.

Tables are part of HTML 3.2, so you should use a Web browser that supports the table tags included in HTML 3.2. Most recent graphical Web browsers should support these tags. Netscape Navigator 2.0 or greater or Internet Explorer 3.0 or greater are suitable for doing this tutorial.

I'll also be introducing a couple of new HTML 4.0 tables features. To be able to do those parts of the tutorial, you should use the latest version of Netscape Navigator or Microsoft Internet Explorer. I've tested out this tutorial with Navigator 4.04 and Internet Explorer 4.01. If you are using an earlier browser than these, feel free to skip the few HTML 4.0 sections I've included.

Run the text editor you want to use to edit HTML files. As mentioned earlier, I recommend using Notepad until you master the fundamentals of HTML. In Windows 3.1, you can usually find Notepad in the Accessories window in Program Manager. In Windows 95, you can find it on the Start Menu, under Programs and Accessories.

Loading Your Starting Template

Load the starting template you saved this morning, C:\HTML\START.HTM. It should look like the following listing (if you didn't save the template, just retype it now):

```
<HTML>
<HEAD>
<TITLE>Your Title: Describe Your Title</TITLE>
</HEAD>
<BODY>
</BODY>
</HTML>
```

Save the scratch pad file that you'll be using in this afternoon's tutorial. In Notepad, select File and Save As. Change the folder where you are going to save your file to C:\HTML, then save your file as SCRATCH3.HTM.

Working with the TABLE Tag

In doing this tutorial, you'll be creating two tables. In the first table, you'll learn all the standard HTML 3.2 table tags, along with a couple of the new HTML 4.0 table tags. I'll even be showing you how to apply some styles to your table. With each new example, just modify the same table you are creating—no need to create a separate table for each example. In the second table, you'll learn how to create a 3-D icon bullet list using tables so you have no limit on the number of indented lines following the bullet. Feel free to save your file after each example and hop over to your Web browser to see what it looks like.

TIP

■ ■

With the example files you copied from the CD-ROM, you'll find a file, TUTOR3.HTM, that shows all the examples covered in this tutorial as separate tables. Don't bother to copy and paste each example as a separate table. Instead, make all the changes in a single table file and use TUTOR3.HTM for future reference on how to implement each feature.

■ ■

The TABLE tag needs to bracket your table. All other tags or text to be included in your table should be nested inside the TABLE tag. Enter this HTML nested in the BODY tag:

```
<BODY>
<TABLE>
</TABLE>
</BODY>
```

Defining Columns and Rows

You can use the TR (Table Row) and TD (Table Data) tags to create a grid of rows and columns. Here's an example:

```
<TABLE>
<TR><TD>1A</TD><TD>1B</TD><TD>1C</TD><TD>1D</TD></TR>
<TR><TD>2A</TD><TD>2B</TD><TD>2C</TD><TD>2D</TD></TR>
</TABLE>
```

Notice that the <TR> start tag and the </TR> end tag bracket each row. See Figure 4.1 for what this looks like in a Web browser.

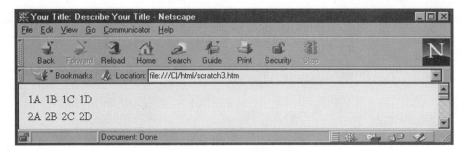

Figure 4.1

A table can
consist of columns
and rows.

Adding and Controlling Borders

A table hardly looks like a table without a border. Including a BORDER attribute inside the TABLE tag does the trick. Here's an example:

```
<TABLE BORDER="1">
<TR><TD>1A</TD><TD>1B</TD><TD>1C</TD><TD>1D</TD></TR>
```

See Figure 4.2 for what this change looks like in a Web browser.

HTML 3.2 also recognizes the BORDER attribute by itself, while HTML 4.0 recognizes the BORDER="border" attribute value. Both of these should have exactly the same result as BORDER="1". As long as a browser recognizes the BORDER attribute by itself, you could use BORDER="buster" and still get the same results.

Increasing the value of the BORDER attribute has a result you might not expect: it increases the thickness of the outer border of the table, displaying it in 3-D relief. It does not affect the appearance of the interior lines of the table. Increase the BORDER to six pixels:

```
<TABLE BORDER="6">
<TR><TD>1A</TD><TD>1B</TD><TD>1C</TD><TD>1D</TD></TR>
```

See Figure 4.3 for what this change looks like in a Web browser.

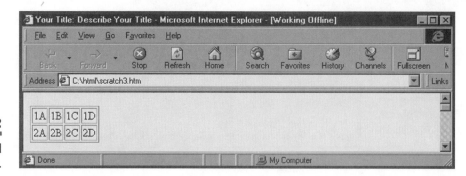

Figure 4.2

You can add borders to a table.

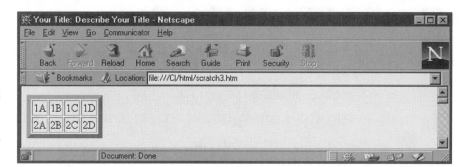

Figure 4.3

Table borders go 3-D when you boost their thickness.

Setting Spacing and Padding

Your table looks a bit cramped, don't you think? The CELLSPACING attribute adds space between cells, whereas the CELLPADDING attribute adds space within each cell. Add six pixels of spacing and padding, like this:

```
<TABLE BORDER="6" CELLSPACING="6" CELLPADDING="6">

<TR><TH>A</TH><TH>B</TH><TH>C</TH><TH>D</TH></TR>
```

As shown in Figure 4.4, both the space between the cells and the padding within the cell have been increased.

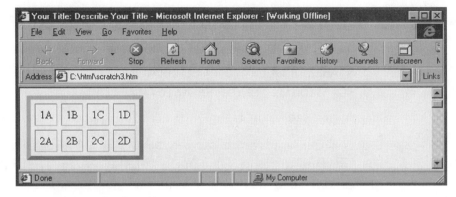

Figure 4.4

You can add space between cells and padding within cells.

Defining Column Headings

What's a table without column headings, right? The TH (Table Heading) tag works just like the TD (Table Data) tag, except it defines a particular cell as a heading cell rather than as an ordinary data cell. To create a row of three column headings at the top of your table, use the TR tag to define a row and then, instead of using TD tags, insert TH tags to define the cells, like this:

```
<TABLE BORDER="6" CELLSPACING="6" CELLPADDING="6">
<TR><TH>A</TH><TH>B</TH><TH>C</TH><TH>D</TH></TR>
<TR><TD>1A</TD><TD>1B</TD><TD>1C</TD><TD>1D</TD></TR>
```

As Figure 4.5 shows, table headings automatically show up in centered boldface type.

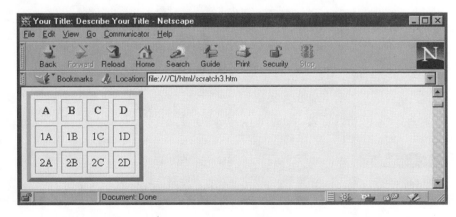

Figure 4.5

Table headings are automatically bolded and centered.

Adding a Caption

The CAPTION tag allows you to specify a caption for your table:

```
<TABLE BORDER="6" CELLSPACING="6" CELLPADDING="6">
<CAPTION>I. Table Example</CAPTION>
```

As you can see in Figure 4.6, a caption appears above the title by default.

You can display the caption below the table by setting an ALIGN=
"bottom" attribute value in the CAPTION tag. The HTML 4.0 specifications state that you should also be able to use ALIGN="left" or
ALIGN="right" to display the caption either to the left or right of the
table. Neither Navigator nor Internet Explorer currently supports this,
however. (Internet Explorer left- and right-flushes the caption in the
caption cell, while Navigator ignores these attributes entirely.)

Centering a Table

To center the table, just insert an ALIGN="center" attribute value in the
TABLE tag:

```
<TABLE ALIGN="center" BORDER="6" CELLSPACING="6" CELL-
PADDING="6">
<CAPTION>I. Table Example</CAPTION>
```

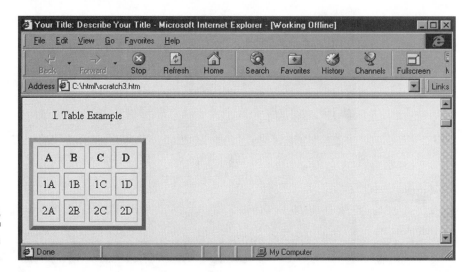

Figure 4.6

You can add a
caption to a table.

Figure 4.7 shows how this will look. Alternatively, you can get the same result by putting your table inside a CENTER tag, or by placing it in a center-aligned paragraph. To indent your table rather than center it, place it inside a BLOCKQUOTE tag.

TIP

Tables are inline elements that function like images created with the IMG tag. Just as with inline images, you can flow text around a table by inserting an ALIGN="left" or ALIGN="right" attribute value in the TABLE tag. (ALIGN="left" will flow text around the right-side of a table, while ALIGN="right" will flow text around the left-side of a table.) You can flow text around any element, including another table. Make sure that you insert a BR tag with the appropriate CLEAR attribute value ("left", "right", or "all") where you want the flowing to stop. Navigator recognizes the HSPACE attribute in the TABLE tag, but Internet Explorer doesn't, which renders doing this much less useful. Figure 4.8 shows two tables displayed side-by-side, with ALIGN="left" set in the first table and ALIGN="right" set in the second table. A BR tag with a CLEAR="all" attribute value set follows the second table.

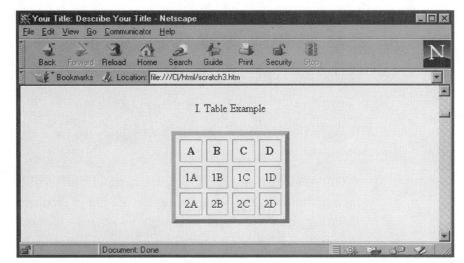

Figure 4.7

You can center a table by inserting the ALIGN="center" attribute value in the TABLE tag.

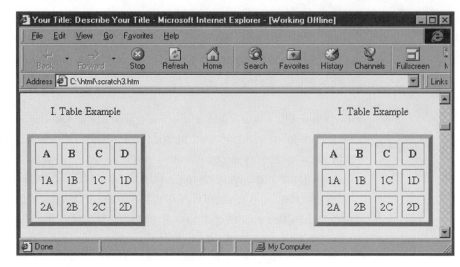

Figure 4.8

You can display two tables side by side by using the ALIGN="left" and ALIGN="right" attribute values.

Setting Table Width and Height

You can include WIDTH or HEIGHT attributes to specify the size of your table. You can use either absolute values (number of pixels) or relative values (percentages). Go back to the original table you are working on (don't use the side-by-side tables you pasted in for the previous tip example), and specify a width of 75 percent, like this:

```
<TABLE ALIGN="center" BORDER="6" CELLSPACING="6" CELL-
PADDING="6" WIDTH="75%">

<CAPTION>I. Table Example</CAPTION>
```

Figure 4.9 shows the table occupying 75 percent of the browser window's width.

You can also set the HEIGHT attribute in the TABLE tag, although it is generally less useful than setting the WIDTH attribute. You can use it to increase the row heights in a table by setting an absolute value (number of pixels) for the height of the table that is greater than the normal height.

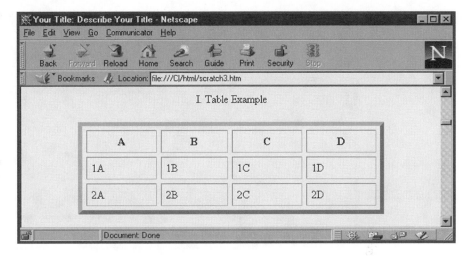

Figure 4.9

You can set the width of a table to a percentage, here 75 percent, of a browser window.

Adding Row Headings

Now you can add some row headings. To create a row heading, you just add a TH cell (instead of a TD cell) at the start of a table row, like this:

```
<TABLE ALIGN="center" BORDER="6" CELLSPACING="6" CELL-
PADDING="6" WIDTH="75%">

<CAPTION>I. Table Example</CAPTION>

<TR><TH></TH><TH>A</TH><TH>B</TH><TH>C</TH>
<TH>D</TH></TR>

<TR><TH>Row 1:</TH><TD>1A</TD><TD>1B</TD><TD>1C</TD>
<TD>1D</TD></TR>

<TR><TH>Row 2:</TH><TD>2A</TD><TD>2B</TD><TD>2C</TD>
<TD>2D</TD></TR>

</TABLE>
```

As Figure 4.10 shows, row headings are formatted just like column headings (they are both TH tags, after all)—centered and bolded.

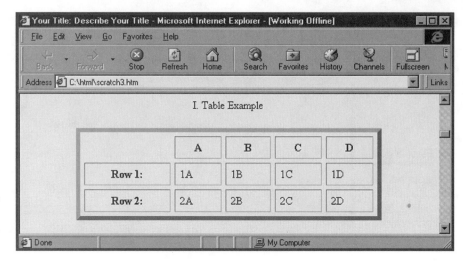

Figure 4.10

You can also
add row headings
to a table.

Horizontally Aligning Cell Contents

The text in the row headings and the data cells is left-aligned. Use the ALIGN attribute to set right-alignment for the bottom two rows of the table:

```
<CAPTION>I. Table Example</CAPTION>

<TR><TH></TH><TH>A</TH><TH>B</TH><TH>C</TH><TH>D</TH></TR>

<TR ALIGN="right"><TH>Row 1:</TH><TD>1A</TD><TD>1B</TD>
<TD>1C</TD><TD>1D</TD></TR>

<TR ALIGN="right"><TH>Row 2:</TH><TD>2A</TD><TD>2B</TD>
<TD>2C</TD><TD>2D</TD></TR>
```

See Figure 4.11 to see the new alignment for the row headings.

You can use the ALIGN attribute to horizontally align the contents of table rows (TR), table headings (TH), and table data cells (TD). Possible values are "left," "center," and "right." Center-alignment is the default for TH cells and left-alignment is the default for TD cells.

The HTML 4.0 specification also provides for the CHAR attribute, which would let you align columns along a decimal point or other character. Unfortunately, neither Navigator nor Internet Explorer supports this.

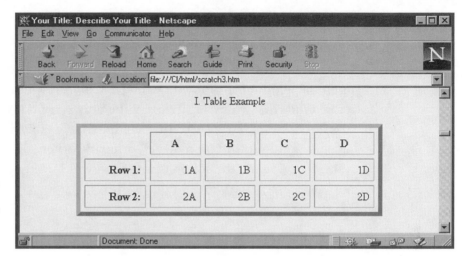

Figure 4.11

The bottom two rows of the table are right-aligned.

Setting Column Widths

By inserting a WIDTH attribute in the top cell of a column, you can specify the width of the entire column. Column widths can be set in either percentages or pixels.

The columns of your table are fairly equal in width. Only the first column, where the row header cells are, is somewhat wider than the other columns. A browser will expand or contract the columns depending on their contents (that's why the first column is wider—its contents take up more horizontal space). In other words, you can't depend on any column remaining the same width once you have started to fill it in with real data.

Since there are five columns in your table, set each column to an equal width by inserting a WIDTH="20%" attribute in each of the TH tags in the top row of the table:

```
<CAPTION>I. Table Example</CAPTION>

<TR><TH WIDTH="20%"></TH><TH WIDTH="20%">A</TH>
<TH WIDTH="20%">B</TH><TH WIDTH="20%">C</TH>
<TH WIDTH="20%">D</TH></TR>
```

The percentage for setting equal column widths will depend on the total number of columns. If your table had six columns, you would set each to

16% (100 divided by 6). Figure 4.12 shows what percentage-based column widths look like. I'll spare you the pixel version.

Column widths set in percentages will expand or contract depending upon the width of the browser window. Column widths set in pixels will remain the same width, regardless of the browser window width. Nothing stops you from setting the first column of a table in pixels and the remaining columns in percentages, or in any other combination that you want. If you set all the columns to a fixed width using pixels, you should not set a percentage width in the TABLE tag.

Inserting an Image

You can insert an image inside a table cell. The following HTML inserts a graphic, **ONE.GIF**, inside the upper-left corner cell (this graphic was used in the HTML tutorials so it should already be available):

```
<CAPTION>I. Table Example</CAPTION>

<TR><TH WIDTH="20%"><IMG SRC="one.gif"></TH><TH
WIDTH="20%">A</TH><TH WIDTH="20%">B</TH><TH
WIDTH="20%">C</TH><TH WIDTH="20%">D</TH></TR>
```

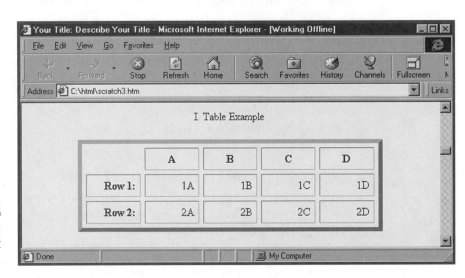

Figure 4.12

Each column of the table has been set to a width of 20%.

As Figure 4.13 shows, a graphic image of the number "1" has been inserted in the top left cell.

Vertically Aligning Cell Contents

You can use the VALIGN tag set to "top," "middle," or "bottom" to set the vertical alignment of a table row (TR), table heading (TH), or table data (TD) cell. Middle alignment is the default. Set the top row to bottom alignment:

```
<CAPTION>I. Table Example</CAPTION>

<TR VALIGN="bottom"><TH WIDTH="20%"><IMG
SRC="one.gif"></TH><TH WIDTH="20%">A</TH><TH
WIDTH="20%">B</TH><TH WIDTH="20%">C</TH><TH
WIDTH="20%">D</TH></TR>
```

As Figure 4.14 shows, the top row of the table is bottom-aligned.

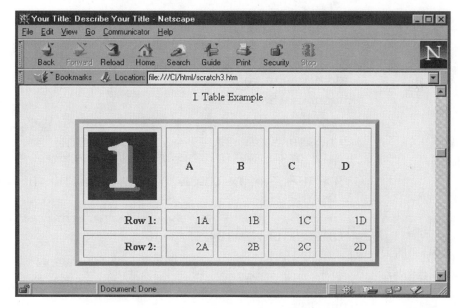

Figure 4.13

You can insert an inline image inside a table cell.

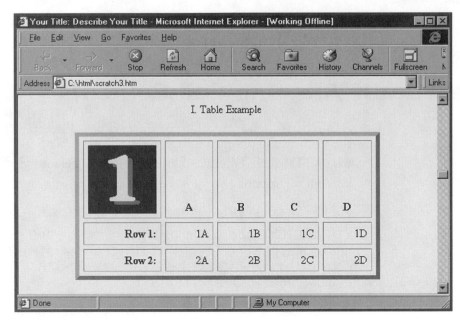

Figure 4.14

You can vertically align cell contents.

Spanning Columns

The COLSPAN attribute lets you create cells that span across columns. Add a row to your table that includes two cells that span across two columns each, like this:

```
<TR><TH VALIGN="bottom" WIDTH="20%"><IMG SRC="one.gif">
</TH><TH WIDTH="20%">A</TH><TH WIDTH="20%">B</TH>
<TH WIDTH="20%">C</TH><TH WIDTH="20%">D</TH></TR>
```

`<TR><TH></TH><TH COLSPAN="2">A & B</TH><TH COLSPAN="2">C & D</TH></TR>`

```
<TR><TH ALIGN="right">Row 1:</TH><TD>1A</TD><TD>1B</TD>
<TD>1C</TD><TD>1D</TD></TR>
```

Figure 4.15 shows the result of inserting a new row including three cells: a blank cell in the first column, then two following cells spanning two columns each.

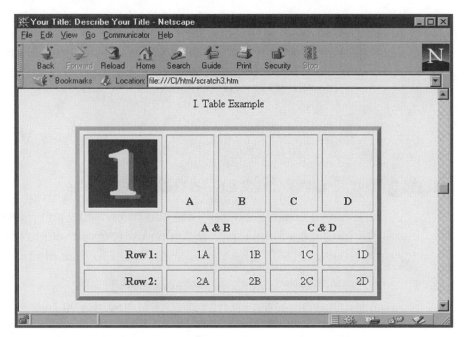

Figure 4.15

Table cells can span columns.

To span additional columns, specify the number with the COLSPAN attribute. Just make sure you don't exceed the total number of columns in the table. For instance, this example amounts to three cells spanning five columns (1 + 2 + 2 = 5).

Spanning Rows

You can not only create cells that span columns, you can create cells that span rows. To create a cell that spans rows, use the ROWSPAN attribute to specify the number of rows to span. This gets a little tricky: the cells to be spanned need to be removed from any following rows. In the following example, the cell that you need to delete is marked with strikethrough:

```
<CAPTION>I. Table Example</CAPTION>
```

```
<TR VALIGN="bottom"><TH ROWSPAN="2" WIDTH="20%"><IMG
SRC="one.gif"></TH><TH WIDTH="20%">A</TH><TH
WIDTH="20%">B</TH><TH WIDTH="20%">C</TH><TH
WIDTH="20%">D</TH></TR>
<TR><TH></TH><TH COLSPAN="2">A & B</TH><TH
COLSPAN="2">C & D</TH></TR>
```

As Figure 4.16 shows, the cell with the graphic "1" in it now spans two rows.

Changing Font Sizes and Colors

You can change the font size and color of the contents of a table cell by inserting a FONT tag bracketing the text you want to be affected. Set the font size to "7" and the color to "blue" for one of the cells:

```
<CAPTION>I. Table Example</CAPTION>

<TR><TH ROWSPAN="2" WIDTH="20%"><IMG
SRC="one.gif"></TH><TH WIDTH="20%"><FONT SIZE="7"
COLOR="blue">A</FONT></TH><TH WIDTH="20%">B</TH><TH
WIDTH="20%">C</TH><TH WIDTH="20%">D</TH></TR>
```

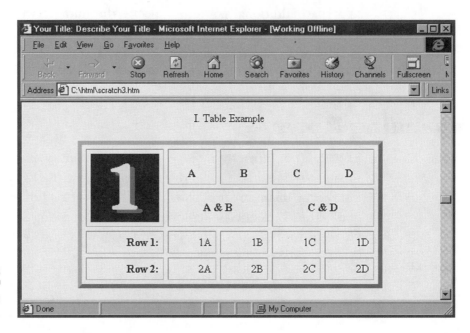

Figure 4.16

Table cells can also span rows.

As Figure 4.17 shows, your first row heading has grown considerably and turned blue (you should check the color out in your own browser, though).

Assigning Background Colors

You can assign a background color to an entire table, a row within a table, or a single cell. A table can be made more readable by assigning different background colors to row heading cells and row cells.

Assigning a Background Color in the TABLE Tag

Navigator and Internet Explorer do not handle assigning a background color to an entire table in the same fashion. In fact, the most recent version of Internet Explorer doesn't even handle this the way earlier versions of Internet Explorer did. Navigator will display the backgrounds of the table's cells in the background color, but not the borders between the cells. Internet Explorer also fills in the borders with the background color. Earlier versions of Internet Explorer fill in the background of the caption with the specified color. In other words, if you want to be sure that your

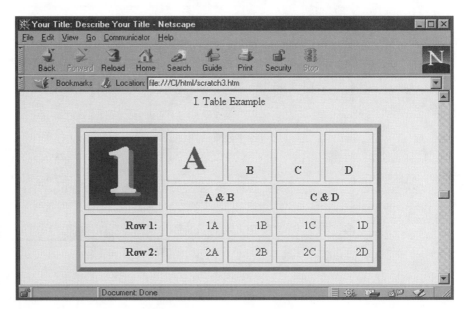

Figure 4.17

You can assign different font sizes and colors to text inside a table cell.

table is displayed at least similarly in these different browsers, you should probably avoid setting a background color in the TABLE tag. To see what it does, use the BGCOLOR attribute to set a background color in the TABLE tag (you can delete it later), like this:

```
<TABLE BGCOLOR="aqua" ALIGN="center" BORDER="6"
CELLSPACING="6" CELLPADDING="6" WIDTH="75%">

<CAPTION>I. Table Example</CAPTION>
```

Internet Explorer, as shown in Figure 4.18, displays a background color inserted in the TABLE tag behind the whole table. If you want to set the background color in the TABLE tag, you should set background colors in the TR, TH, and TD tags, as shown.

Navigator, as shown in Figure 4.19, displays a background color inserted in the TABLE tag only inside the table's cells.

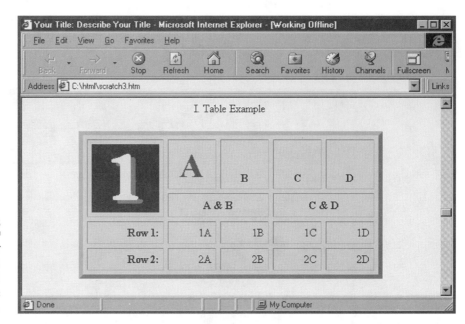

Figure 4.18

Internet Explorer displays a background color behind the whole table.

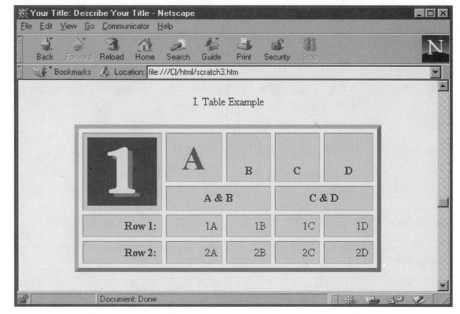

Figure 4.19

Navigator displays
a background color
only within the
table's cells.

Assigning a Background Color in the TR, TH, and TD Tags

You can assign background colors to individual table rows (TR tags), as well as to individual table heading (TH) and table data (TD) cells. The following will assign the color lime to the top row, red to the top-left TH cell (the one with the image in it), olive to the second row, and yellow to the bottom two rows (notice that BGCOLOR="aqua" should be deleted):

```
<TABLE BGCOLOR="aqua" ALIGN="center" BORDER="6"
CELLSPACING="6"  CELLPADDING="6" WIDTH="75%">

<CAPTION>I. Table Example</CAPTION>

<TR BGCOLOR="lime"><TH BGCOLOR="red" WIDTH="20%"
ROWSPAN="2"><IMG SRC="one.gif"></TH><TH
WIDTH="20%"><FONT SIZE="7"
COLOR="blue">A</FONT></TH><TH WIDTH="20%">B</TH><TH
WIDTH="20%">C</TH><TH WIDTH="20%">D</TH></TR>
```

```
<TR BGCOLOR="olive"><TH COLSPAN="2">A & B</TH><TH
COLSPAN="2">C & D</TH></TR>

<TR BGCOLOR="yellow"><TH ALIGN="right">Row 1:</TH>
<TD>1A</TD><TD>1B</TD><TD>1C</TD><TD>1D</TD></TR>

<TR BGCOLOR="yellow"><TH ALIGN="right">Row 2:</TH>
<TD>2A</TD><TD>2B</TD><TD>2C</TD><TD>2D</TD></TR>
```

As shown in Figure 4.20, different background colors appear behind one of the table cells, as well as the top, second, and last two table rows. You'll need to hop over to your Web browser to see what this looks like.

Removing Borders and Cell Spacing

You might think that you could get rid of the spacing and borders just by removing the BORDER and CELLSPACING attributes in the TABLE tag. Not so. To get rid of them completely, you have to set the attribute values to zero, like this:

```
<TABLE ALIGN="center" BORDER="0" CELLSPACING="0" CELL-
PADDING="6" WIDTH="75%">

<CAPTION>I. Table Example</CAPTION>
```

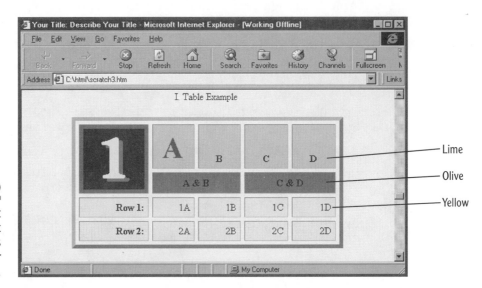

Figure 4.20

You can set different background colors for rows or individual cells.

As shown in Figure 4.21, the borders and spacing between the table cells have completely disappeared.

Using Background Images

You can also use background images in tables using the BACKGROUND attribute. However, this gets a bit tricky, because Navigator and Internet Explorer don't do this in the same way. While both Navigator and Internet Explorer allow you to specify a background image in the TABLE, TH, and TD tags, the details are substantially different:

❍ Just as the case with a background color, Internet Explorer displays a background image set in the TABLE tag behind the entire table, including behind the cell spacing. Navigator puts it only behind the individual cells.

❍ Internet Explorer does not recognize background images specified in the TR tag, but Navigator does. To specify a background image for a table row that will show up in both browsers, you need to specify it for each individual cell (TH or TD) in the row.

Figure 4.21

You have to set BORDER and CELLSPACING to zero to completely get rid of them.

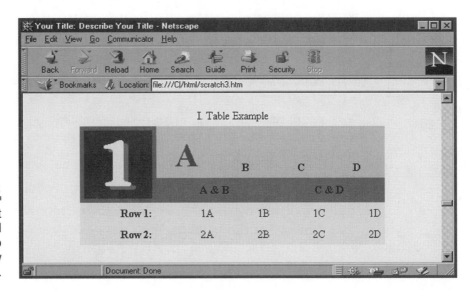

✿ In Navigator, a background image specified in the TABLE tag takes precedence over any background colors set in the rows, heading cells, or data cells. In Internet Explorer, it is the other way around. Thus, if you want to specify a background image in the TABLE tag that will display identically in both browsers, get rid of any BGCOLOR attributes elsewhere in the table.

For these reasons, you may be smart to avoid setting background images in tables. While the BGCOLOR attribute is a standard HTML attribute in both HTML 3.2 and 4.0, the BACKGROUND attribute isn't, most likely because of the wide variance between how the two main browsers interpret it. Still, if you want to check it out, specify a background image in the TABLE tag, reset the BORDER and CELLSPACING attributes as shown, and delete any BGCOLOR attributes, like this:

```
<TABLE BACKGROUND="backgrnd.gif" ALIGN="center"
BORDER="1" CELLSPACING="6" CELLPADDING="6" WIDTH="75%">

<CAPTION>I. Table Example</CAPTION>

<TR BGCOLOR="lime" VALIGN="bottom"><TH BGCOLOR="red"
ROWSPAN="2" WIDTH="20%"><IMG SRC="one.gif"></TH><TH
WIDTH="20%"><FONT SIZE="7"
COLOR="blue">A</FONT></TH><TH WIDTH="20%">B</TH><TH
WIDTH="20%">C</TH><TH WIDTH="20%">D</TH></TR>

<TR BGCOLOR="olive"><TH COLSPAN="2">A & B</TH><TH
COLSPAN="2">C & D</TH></TR>

<TR BGCOLOR="yellow" ALIGN="right"><TH>Row 1:</TH>
<TD>1A</TD><TD>1B</TD><TD>1C</TD><TD>1D</TD></TR>

<TR BGCOLOR="yellow" ALIGN="right"><TH ALIGN="right">
Row 2:</TH><TD>2A</TD><TD>2B</TD><TD>2C</TD>
<TD>2D</TD></TR>

</TABLE>
```

Figure 4.22 shows what this looks like in Internet Explorer, and Figure 4.23 shows what this looks like in Navigator.

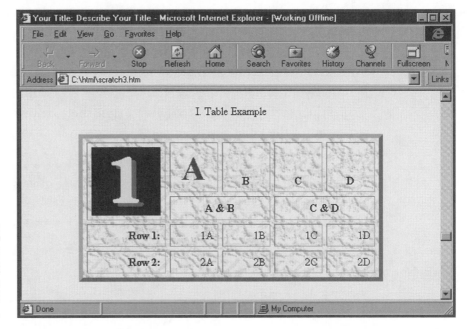

Figure 4.22

A background image in Internet Explorer is displayed behind the whole table.

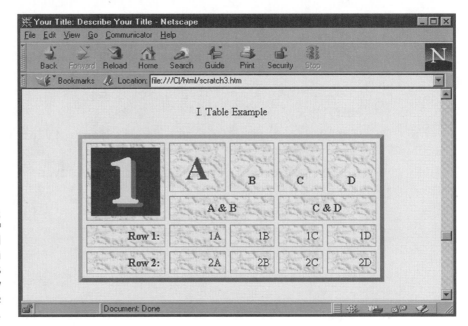

Figure 4.23

A background image in Navigator is displayed only behind the table cells.

Defining Table Head, Body, and Foot Sections

HTML 4.0 has three new table tags, THEAD, TBODY, and TFOOT. You can use them to define different sets of rows as the head, body, and foot of your table. By themselves, these tags do nothing. To get them to strut their stuff, you've got to define a style sheet that will specify how the sections of the table nested in these tags are to be displayed.

 NOTE   THEAD, TBODY, and TFOOT are supported only by Internet Explorer 4.01. Navigator 4.02 does not recognize these tags.

Creating the Style Sheet

The following is just a sample style sheet meant to give you some idea of the possibilities. For links to where you can find more information on using style sheets, see Appendix A, "The Web Resources Directory." Nest the following style sheet in the HEAD element:

```
<HTML>
<HEAD>
<TITLE>The Table Tutorial</TITLE>
<STYLE type="text/css">
THEAD {font-family: sans-serif; font-style: bold; font-size: 200%; color: maroon}
TBODY {font-family: monospace; font-style: bold; font-size: 125%; color: navy}
TFOOT {font-family: sans-serif; font-style: italic}
TR.head {background: lime}
TR.data {background: yellow}
TR.foot {background: #FF8000}
</STYLE>
</HEAD>
```

You'll notice that for the background colors for TR.head, TR.data, and TR.foot, I've used both color names from the 16 standard colors and an RGB color code, #FF8000, that is actually the hex code for the color "orange," which is *not* included in the 16 standard colors. The 4.0+ versions of both Internet Explorer and Navigator both recognize "orange" as a color name, as well as many additional color names (they just aren't part of standard HTML).

Using TBODY by Itself

If no THEAD or TFOOT sections are included in a table, the TBODY start and end tags may be omitted. In that case, all you have to do is define TBODY in your style sheet to have its properties automatically applied to your table.

Remove the background image you set in the last example:

```
<TABLE BACKGROUND="backgrnd.gif" ALIGN="center"
BORDER="1" CELLSPACING="6" CELLPADDING="6" WIDTH="75%">

<CAPTION>I. Table Example</CAPTION>
```

As shown in Figure 4.24, the TBODY properties defined in the style sheet (here a bold monospace font set to navy and scaled to 125% in size) are applied to the whole table, even though the TBODY tag has been omitted.

Actually, this beats using the FONT tag to assign font colors within a table, which you have to set within every cell where you want it to take effect. A bit laborious, in other words, if all you want to do is reset the font size and color for all the cells. Now, if only Navigator would support the TBODY tag!

Using THEAD, TBODY, and TFOOT Together

To have one or more rows in your table show up with the properties defined in the style sheet, just bracket them in the THEAD, TBODY, or

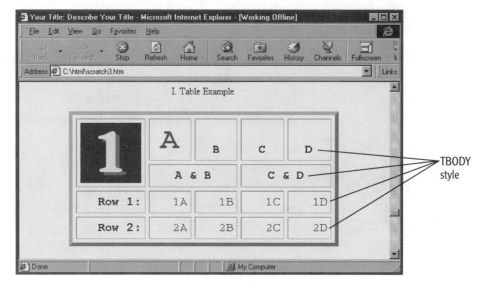

Figure 4.24

TBODY style
properties will be
applied to the
whole table, even
though THEAD,
TFOOT, and TBODY
are absent.

TFOOT tags. In the following example, apply the THEAD, TBODY,
and TFOOT tags to your table, add CLASS attributes to the TR tags, and
add an additional table row (for the table foot):

```
<TABLE ALIGN="center" BORDER="1" CELLSPACING="6" CELL-
PADDING="6" WIDTH="75%">
```

```
<CAPTION>I. Table Example</CAPTION>
```

<THEAD>

```
<TR CLASS="head" VALIGN="bottom"><TH ROWSPAN="2"
WIDTH="20%"><IMG SRC="one.gif"></TH><TH WIDTH="20%">
<FONT SIZE="7" COLOR="blue">A</FONT></TH><TH WIDTH="20%">
B</TH><TH WIDTH="20%">C</TH><TH WIDTH="20%">D</TH></TR>
```

```
<TR CLASS="head"><TH COLSPAN="2">A & B</TH><TH
COLSPAN="2">C & D</TH></TR>
```

</THEAD>

<TBODY>

```
<TR CLASS="data" ALIGN="right"><TH>Row 1:</TH>
<TD>1A</TD><TD>1B</TD><TD>1C</TD><TD>1D</TD></TR>
```

```
<TR CLASS="data" ALIGN="right"><TH ALIGN="right">Row 2:
</TH><TD>2A</TD><TD>2B</TD><TD>2C</TD><TD>2D</TD></TR>
</TBODY>
<TFOOT>
<TR CLASS="foot"><TD COLSPAN="5" ALIGN="center">This is
the table foot.</TD></TR>
</TFOOT>
</TABLE>
```

As shown in Figure 4.25, the latest version of Internet Explorer applies the properties defined in the style sheet to the different sections of the table when it displays it.

 TIP ■■
You can define as many TBODY sections as you want within a single table. The only requirement is that a TBODY section have at least one table row in it. (You should not define more than one THEAD or TFOOT section, however.)
■■

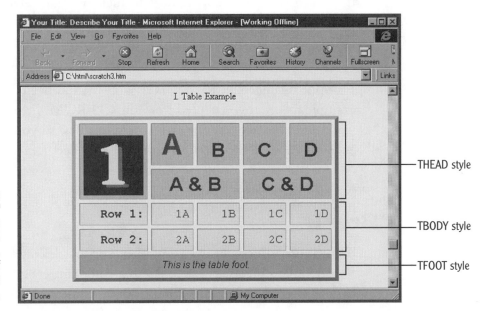

Figure 4.25

You can define styles that will render the head, body, and foot of your table in the format you prefer.

Other Table Tags

There are only a few table tags and attributes I haven't covered in this tutorial. HTML 4.0 has added the FRAME, RULES, COLGROUP, COL, and CHAR tags. Only the FRAME and RULES tags are supported by Internet Explorer. Navigator doesn't support any of these tags. The CHAR tag would allow vertical alignment on a decimal point, which would be handy. Internet Explorer also supports a number of additional table tags, BORDERCOLOR, BORDERCOLORDARK, and BOR-DERCOLORLIGHT, that have not yet been included in official HTML. See Appendix A, "The Web Resources Directory," for links to the latest HTML 4.0 specifications, references, and guides, where you can find out about these and other HTML tags.

Saving Your Work

Save the HTML file you just created. You can use it later as a reference. When you first saved it, you named it SCRATCH3.HTM. If more than one person is going to be doing this tutorial and you want to make sure that it doesn't get overwritten, you might want to give it a new name, such as using your first initial and last name for the file name (JMILLER3.HTM, for instance, if your name is John Miller). Once you've saved your scratch pad file, go ahead and exit Notepad.

For your reference, a file, TUTOR3.HTM, has been included with the example files that you copied from the CD-ROM. It includes all the previous examples broken out into separate tables, so you can have a reference for each of the features covered here. Feel free to pull it up into Notepad or check it out in your browser.

Take a Break

Wow, if you've been at it all day long, you are definitely a long-distance runner! Take a breather! Then, if you are not entirely out of breath, come back in five or ten minutes for a little mini-tutorial I've added on creating fancy 3-D icon bullet link lists using tables. If you are just plain tuckered out, feel free to call it a night. I'll see you bright and early tomorrow morning for the start of the Sunday Morning session, "Planning Your First Web Page." You can come back later to complete this tutorial.

Creating Icon Bullet Link Lists

In the Intermediate HTML Tutorial, I showed you a couple of different methods for creating icon bullet lists. The preferred method worked fine, except it was limited to indenting only two lines of text. The method I'll be showing you here for using tables to create an indented icon bullet list can have as many lines of indented text as you want.

Loading Your Starting Template

You should start here with a fresh Notepad window. Rerun Notepad to get a new empty Notepad window, then load the starting template you saved this morning, C:\HTML\START.HTM. It should look like the following listing (if you didn't save the template, just retype it now):

```
<HTML>
<HEAD>
<TITLE>Your Title: Describe Your Title</TITLE>
</HEAD>
<BODY>
</BODY>
</HTML>
```

Saving Your Scratch Pad File

Save your scratch pad file that you'll be using in this afternoon's tutorial. In Notepad, select File and Save As. Change the folder where you are going to save your file to C:\HTML, then save your file as SCRATCH4.HTM.

Creating the Example Table

To create an icon bullet link list using tables, enter the following HTML:

```
<TABLE WIDTH=100%>

<TR VALIGN="top">

<TD WIDTH="20"><P><IMG SRC="redball.gif" VSPACE="3">
</TD><TD><A
HREF="http://www.li.net/~autorent/yoyo.htm">Jon's Yo-Yo
Kingdom</A> Claims to have the largest Yo-Yo link list
on the Web. This is more text just to show that you can
indent as much text as you wish. This is more text just
to show that you can indent as much text as you
wish.</TD></TR>

<TR VALIGN="top">

<TD><P><IMG SRC="redball.gif" VSPACE="3"> </TD><TD><A
HREF="http://pages.nyu.edu/~tqm3413/yoyo/index.htm">Tomer's
Page of Exotic Yo-Yo</A> Dedicated to the "little-known,
original, unusual, difficult, or otherwise interesting
tricks." This is more text just to show that you can
indent as much text as you wish. This is more text just
to show that you can indent as much text as you
wish.</TD></TR>

</TABLE>
```

Figure 4.26 shows what this should look like in your browser.

Figure 4.26

Using tables, you can create an indented icon link list with no limit on the number of indented lines.

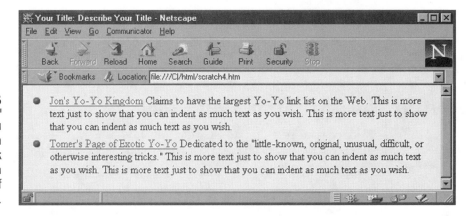

In this example, there are a number of things you should pay attention to when creating indented icon link lists using tables:

- The TR tags include VALIGN="top" to set the vertical alignment. Without this, the icon bullet images would be middle-aligned, which is not what you want. You could also set this attribute value in the TD tag containing the icon bullet graphic.

- A WIDTH attribute value of 20 pixels is set in the first cell of the top row to specify the width of the first column. This width can be increased or decreased to suit your taste.

- A P tag is inserted in the first cell of each row with a space also inserted at the end of the same cell. This makes allowance for older Web browsers that don't support displaying tables. The P tag will cause them to display each table row as a separate line, and the space will be inserted between the icon graphic and the following text. Otherwise, adding the P tag and inserting the space will have no effect on the display of the table in a tables-compatible Web browser.

- The IMG tags for the icon bullet graphics include a VSPACE (Vertical Space) attribute of 3 pixels. It is seldom that an icon bullet will line up even with a following line of text. You can add or subtract pixels in the VSPACE attribute in the IMG tag to adjust the position of the icon bullet relative to following text.

Saving Your Work

Save the HTML file you just created. You can use it later as a reference. When you first saved it, you named it SCRATCH4.HTM. If more than one person is going to be doing this tutorial and you want to make sure that this file doesn't get overwritten, you might want to give it a new name, such as using your first initial and last name for the file name (JMILLER4.HTM, for instance, if your name is John Miller).

What's Next?

You should now be comfortable including tables in your Web pages. If you completed the whole tables tutorial, you not only learned everything you need to know to create effective tables, you also learned how to use some of the latest HTML 4.0 table tags in conjunction with a snazzy style sheet. And you also learned how to create fancy 3-D icon bullet link lists with tables.

You can find out more about applying styles to your Web pages in Appendix A, "The Web Resources Directory." You'll also find a shareware software program, CoffeeCup StyleSheet Maker++, on the CD-ROM that can automate creating style sheets for your Web pages. For even more tools that can assist you in creating style sheets, look in Appendix B, "The Web Tools Directory."

If you managed to do all three Saturday tutorials, you're definitely a super HTML hotshot! Get a good night's sleep. I'll see you tomorrow, when you'll plan and create your first Web page.

Planning Your First Web Page

- Defining Your Objective
- Devising Your Outline
- Selecting an Example Web Page
- Creating Your Mock-Up Text File

Before you start creating your first Web page, you need to do some planning. I've broken down the planning process into a series of steps. To make things easier for you, I'll be providing three example Web pages. I'll be asking you to select one as a guide for planning and organizing your own material.

You won't actually be working with the example files in this session, but when you get around to selecting the Web page you want to use as a model, you will want to pull them up in your browser and take a closer look at them. I'll also present screen grabs for easy reference—but paper never captures the feel of looking at a live screen. You'll want to see what the example pages look like and check out how they work.

Creating Your Working Folder

Although you can continue using the C:\HTML folder as your working folder, you should start fresh. The reasons for doing so are several:

✪ You'll be using example Web pages and attendant graphic files in creating your first Web page. You'll have an easier time of it if these files are not mixed in with the example graphics and scratch pad files you used in doing the tutorials.

✪ You will probably want to use this new working folder for any future Web pages you want to create—another reason to keep it separate from the working folder for the HTML tutorials.

✿ More than one person can make use of the C:\HTML working folder
for doing the HTML tutorials (you just need to give your scratch pad
files unique file names), but if many people want to use the same
computer to create their Web pages, each person will need to have a
unique working folder for doing the planning and creating sessions.

So, if you choose to create a new working folder now (my recommendation), create a C:\PAGES folder. You can name your working folder whatever you want, but in today's planning and creating sessions, I'll be referring
to this folder as C:\PAGES. Use Windows Explorer in Windows 95 or File
Manager in Windows 3.1 to create your C:\PAGES working folder.

Using the Prima Interface to Install the Example Web Pages

On the CD-ROM, I've included example Web pages, along with attendant graphic files, for you to use in this planning session, as well as in the
creating session that follows this afternoon. You can use the interface on
the CD-ROM to install these files by doing the following:

1. Insert the CD-ROM in your CD-ROM drive.

2. For Windows 3.1 only:

   A. Run File Manager and select File, Run to open the Run
      window.

   B. In the Command Line text box, type **D:\primacd.exe** (where
      D:\ is the CD-ROM drive)

3. At the opening screen of Prima's CD-ROM interface:

   A. Click on Book Examples.

   B. Click on Web Pages in the center menu.

4. The Install radio button should already be selected. Click on OK
   to install the example Web pages and attendant graphic files.

5. At the WinZip Self-Extractor window, click on OK.

6. In the Unzip to Folder text box, enter **C:\PAGES** as your working folder (or C:\HTML if you are using that as your working folder). Click on Unzip. Click on OK when told that the files have been unzipped, and then click on Close.

NOTE If you don't have a CD-ROM drive, all the example Web pages and their attendant graphic files are available for download from this book's Web site at `http://www.callihan.com /create2/`. Just unzip the files into your working folder (C:\PAGES).

Thinking Ahead

It is up to you what else you may need to plan your first Web page. You might want to do it all inside Notepad, or you may want to use your favorite word processor. You might want to use butcher paper taped to a wall. Or a yellow legal pad. Use whatever best gets the juices flowing. Eventually, you'll want to tie everything together in one file in Notepad, which you'll then use as the basis for creating your Web page.

In the "Assembling Your Materials" section, you will have the option of taking a stab at creating your own custom banner graphic. I've included an example banner graphic with the example Web pages and, just in case you don't like the way that one looks, I've included another one with the example Web page files. Even if you decide to create your own custom banner graphic to give your page a personal touch, you shouldn't spend a lot of time doing it—that is, if you want to get this thing planned in a single morning!

Getting Oriented

Planning your first Web page, as with planning *any* Web page, is a process. This can be a very free-form, open-ended process, or it can be a fairly organized and orderly one. I've broken down a suggested planning process into seven basic stages.

For this first time, I recommend that you follow the steps in the order I present them. Later, when you get into planning more Web pages, feel free to rearrange these steps as you see fit—or devise an entirely different planning process, if you wish.

How you want to go about doing these steps is pretty open. Starting out, use whatever works best for you, which might be your favorite word processor, Notepad, a yellow legal pad, the back of an envelope, a restaurant napkin, or butcher paper taped to the wall. At least by the end of this process, you'll be pulling it all together in your word processor or text editor.

The final product will be a *mock-up* text file that you'll need to export out as an ASCII text file (a "Text Only" file, if you are using Word for Windows). This text file will include the text you want to use plus references to anything else you want to have in your Web page.

The mock-up should be organized and arranged according to the relative order, precedence, and position in which you want text or other objects to appear in your Web page. Optionally, if you are planning on creating a multiple-page Web site, you may also want to draw a map that will help clarify the relationships between your different Web pages (although I recommend you hold off trying to create a multiple-page Web site until you've completed a single Web page).

Here's a breakdown to give you a better idea of what you'll be doing this morning:

- **Define Your Objective.** You begin by defining your objective. In this case, your objective amounts to what you want to do. If you don't already have a pretty good idea of what you want to do, you might follow one of the suggestions for brainstorming provided in these sections.

- **Do an Outline.** You then take your objective and break it down into its main constituent parts, creating an outline, defining the basic structure and order of precedence of your material.

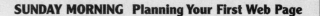

- **Select a Web Page Example.** I've included three generic Web page examples that you can use as guides or templates in planning and creating your first Web page. For this first time through, you should choose whichever of the first two Web page examples that best fits what you want to do. Generally, if your Web page is going to be fairly simple (and there is nothing wrong with starting out simple!), you should choose the first Web page example. If what you want to do is a bit more complicated than what the first Web page example will afford, try the second Web page example. After you have created your first Web page, you can come back and use the third Web page example to help you create your first multi-page Web site. Later, once you've become more adept at creating your own Web page designs, you can dispense with this step and design your own templates.

- **Assemble Your Materials.** Next, sketch out what you want to do in more detail, developing and writing some text to go with your outline. You can also take the opportunity here to decide on a banner or logo graphic for your page, but you might want to consider using the sample banner I provide. After you become a more experienced Web publisher, you'll select or create a background image, create and convert graphs, charts, or diagrams, define a form, design a table, delineate frames, create an animated GIF, decide on streaming audio, animation, or video, and so on. Don't worry, models are provided for organizing your text and plugging in your banner graphic and hypertext links.

- **Gather Your URLs (Optional).** Part of what makes a Web page are links to other Web pages. If you want to include a list of links, for instance, connecting to other Web pages or sites out on the Web, you need to gather the URLs (Web addresses) you want to use. You should try to gather as many of the URLs as you can for links you want to use *before* you start to create your first Web page. This section will cover some methods to easily assemble a collection of URLs for your Web page.

✪ **Create Your Mock-Up File.** Here you'll pull together in a single mock-up text file the different elements you want to include in your Web page, placed in the rough position and order in which you want them to appear, including any text you want to use, references to any graphics you want to use, and URLs for any hypertext links you want to include.

✪ **Draw a Map (Optional).** You probably won't be drawing a map this morning, since you are just planning a single page. Once you get around to planning and creating a multiple-page Web site, however, this section will come in handy. Some sort of map, if only a mental picture, should be part of planning any Web site. Although an outline captures the static structure of a Web page or Web site, a map delineates the dynamic relationships within and between your Web pages.

Don't get bogged down! This section breaks up the planning process into a series of tasks that you can perform easily, but they still take time. Do your best, but don't take more than 20 to 40 minutes on any one task. The main point here is not to plan your ultimately perfect Web page in depth, but to get a taste of what a real planning process might be like.

Defining Your Objective

First, you must define what you want to do. One way is to try to boil it down to an objective—the purpose of your undertaking. (This is sometimes called a mission statement, but that just seems a bit too formal for this activity.) Don't assume that you already know your objective. Even worse than thinking you know all the answers is thinking you know all the questions! The questions you need to identify are short but not easy. In fact, you can put them each in one word: Why, Who, What, and How.

Your first question should simply be, "Why do I want to create a Web page?" Try to think of all the reasons. Write them down in a list. These reasons can be fairly general—it is good to start out with the general, then

refine it to something more specific as you go along. For instance, you may simply want to communicate and express yourself. Or you may want to sell a product or offer a service. You may want to explore a new opportunity, learn, grow, experiment, and challenge yourself. You may want to connect and network with colleagues and associates. Define your larger frame focus. And don't just stop at the first answer. Think up at least three reasons for creating a Web page, prioritizing them in a list, from most to least important.

Your second question should be, "Who am I trying to reach?" The Web is all about connecting, but nobody is compelled to connect with anyone else. If people choose to connect with you, they generally do so of their own accord. Push promotion strategies have never worked very well on the Web, with some glaring exceptions (spam e-mail, for one).

Pull strategies do work. Offer information, resources, even entertainment. What pulls people to your site or page and keeps them coming back generally isn't that you happen to be selling a product or offering a service, but that you offer value-added resources. Think of what you can offer, what you have to give. Target that relative to the audience you would like to attract. Then provide links to descriptions of your company, products, and services. That's what works.

NOTE You shouldn't confuse this with all the talk about "push" technologies that you hear about on the Web. Although they are somewhat related, what I'm referring to are a couple of old-line marketing terms that, in fact, predate the Web or the Internet. Cold calling is a push strategy, as is putting up a billboard, advertising in a magazine, and distributing a catalog. A pull strategy might be a sidewalk sale, free entertainment, sponsoring a public service announcement, or distributing a brochure on health risks. *Pull* means giving people a reason to visit you ("Free balloons! Free pop!"). So, think in terms of what you have to offer, what others may want or need, and not just of what you are trying to sell. Be creative. Be giving.

The third question should be, "What am I trying to achieve?" It is very easy to confuse this question with the first question, the Why question. The Why question has to do with reasons, with what compels you in a particular direction or course, while the What question has to do with specific actions or results you want to facilitate. Here you need to zero in on specific actions or results that you want to happen. For instance, you might find that you want to facilitate communication with clients or potential customers, disseminate industry information, educate and inform the public, receive feedback from customers or clients, entertain friends and neighbors, display your talents or skills, lobby for a political position (or argue for a philosophical one), or schmooze with professional colleagues. With the Why question, you defined your larger frame, while here you need to get down to specific things you want to occur. As with the Why question, don't just stop with a single answer, but make a list of at least three fairly specific things (actions or results) you'd like to see happen, then prioritize them from most important to least important. And don't forget the Who! Correlate the Why with the Who to come up with a pretty good idea of what your What is.

The fourth question should then be something like, "How do I want my page to implement my Why, Who, and What?" The How here will be the actual form or forms that your Web page or pages will take to achieve the ends you want. Don't be afraid to be specific. This could be just about anything, including a personal page, an online résumé, your own link-o-rama, an informational page on a hobby, a subject of interest, a field of expertise, a catalog of products, a price list, a description of services, a glossary, a time line, a FAQ (Frequently Asked Questions) page, a customer response form, a survey, a book review or paper, an online newsletter, a collection of poems, or an online brochure for your organization, business, or project. Once again, make a list of at least three ways in which you would like to achieve your desired results, then prioritize them from the one you think would be the most effective. Once you get around to creating your first multi-page Web site, you'll probably end up combining several different How answers together.

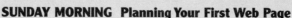

Finally, try pulling it all together in a single concise statement. In other words, correlate the Why and the Who to come up with your What and then let that What determine your How. Put it all together and you have your objective. Sounds simple, right? You wish! Simplicity is not simple.

Stay flexible and open! You can spend so much time creating an objective that you end up being hesitant to change or alter it in response to changing realities—which is why I've chosen to call it an objective here, rather than a mission statement. Don't get too hung up on your objective. Try to make it an aiming point, a working hypothesis, not a stone around your neck. Feel free to change it as you go.

Remember, right now you're only creating an objective for one page. You probably would come up with a different objective if it were for an entire Web publishing enterprise or undertaking. Tie that into the mission statement of your company, organization, or agency, and you'll probably come up with yet another objective.

TASK #1: Define Your Objective

Ask yourself the four one-word key questions and then combine your answers to form a single statement. This statement then becomes your objective.

Develop this statement in a medium with which you're comfortable—your word processor or your text editor, or on a pad of paper—whatever works. Don't take forever doing this, though. This is just a starting point, not a destination. The idea is to get some kind of grip on where you're coming from and where you're trying to go.

Devising Your Outline

Whereas an objective expresses the intentions, purposes, and goals of your project as a whole, an outline organizes it into divisions and subdivisions, establishing the hierarchy and sequence of the material you want to present.

Your outline doesn't have to be complicated or even complete, but it should at least break your objective down into its basic components, even if only just A, B, and C. As with your objective, your initial outline should not be carved in stone. It may not take full form, for instance, until you are well into the next phase, assembling your materials. Some people prefer to create an outline right off the bat. Others need to sketch out their ideas first, from which they can then create their outline.

TASK #2: Do Your Outline

For now, use your objective as the top level of your outline, then break out beneath it the different components. These components define and order how you want to execute your objective, providing a structure for the information you're going to want to present to a viewer of your Web page. If you want, write a brief description of each component.

Selecting an Example Web Page

I've placed this step here to help you visualize the Web page you are going to plan and create today. At the start of this session, you copied three Web page examples from the CD-ROM to your working folder. This afternoon, you'll be using one of these as a template or guide as you create

your first Web page. This morning, you won't actually be working with the files, but you should pull them up and review them in your browser. I also show you each Web page example in figures that you can use for easy reference while planning your Web page.

Once you become more adept at designing your own Web pages, you can skip this particular step. Think of the Web page examples presented here as training wheels that you can dispense with once you learn how to ride on your own.

I've included three Web page examples that you can choose from:

- **A Web Page Using a Link List.** This is the simplest of the three example Web pages. It includes a list of external links connecting to other pages out on the Web.

- **A Web Page Using Subsections.** This example Web page is a little more complex, providing a table of contents (a *menu*) of internal links that jump to different subsections within the same page.

- **A Web Site Using Subpages.** You should use this example Web page only after trying out one of the first two. It provides a menu of external links that functions as an index to a multi-page Web site, allowing the user to jump to different subpages.

NOTE Content, content, content. All the whiz-bang graphics aside, what still matters more than anything else is simply content—straightforward, honest information. What the Web doesn't need more of are loads of narcissistic, self-congratulatory, bandwidth-hogging but otherwise empty Web pages. Before doing a Web page on a certain subject, do a few searches on the Web using Open Text, Webcrawler, Yahoo!, or some other search engine to find out whether someone else has already done what you want to do. If so, just create a link to it rather than cover the same ground.

TASK #3: Select Your Web Page Example

Choose one of the following Web page examples to use as a model in assembling the materials for your Web page. Use the third example only if you have already created your first Web page using one of the first two and are ready to plan and create your first multi-page Web site.

Example #1: A Web Page Using a Link List

This very basic Web page example includes a banner graphic, a level-one heading, an introductory paragraph, a list, and an address block.

The list can either be a "list of particulars" or a link list to other Web pages. An example of using this with a plain list (no links) would be to create a "business card" where you describe your business in the introductory paragraph, then follow that with a list of products, services, or qualifications. A different kind of example of a page using a link list with other pages on the Web would be a page that describes a hobby, professional expertise, or area of interest, followed by a list of links to other pages on the Web that share the same theme. (See Figure 5.1.)

Pull this up in your browser to get a closer look. If you copied the example Web page files at the start of this session, you should find it in your working folder as BASIC-1.HTM.

Example #2: A Web Page Using Subsections

This is a more complex example, but it's still just a single page. Like the first Web page example, it includes a banner graphic, a level-one heading, and an introductory paragraph. However, the link list here, instead of linking to other Web pages, functions as a table of contents that jumps to the subsections of the document, using internal links rather than external ones. You probably would want to use this example if your outline is more complicated. Think of the subsections as corresponding to the subsections of your outline. (See Figure 5.2.)

Figure 5.1

The first Web page example, best for a relatively simple page, contains a banner graphic, a level-one heading, an introductory paragraph, a link list, and an address block.

Figure 5.2

The second Web page example, for a more complex page, contains a banner graphic, a level-one heading, an introductory paragraph, a table of contents that jumps to a series of subsections, and an address section.

Pull this up in your browser to get a closer look. Test drive the table of contents, jumping to the different subsections. You should find it in your working folder as BASIC-2.HTM.

Example #3: A Web Site Using Subpages

I don't recommend that you use this Web page example the first time through. Get your feet wet with one of the first two Web page examples, and then, when you feel ready, come back and try this example. Generally, if the material you want to present is extensive, you should consider breaking the page's subsections into separate subpages. Any time a page extends beyond three or four screens, you should consider breaking it up into more than one page.

One of the advantages of breaking up a long Web page into a main page and subpages is that visitors to your Web site need only load the home page and the particular subpage they're interested in seeing, rather than wait for the whole document to load, before they can get at the part they want to read.

On the other hand, breaking up the whole document into pieces can penalize visitors who want to view the whole thing, forcing them to reconnect to the server to retrieve each subpage. Another disadvantage is that a Web document that's broken up into a main page and subpages can't be printed in a single operation. It must be printed in separate pages—and the longer a Web document, especially if it contains mostly text, the more likely that a viewer will want to print it out to read more comfortably or save it for later.

A compromise that you see fairly frequently on the Web is to do both— to break up the site into subpages, but include a link to another version that is all in one page and uses subsections.

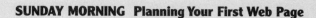

You might also want to create a home page linked to subpages if you've created a number of different loosely related or unrelated Web pages that you want to link together through an index page. It's fairly common on the Web to see personal pages done this way, linking to and serving as indexes for other more specialized pages possibly created for business or other purposes. See Figure 5.3 for an example of a home page linked to a number of subpages.

Pull this up in your browser to get a closer look. Test drive the index link list, clicking on the first link in the list to check out the jump to the subpage. Check out the loop-back link from the subpage to the main page. I've only included one subpage with this example, so the links to the other subpages in the list won't work unless you create additional subpages. You should find the main page for this example Web page in your working folder as BASIC-3.HTM.

A subpage is just another Web page. Figure 5.4 shows a basic subpage, which doesn't even have a banner graphic. If you use a subpage rather than add subsections to your home page, then what would have been the level-two subheadings serve as the level-one headings at the top of your subpages.

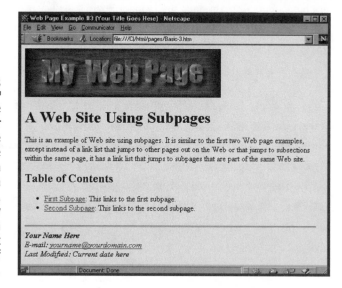

Figure 5.3

The third Web page example, best for an even more complex multi-page Web site, contains a banner graphic, a level-one heading, an introductory paragraph, and an "index" link list that jumps to a series of subpages.

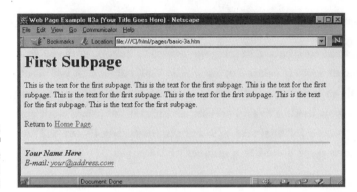

Figure 5.4

A subpage for the
Web site introduced
in Figure 5.3

I've only provided one example subpage here, but you probably want to use several subpages. Use this one as a model for any other subpages you want to create.

You should find this in your working folder as BASIC-3A.HTM. Feel free to pull it up in your browser directly. However, you'll get a better idea of how it works if you click on the link to the first example subpage in the main page.

TIP

I haven't included a banner graphic in the sample subpage. Coordinating your graphics between your main page and your subpages, however, is a good way to give a Web site a common look and feel. One trick is to use a smaller version of the banner graphic that heads your main page.

Notice that the subpage example includes a loop-back link at the bottom of the page that returns viewers to the home page. Check it out to see how it works. When you use subpages, always include a loop-back link to your home page. Visitors don't necessarily come through your home page to get to a subpage. If they have the URL on their hotlist or bookmark list or have gotten it from a search engine, they go directly to your subpage. Without a loop-back link they would have no way to get to your home page—hitting the Back button won't work.

Take a Break

You've defined your objective, done your outline, and selected the Web page example you want to use—hey, that's a lot of brain work! If you haven't eaten anything yet, you might want to get a bowl of cereal or some other sustenance, because there's plenty more to do if you want to install your first Web page today. So, give the noggin a rest, get a bite if you're hungry. I'll see you back in five or ten minutes, when you'll assemble your materials and pull together your mock-up text file.

Assembling Your Materials

In this stage, you should start to put together the different bits and pieces that will actually compose your Web page. For instance, you may want to think of a title and type or write an introductory paragraph, as well as any other text you want to create. For this first time through, I recommend that you stick to just including a banner graphic. If you don't already have a graphic handy that you want to use, just plug in the sample banner graphic that is included with the example Web pages as a placeholder until you get around to creating exactly the right graphic for yourself.

Eventually, you are probably going to want to include other images in your Web pages—a snapshot of your kids, a photo of your dog or cat, or one of your kid's drawings or finger paintings.

If you already have a scanner or digital camera, you have no difficulty in getting images to include in your Web pages—you just need to convert them to JPG format (recommended for photos). If you don't have a scanner or digital camera, there is no need to immediately go out and plump down the plastic just to get a means for including images in your Web pages. Most copy shops now offer scanning services—you just have to convert the scans to JPG or GIF format. Also, if you get a roll of film developed through Kodak, you can request to have your pictures put on a Photo-CD. Then you just need to convert your photos (using Paint Shop Pro, for instance) from the Photo-CD format to JPG format.

Don't spend a whole lot of time right now trying to get a bunch of images together to include in your first Web page. For now, the most you should probably try to do is to create a custom banner graphic.

TASK #4: Write a Title and Introductory Paragraph

Think of a title that you want to have displayed at the top of your Web page, then write an introductory paragraph. This should describe your Web page in a nutshell.

If you use your word processor, you'll need to save your file as a straight text file (in Word for Windows, select "Text Only" as the file type). If you want to use a yellow legal pad, or a napkin, for that matter, you should still type your finished text into a file in your word processor or text editor when you are happy with it. Just keep the crumbs from between the keys!

One thing you may want to keep in mind here is that many search engines index Web pages according to what they find in the first paragraph. So try to include a number of keywords that people might use in doing a search for a page like yours.

If you chose the second Web page example to use as your model, you should also think of some subsection headings you want to use, and write an introductory paragraph (keep them short!) for each.

Go ahead and save the Notepad file you create here as TEXT.TXT (or whatever name you want, just so you remember what you call it).

 NOTE As you know, I don't recommend that you try to use the third Web page example to create a multi-page Web site the first time through. If you have already created your first *single* Web page and have come back to try your hand at creating a multi-page site, you should create separate text files containing the title and the introductory paragraph for each separate Web page you want to create.

TASK #5: Create Your Banner Graphic (Optional)

I've provided a sample banner graphic for you, so if you don't have one of your own and don't want to take the time right now to create one, feel free to skip the rest of this task. You can use the sample banner graphic as a placeholder until you get around to scanning or creating the graphic you want to use.

If you do have a graphic handy that you want to use, you may need to convert it to GIF or JPG format. Paint Shop Pro, available on the CD-ROM, can convert graphics from many other formats (such as PCX or TIFF) to GIF or JPG. You may also need to resize the graphic so that it will fit within a browser window—make sure your graphic is less than 600 pixels wide, and you may want to reduce the width even further.

You can create your own custom banner graphic at this time. Just use Paint Shop Pro or another photo-paint program that can create GIF or JPG format graphics. Don't take all day to do it! Just something to give a personal touch to your page. You might, for instance, try setting the text for your level-one heading in a fancy font. Preferably, keep it to less than 500 pixels wide, 200 pixels high.

If you create your own banner graphic or want to convert and resize a graphic you already have, just save the final graphic you create as a GIF file in your working folder so it will be handy when you get around to creating your first Web page this afternoon. Name it MYBANNER.GIF, or something like that.

Although I recommend that you stick to just adding a banner graphic to your first Web page, you may have other graphics you want to include. If you already have these graphics handy in electronic form, all you need to do is convert them to GIF or JPG files and resize them to fit on your Web page. Feel free to take the time to do that, if you wish. Just don't take a whole lot of time trying to scan or create original graphics, or you'll still be working at breakfast tomorrow.

Gathering Your URLs (Optional)

This is really part of the "assembling your materials" process, but it is important enough to break it out as a separate step. If you have chosen the first Web page example, you'll probably want to include a list of links to other Web pages. If you have chosen one of the other Web page examples, you may still want to include links to other Web pages, either as link lists or as *in-context* links inserted in your text.

If you are using the first Web page example, you can use the example link list I include with it. (If you are using the second or third Web page examples and want to play with including a list of URLs in one or more of your subsections or subpages, you can copy in the example link list from the first Web page example.) You'll also find lots of URLs you can use in Appendix A, "The Web Resources Directory," and Appendix B, "The Web Tools Directory." However, in case you want to take the time right now to gather your own URLs, this section covers some methods you can use in your hunting expedition.

TIP You may not have the slightest idea what hypertext links you want to include in your Web page. A good way to gather a list of URLs to use in your Web page is to go to Yahoo! (http://www.yahoo.com) and do a search using a keyword or keywords that describe your page. Yahoo! should return one or more categories of links that match your query.

Gathering URLs as You Surf

The easiest way to gather your URLs is simply to connect to the Web, go to the Web page you want to link to, and grab its URL. Here's how to do it.

1. First, run Notepad. You'll be pasting your URLs into a text file, then saving them for later use.

2. Connect to the Internet and run your Web browser.

3. Display the Web page you want to link to in your Web browser (see previous tip for using Yahoo! to find links).

4. Right-click on the URL (in the Location box in Navigator or in the Address box in Internet Explorer). This should highlight the URL and open up a drop-down menu. Select Copy.

5. Hop over to Notepad and press Ctrl+V to paste in the URL you just copied.

6. Following the URL, type in the title of the Web page you are linking to (you can copy and paste this from the Web page, if it is available there). Optionally, type in some additional text describing the Web page. These will later form the link text and descriptive text for your link list.

7. Repeat these steps for any other URLs you want to include in your Web page. When you finish, you should have a list of URLs in your Notepad file, along with titles for the links and, optionally, text describing each link. When you have enough URLs for your Web page (a half-dozen or so should do), just save your Notepad file as LINKS.TXT in your working folder.

Using Your Bookmarks or Favorites to Get URLs

If you have been surfing the Web using Navigator or Internet Explorer, you probably have collected a pretty good selection of bookmarks in Navigator or favorites in Internet Explorer. Your bookmark or favorites list can be an excellent source for URLs that you might want to include in your Web pages. The following is a quick rundown on how to do this in Navigator or Internet Explorer.

Using Navigator Bookmarks

1. Run Notepad. You'll be pasting the URLs you gather into a text file that you'll save for later. (If you already created LINKS.TXT in the previous section, you can just reopen that file here.)

2. Run Navigator (no need to log on to the Internet). Click on the Bookmarks button, then select Edit Bookmarks.

3. Right-click on a bookmark that you want to use, and then select Copy Link Location.

4. Hop back over to Notepad and press Ctrl+V to paste in the bookmark's URL. Following the URL, type in a title for the URL that you want to use as the link text (you may want to hop back over to Navigator and check out what is listed for the bookmark). You can also add some descriptive text. Save (or resave) your Notepad file as LINKS.TXT in your working folder.

TIP

Navigator stores its bookmarks in an ordinary HTML file, BOOKMARK.HTM. You can open this file in your browser, then easily copy and paste both the URLs and the link text. Different versions of Navigator may store this file in different locations. (To find out where your BOOKMARK.HTM is, in Windows 95, click on the Start button, then select Find, Files or Folders. In Windows 3.1, run File Manager and select File, Search.) Once you have loaded BOOKMARK.HTM into Navigator, just right-click on the link, select Copy Link Location, then hop over to Notepad and press Ctrl+V to paste in the URL. To copy the link text for the link, just position your mouse to the left or right of the link text, then click and drag with your mouse to highlight it (clicking on the link text won't work—it activates the link). Press Ctrl+C to copy it, then hop over to Notepad and press Ctrl+V to paste it in.

Using Internet Explorer Favorites

1. Run Notepad. You'll be pasting the URLs you gather into a text file that you'll save for later. (Note: If you already created LINKS.TXT in the previous section, you can just re-open that file here.)

2. Run Internet Explorer (no need to log on to the Internet). Select Favorites, Organize Favorites. Open up one of the folders (Links, for instance).

3. Right-click on one of the favorites listed, then select Properties. Select the Internet Shortcut tab. The Target URL should already be highlighted. Just press Ctrl+C to copy it to the Clipboard.

4. Hop back over to Notepad and press Ctrl+V to paste in the URL. Following the URL, type in a title for the URL that you want to use as the link text (you may want to hop back over to Internet Explorer and check out what is listed for the favorite). You can also add some descriptive text. Save (or resave) your Notepad file as LINKS.TXT in your working folder.

● ●

NOTE   Some feel you should request permission before you link to someone else's Web page. I think that advice is a bit extreme, with its rationale dating back to when most Web hosting arrangements came with very skimpy traffic allowances. These days, I don't know of anyone who doesn't want all the links they can get. Feel free, however, to let someone know that you think their page is informative, well-designed, or just plain great—most Web authors are gluttons for appreciation. Let them know that you are placing a link to their page on yours. Ask if they'd like to link back to you—getting reciprocal links is an excellent way to build up your own Web traffic. I always try to give full credit for any Web page I link to, including the title of the full Web site if I'm linking to a subpage, plus the name of the author, or the name of the organization/company responsible for creating the site.

● ●

TASK #6: Snag Some URLs (Optional)

I've provided sample URLs in the example Web pages that you can use as place-holders, so if you are running short on time, you can skip this task if you wish. You'll want to come back later, however, and gather the actual URLs you want to use in your Web page—these aren't useful links for the long haul.

If want to take the time right now to gather your own URLs, go up on the Web and use one of the techniques discussed in the previous sections to copy the URLs you want to use to the Clipboard, then paste them into a Notepad file. Gather at least a half-dozen URLs that you want to use, along with the link text and description text for each link. Save the file as LINKS.TXT in your working folder. You'll use it in the next step when you create your mock-up text file.

Creating Your Mock-Up Text File

Your mock-up text file should include everything you want in your Web page—any text you have written (such as your title, introductory paragraph, or other text), file names of any graphics you want to use, any URLs you want to include either as in-context links or as a list of links, an address section including your name, company name (if applicable), and e-mail address. A good part of this you may already have created or gathered while doing the previous tasks.

Some of it may still need to be determined, such as the file name for a graphic you have yet to scan or create. Some of it may still be scrawled on that yellow legal pad, or on that napkin, and will finally need to be typed in. The basic idea here is to pull everything together in one file, in the rough order and precedence in which you want it to appear in your Web page. Use your outline (created in Task #2) and the example Web page you chose (in Task #3) as guides for how to organize your mock-up text file. Put in everything *except* the HTML codes. You'll be adding the HTML this afternoon. Right now, don't worry about the code—just focus on the content and organization of your Web page.

As you gather your materials, you may find that your outline, or even your objective, has changed. A creative process is a fluid one. Feel free to change your course. Sometimes, not until you're pulling all the pieces together do you realize what you really want. Although what is being presented here is a highly condensed version, a large part of any planning process involves a good amount of research, and as an e-mail signature I once saw said, "If you know what you are doing, it isn't research!"

What you want to end up with here is a somewhat fleshed-out draft that at least has everything put roughly into place, even if it's in the form of a "To be determined," "Need to create logo graphic," "Get photo of dog," "Write product description," "Create chart of sales figures," or similar notation.

TASK #7: Create Your Mock-Up Text File

Here you should pull together all the results from the previous tasks into a single text file, your mock-up text file. Feel free to do this in your word processor, or you can go directly to working with Notepad. If you use your word processor, you'll need to save your final result as an ASCII text file (a "Text Only" file in Word for Windows).

If you are using your word processor, you should open any files you've created in the previous tasks into separate windows, then copy and paste to arrange them in the order in which you want them in your final Web page. If you have been working in Notepad, just run a copy of Notepad for each of the files you've created in the previous tasks.

The pieces you may want to pull together here should at minimum be: the outline you created in Task #2 and the title, introductory paragraph, and any other text you created in Task #4. Optionally, you'll also want to have the file names of any graphics, probably just your banner graphic, that you created in Task #5; and any URLs you gathered in Task #6. You should also have the Web page example you selected in Task #3 open in your browser, so you can use it as a guide for pulling all these pieces together.

At minimum, if you have chosen the first Web page example as your model, you will want to end up with a file containing the following:

1. A reference to the file name of the banner graphic you want to use (just put in "Add sample banner," if you want to use the sample banner graphic I provide).

2. The title that you want to appear at the top of your Web page.

3. Your introductory paragraph.

4. A list of URLs you want to use for your link list (just put in "Add sample link list," if you want to use the sample link list I provide). You should also insert any URLs you want to use as in-context links into your introductory paragraph in the positions where you want them to appear.

5. Information you want in your address block, as well as any contact information. You should at least include your name and e-mail address here. Optionally, you could include your company name (if applicable), an 800 number, your phone and fax numbers, and so on.

If you are using the second Web page example, you will also need any subtitles and subsection text. Also, you may want to include separate link lists in some or all of your subsections—you'll need to break out the URLs you gathered and arrange them under the subsections where you want them to appear.

If you are using the third Web page example (meaning this is at least your *second* Web page!), you should create a mock-up text file for each page you are creating (your main page and your subpages).

After you create your mock-up text file, save it in your working folder as MOCKUP.TXT. (If you are creating your mock-up text file in your word processor, you should save it as a straight text file ("Text Only" in Word for Windows), giving it a .TXT extension. If you used the third Web page example to plan a multi-page Web site, you will need to save a text file (MOCKUP.TXT) for your main Web page and text files for each of your subpages (MOCKUP1.TXT, MOCKUP2.TXT, and so on, or you can give separate descriptive names to your subpages, such as PRICES.TXT, PRODUCTS.TXT, and so on).

Drawing a Map (Optional)

You only need to work through this section if you're creating a multi-page Web site. You can create a map for a single Web page, but in most cases it won't be complex enough to be worthwhile. So if you are not creating a multi-page Web site and are running short on time, feel free to skim or skip this section.

An outline defines the static structure of your document but does little to highlight and define any dynamic interrelations within your document. This is fine for paper, which doesn't do interrelations very well anyway. However, the advantage of a hypertext document is that it is dynamic, allowing many different ways to approach and peruse the information you provide. Your map may closely mirror your outline, or it may sharply diverge from it, opening up links between sections that might otherwise remain separate from each other.

This map can be a simple chart like an organizational chart, using boxes and lines. It can be a flow chart or a storyboard. Whatever approach you choose to take, it's important that you capture in it the dynamic relationships within and between different parts of your document.

The map of one multi-page site can take many different forms. The important thing is to be able to visualize the layout and relationships in your site. You might map your site in the form of an organization chart, as shown in Figure 5.5

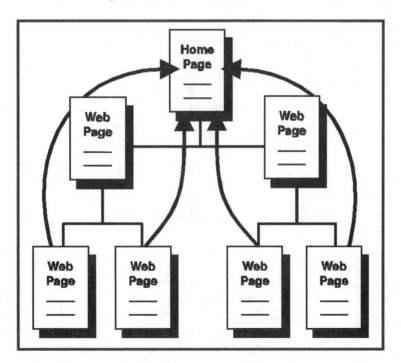

Figure 5.5

A Web site plan can look like an organization chart.

Or, if you're a technical type, you might want to do a flow chart. Another kind of map can be described metaphorically as a train. A train map might be a good approach for something that uses sequential chapters. In this type of map, your Web pages are like a string of box cars, as shown in Figure 5.6.

Another approach is to have your home page be the hub of a wheel, with the subpages along the rim, as shown in Figure 5.7.

And if you want to create a more complex site, you might want to create a more elaborate map, resembling a tree—with a trunk, branches, and subbranches, like the one pictured in Figure 5.8.

Figure 5.6

A Web site plan can be organized like a train.

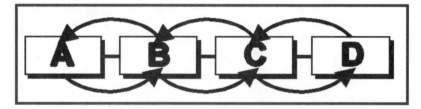

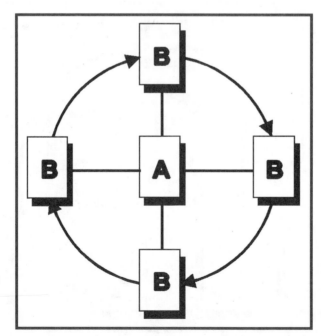

Figure 5.7

A Web site plan can take the form of a hub and wheel.

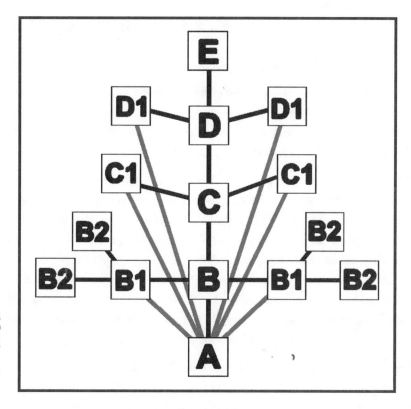

Figure 5.8

A more complex
Web site plan
might be laid out in
the form of a tree.

You could visualize your Web site map in many other ways. The last few figures represent only a few of the possibilities, and in quite broad terms. In planning your Web page, there is no need to try to draw up a map. Maps are most useful for creating more elaborate, multi-page Web sites. Still, even if you're only creating a single page, you might want to try to visualize the kinds of dynamic interrelationships you can activate through links. For instance, if you're creating a Web page using subsections using the second example, in addition to the table of contents linking to the different subsections, you can include a loop-back link at the end of each subsection to return the reader to the table of contents. Additionally, at the bottom of the page, you might provide a link back to the top of the page. You can also include in-context links within the paragraph sections that will jump to different subsections.

TASK #8: Draw a Map (Optional)

You only need to do this if you have already created your first Web page and are trying your hand at using the third Web page example to create a multi-page Web site. This is probably best done the old-fashioned way, with pen and paper. However, if you want to use a drawing or CAD program, that's okay too.

Don't just settle on the first map you think up. Try to picture two or three possible maps, and don't just stick to the examples shown here—you want a map that really suits the site you want to create. Visualize, in other words. Use different color pens to help distinguish the different relationships between your pages: one color to map out any hierarchical (top-down) or static relationships, and another color to map out any dynamic relationships between pages that are not explicit in your hierarchical plan. Alternatively, use another color pen (if you have one!) to draw in any loop-back links you want to include. The idea is to be able to see how your Web site will be structured both statically and dynamically.

Be prepared to reorganize! Seeing the dynamic interactions within your Web site almost always leads to at least one forehead slap ("Of course!"). Don't be afraid to redo your outline to match your visualization. Try to simplify, making sure that everything that is important in your site is only a hop, skip, and jump away. Don't bury that price list ten levels deep! And don't be surprised if you end up redefining your objective—in many ways, you don't really know what you are doing until you can visualize it.

What's Next?

Before moving on to this afternoon's session, you should have defined an objective, done an outline, and gathered and organized your materials. The latter includes writing the text for your Web page, as well as creating a banner graphic and gathering any URLs you want to use. The end product of this process should be a mock-up text file that contains the text you want to include in your Web page, references to the file names of any graphics you want to use (probably just a banner graphic), and any URLs inserted in the positions where you want them to appear. You'll use this mock-up this afternoon as the raw material for the Web page you create.

First time through, for the purposes of this book, your mock-up should closely match one of the basic Web page example formats. The actual content, however, is entirely subject to your discretion. You can copy it out of the encyclopedia, if you want, just for the sake of practice, or you can come up with something original.

Is it lunchtime? Or pretty close? Take a break and grab a bite to eat. But don't take too long. See you back soon for the Sunday Afternoon session, when you'll finally create your first Web page.

Creating Your First Web Page

- ✿ Setting Up an Example Web Page
- ✿ Inserting a Banner Graphic
- ✿ Creating a Table of Contents
- ✿ Extra Options for the Whole Page

I know you want to jump right in and see your own stuff on a Web page—and you should be ready by now, assuming you've completed at least the reading assignment that was scheduled for Friday evening, the Basic HTML Tutorial that was scheduled for Saturday morning, and the session that was scheduled for this morning. If you've missed any of those sessions, you should return and pick them up before trying to create your first Web page. Optionally, you may also have completed the Intermediate HTML Tutorial that was scheduled for Saturday afternoon and the Tables Tutorial that was scheduled for Saturday evening, but neither of those tutorials are required for this afternoon's project.

Choosing Your Approach

You can take many approaches to create a Web page. Nothing says you can't, for instance, fold together the planning and creating process, working directly in HTML from the start. For anything other than a fairly simple Web page, however, such an approach tends to be impractical. HTML works by defining structural elements that are common to all Web pages—the more logically organized and structured the material you want to tag, the better.

The approach I'll be presenting here involves using an example Web page as either a template or a guide. Using it as a template involves replacing the sample text with your own, while using it as a guide involves copying its HTML tags and applying them directly to your mock-up text file. The template-or-guide approach is still an option after you finish with this book—when the examples set up for this afternoon seem too basic, there are a few fancier ones on the CD. And you can always download a page you like from the Web and use it as a guide or template for your own.

I've broken up the creation process into three main sections corresponding to parts of the Web page you'll be creating: top, middle, and bottom.

The top section (the banner graphic, level-one heading, and introductory paragraph) and the bottom section (the address block) of all three example Web pages are identical. You would probably include these elements on virtually any Web page you might create, except maybe for the banner graphic.

The middle section of an HTML file is the part that gets interesting. Basically, you can place anything you can dream up and format in HTML in this middle section. However, you should limit your possibilities somewhat, or this session will probably end up looking more like a pretzel than a road map. That's why you should use one of the example files as a model for organizing and planning the material for your Web page—to try to keep things from getting complicated too fast. The following isn't the only way to go about creating a Web page—it's just the best way to go about creating your first Web page within the time constraint of one weekend.

Loading Your Mock-Up Text File

The mock-up text file you created this morning should contain at least a reference to everything you want to put in your finished Web page, including a title, introductory paragraph, any URLs you want to include, an address block with your name and e-mail address, and references to the file names of any images you want to include (most likely, just a banner graphic at this point). This afternoon, you'll be using an example Web page as a model, in combination with your mock-up text file, to create the actual HTML for your first Web page—so you need to have that file open, either to pull text or to add code for your final version.

Setting Up an Example Web Page

You should have copied the example Web page files from the CD-ROM to your hard drive this morning and selected the one you want to use as a model for planning and creating your first Web page this afternoon. In this morning's planning session, you used the example Web page you selected to help you organize and assemble the materials that are going to compose your Web page. This afternoon, you'll be using it either as a guide or a template to create the actual HTML for your Web page.

To use these examples and start creating your first Web page, do the following:

1. Run Windows Notepad.

2. Load the Web page example you have selected from your working folder (if you followed my recommendation in the last session, this will be C:\PAGES). Alternatively, you can just type it in yourself, which can be a good way to familiarize yourself with the example. If you want to use the example files I've already typed for you, they're available as BASIC-1.HTM, BASIC-2.HTM, and BASIC-3.HTM. (BASIC-3A.HTM and BASIC-3B.HTM are example subpage files.)

3. Run another copy of Notepad and load the mock-up text file you created this morning during your Web page planning session. If you followed my suggestion, you saved it as MOCKUP.TXT in your working folder.

4. You can then copy and paste from your mock-up text file to the example Web page file, using it as a template, or you can just use the example Web page file as a guide for adding the HTML tags to your mock-up text file.

5. Save whichever file you are going to use to create your first Web page (your mock-up text file, if you are using the example Web page as a guide, or the example Web page you have selected, if you are using it as a template), giving it a new name. Save it as INDEX.HTM.

The following is the HTML-coded text for the three example Web pages. If you like, you can type the one you want to use into a blank Notepad window. Typing the text and codes may help familiarize you with the example Web page you have selected. You can also use the following sections as a hard-copy reference to what's in the Web page examples, in case you need to retrace your steps.

Example #1: A Web Page Using a Link List

If your Web page is fairly simple (doesn't include subsections), you should use this Web page example as a template or guide.

```
<HTML>

<HEAD>

<TITLE>Web Page Example #1 (Your Title Goes Here)</TITLE>

</HEAD>

<BODY>

<P><IMG SRC="webpage.gif">

<H1>A Web Page Using a Link List</H1>

<P>This is an example of a basic Web page. It contains
a banner graphic, level-one and level-two headings, an
introductory paragraph, a short list of links, a hori-
zontal rule, and an address block. The address block
contains the name of the author of the page, a Mailto
e-mail link, and a date reference.

<H2>A List of Links</H2>

<UL>

<LI><A HREF="http://www.callihan.com/create2/index.htm">
Create Your First Web Page in a Weekend (2nd
Edition)</A>: HTML is for everyone!

<LI><A HREF="http://www.w3.org/">World Wide Web Consor-
tium</A>: Find out the latest about the Web and HTML.

<LI><A HREF="http://www.infohiway.com/faster/homebcs.htm">
The Bandwidth Conservation Society</A>: Save bytes—
don't be a bandwidth hog.
```

```
</UL>
<HR>
<ADDRESS>
<STRONG>Your Name Here</STRONG><BR>
E-mail: <A HREF="mailto:your@address.com">your@address.com
</A><BR>
Last Modified: Current date here
</ADDRESS>
</BODY>
</HTML>
```

If you typed this in yourself, make sure that you save it in your working folder under a name *other than* BASIC-1.HTM. Use MYPAGE-1.HTM or something like that—if any typos have slipped in, you'll be able to check it against the original.

Hop out and run your Web browser, then load the file you just saved. If you want, you can check your screen against Figure 5.1 in the previous session. Skip to the next section, "Loading Your Mock-Up Text File."

Example #2: A Web Page Using Subsections

If your Web page is more complicated, with a number of subsections under subheadings (level-two headings), you should use this Web page example as a template or guide.

```
<HTML>
<HEAD>
<TITLE>Web Page Example #2 (Your Title Goes Here)</TITLE>
</HEAD>
<BODY>
<P><IMG SRC="webpage.gif">
<H1>A Web Page Using Subsections</H1>
```

```
<P>This is an example of a Web page using subsections.
It is similar to the first Web page example, except
that the list of links jumps to subsections within the
same page, instead of to other pages out on the Web.
<UL>
<LI><A HREF="#sub1">First Subsection</A>: This link
jumps to the first subsection.
<LI><A HREF="#sub2">Second Subsection</A>: This link
jumps to the second subsection.
</UL>
<H2><A NAME="sub1">First Subsection</A></H2>
<P>This is the text for the first subsection. This is
the text for the first subsection. This is the text
for the first subsection. This is the text for the
first subsection. This is the text for the first sub-
section. This is the text for the first subsection.
This is the text for the first subsection.
<H2><A NAME="sub2">Second Subsection</A></H2>
<P>This is the text for the second subsection. This is
the text for the second subsection. This is the text
for the second subsection. This is the text for the
second subsection. This is the text for the second sub-
section. This is the text for the second subsection.
This is the text for the second subsection.
<P><HR>
<ADDRESS><STRONG>Your Name Here</STRONG><BR>
E-mail: <A HREF="mailto:your@address.com">your@address.com
</A><BR>
Last Modified: Current date here
</ADDRESS>
</BODY>
</HTML>
```

If you typed this in yourself, make sure that you save it in your working
folder under a name other than BASIC-2.HTM. Use PAGE-2.HTM or
something like that—if any typos have slipped in, you'll be able to check
it against the original.

Hop out and run your Web browser, then load the file you just saved. If you want, check your screen against Figure 5.2 in the previous session.

Example #3: A Web Site Using Subpages

This is the third basic Web page example, the one that uses local links to subpages of your main page. Consider using one of the other pages to create your first Web page. After you've done that, feel free to use this example as a template or guide for creating your first multi-page Web site. (The word *site* here refers to any group of Web pages that are related, sharing a common theme, and linked together.)

You can load BASIC-3.HTM and BASIC3-A.HTM from your working folder, or you can type them in yourself.

Here are the codes for the main page, BASIC-3.HTM:

```
<HTML>
<HEAD>
<TITLE>Web Page Example #3 (Your Title Goes Here)</TITLE>
</HEAD>
<BODY>
<P><IMG SRC="webpage.gif">
<H1>A Web Site Using Subpages</H1>
<P>This is an example of Web site using subpages. It
is similar to the first two Web page examples, except
instead of a link list that jumps to other pages out
on the Web or that jumps to subsections within the
same page, it has a link list that jumps to subpages
that are part of the same Web site.
<H2>Table of Contents</H2>
<UL>
<LI><A HREF="basic-3a.htm">First Subpage</A>: This
links to the first subpage.
<LI><A HREF="basic-3b.htm">Second Subpage</A>: This
links to the second subpage.
</UL>
```

```
<HR>
<ADDRESS><STRONG>Your Name Here</STRONG><BR>
E-mail: <A HREF="mailto:yourname@yourdomain.com">your-
name@yourdomain.com</A><BR>
Last Modified: Current date here
</ADDRESS>
</BODY>
</HTML>
```

If you typed this in yourself, make sure that you save it in your working folder under a name other than BASIC-3.HTM. Use PAGE-3.HTM, or something like that—if any typos have slipped in, you'll be able to check it against the original.

Hop out and run your Web browser, then load the file you just saved. If you want, check your screen against what Figure 5.3 shows in the previous session.

NOTE You may have noticed that this Web page example is almost identical to the first one. The only real difference between the two (other than the sample text) is that this example uses local links to subpages stored in the same directory, rather than links to Web pages that are somewhere else on the Web.

Here are the codes for the subpage, BASIC-3A.HTM. (This page is identical to BASIC-3B.HTM, which is also available with the example Web page files.)

```
<HTML>
<HEAD>
<TITLE>Web Page Example #3a (Your Title Goes
Here)</TITLE>
</HEAD>
<BODY>
<H1>First Subpage</H1>
```

```
<P>This is the text for the first subpage. This is the
text for the first subpage. This is the text for the
first subpage. This is the text for the first subpage.
This is the text for the first subpage. This is the
text for the first subpage. This is the text for the
first subpage.
<P>Return to <A HREF="basic-3.htm">Home Page</A>.
<P><HR>
<ADDRESS><STRONG>Your Name Here</STRONG><BR>
E-mail: <A HREF="mailto:your@address.com">your@address.com
</A>
</ADDRESS>
</BODY>
</HTML>
```

If you typed this in yourself, make sure that you save it in your working folder under a name *other than* BASIC-3A.HTM. Use PAGE-3A.HTM, or something like that—if any typos have slipped in, you'll be able to check it against the original.

Hop out and run your Web browser, then load the file you just saved. If you want, check your screen against what appears in Figure 5.4 in the previous session.

Using Placeholders

If you skipped creating a banner graphic this morning, feel free to use the sample banner graphic from the example Web pages. Also, if you skipped gathering a list of URLs, use the sample list of links from the first Web page example. Use these as placeholders until you come back and create your own customized banner graphic and gather your own list of links. Also, this evening I've included a Graphics Tutorial as a bonus session that will show you how to use Paint Shop Pro to create eye-popping Web art.

You'll also find many URLs in Appendix A, "The Web Resources Directory," and Appendix B, "The Web Tools Directory," that you can use to create a link list for your first Web page.

Saving Your Web Page File

If you haven't already done so, save whichever file you want to use in creating your first Web page. If you are using the example Web page you've selected as a guide for adding the HTML to your mock-up text file, then save your mock-up text file as INDEX.HTM in your working folder. If you are using the example Web page as a template into which you are going to copy and paste parts from your mock-up text file, then save the example Web page you are using as INDEX.HTM in your working folder.

Starting Your Web Page

You're now ready to start constructing your first Web page. Open the basic Web page example you've chosen to use as a template in one copy of Notepad, and the mock-up text file you created this morning in another copy of Notepad.

As stressed earlier, you can use the example Web page you've selected as a template, into which you can plug in the pieces from your mock-up text file, or as a guide listing the HTML tags you'll apply directly to your mock-up text file. For the first time through, you might want to go the template route. Later, after you gain more experience with HTML, you will probably want to directly tag your text files to create your Web pages. The guide route takes a little more explaining, so you'll see several paragraphs in the rest of the session addressing that approach—just ignore anything about inserting tags if you're using the example Web page as a template.

If you're using the basic Web page example you've selected as a guide rather than as a template, you should insert the startup HTML tags into your mock-up text file now:

```
<HTML>
<HEAD>
<TITLE>Insert your title</TITLE>
</HEAD>
<BODY>
```

Insert the following at the bottom of your text file:

```
</BODY>
</HTML>
```

NOTE The following input examples assume that you're using one of the example Web pages as a template rather than as a guide. If you use the Web page example file as a guide in directly tagging your text file, you need to interpret what is shown, realizing that instead of inserting the text into the template, you must insert the HTML codes from the example Web page into your mock-up text file.

CAUTION Many of the features this session presents as "extra options" require the use of an HTML 3.2–compliant Web browser. You should use Netscape Navigator 3.0 or higher or Microsoft Internet Explorer 3.0 or higher. If you want to make use of any extra options that use HTML 4.0 features, you should use Netscape Navigator 4.0 or higher or Microsoft Internet Explorer 4.0 or higher.

Top Section (All Three Example Web Pages)

The following section applies to all three of the example Web pages. It covers creating a title, a banner graphic, a level-one heading, and an introductory paragraph. The following is the top section of the first Web page example, the HTML codes of which are identical to the other Web page examples, although the text in the title, level-one heading, and introductory paragraph may be different:

```
<HTML>
<HEAD>
<TITLE>Web Page Example #1 (Your Title Goes Here)</TITLE>
</HEAD>
<BODY>
```

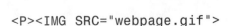

```
<P><IMG SRC="webpage.gif">
<H1>A Web Page Using a Link List</H1>
<P>This is an example of a basic Web page. It contains
a banner graphic, level-one and level-two headings, an
introductory paragraph, a short list of links, a hori-
zontal rule, and an address block. The address block
contains the name of the author of the page, a Mailto
e-mail link, and a date reference.
```

Creating Your Title

You should already have a pretty good idea of what you want to put in here, even if you haven't specifically included it in your text file. Feel free to put in a provisional title for now. Including a short description with your title (no more than 40 to 50 characters) is good practice.

Delete the sample text from within the TITLE tag, then cut and paste the title you want to use from your text file (or just type it):

```
<HTML>
<HEAD>
<TITLE>Insert your title</TITLE>
</HEAD>
```

Inserting a Banner Graphic

You don't have to include a banner graphic at the top of your Web page, but it does add a nice touch.

NOTE   If you haven't created a GIF format banner file or converted a graphic file you want to use (your company logo, for instance), you can use DUMMY.GIF, the banner graphic that is shown in the figure illustrations. It is included with the example Web page files that you copied from the CD-ROM to your hard drive this morning. You can also just keep WEBPAGE.GIF, the sample banner graphic that is already specified in all the example Web page files.

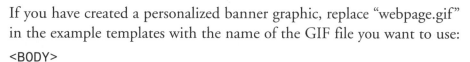

If you have created a personalized banner graphic, replace "webpage.gif" in the example templates with the name of the GIF file you want to use:

```
<BODY>
<P><IMG SRC="Insert the file name of your banner graphic">
```

Figure 6.1 shows what this might look like in a Web browser.

NOTE Since you may insert your own banner graphic and your own mock-up text, the figure illustrations can only approximate what your Web page will look like. To see what your Web page is really going to look like, save your HTML file and hop over to your browser to take a look. You should do so for each example, if only to double-check and debug errors. If your screen doesn't match the figure feature for feature and you can't find an error, it may be that your Web browser doesn't support the particular feature you're trying to use. The latest versions of both Netscape Navigator and Internet Explorer should support all the tags and features that this session presents (except where otherwise noted), but other browsers may not.

For more information on using a banner graphic on your Web page, see "Adding a Banner Graphic" in the Saturday Afternoon session.

Dummy banner graphic

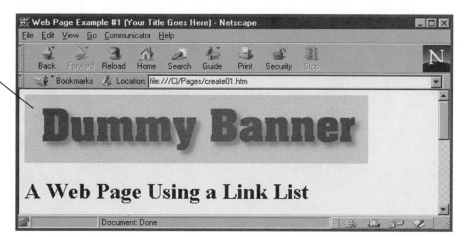

Figure 6.1

A banner graphic is a good way to make your Web page more visually appealing.

Creating a Level-One Heading

The level-one heading is actually a title. You should have only one level-one heading on your page, and you probably have already thought of one for your page during this morning's planning session. If you haven't decided on a title yet, just put in a provisional title—you can always change it later. Try to keep it fewer than 30 characters. Insert your level-one heading as follows:

```
<BODY>
<P><IMG SRC="The name of your banner graphic">
<H1>Insert Your Level-One Heading</H1>
</BODY>
```

Figure 6.2 shows how this might appear in a Web browser.

Creating Your Introductory Paragraph

During this morning's planning session, you probably created an introductory paragraph for your Web page. An introductory paragraph isn't absolutely essential—skipping it doesn't violate any laws. Having an introductory paragraph is a good idea, however, and helps viewers of your page decide whether they want to linger. If you have created an introductory paragraph, insert it as follows:

```
<BODY>
<P><IMG SRC="The file name of your banner graphic">
<H1>Your Level-One Heading</H1>
<P>Insert your introductory paragraph text
```

Figure 6.3 shows what an introductory paragraph might look like in a Web page.

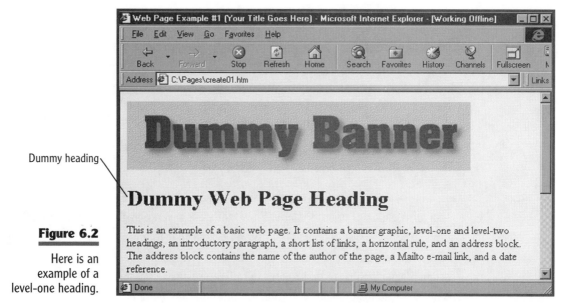

Dummy heading

Figure 6.2

Here is an example of a level-one heading.

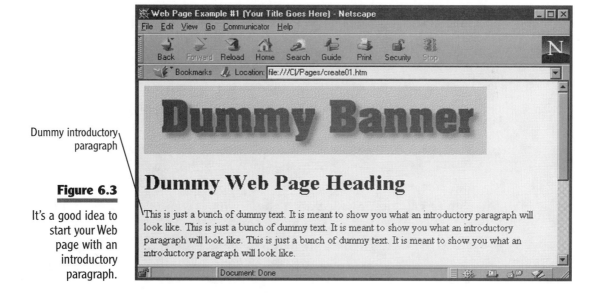

Dummy introductory paragraph

Figure 6.3

It's a good idea to start your Web page with an introductory paragraph.

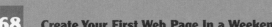

Extra Options

This section presents some things that you might want to try in the top section of your Web page to further enhance or alter its appearance. You don't have to use these options to create your first page—feel free to skip them entirely. If you do choose to experiment with them, save your current Web page file, and then save another version for experimentation. If you find an effect you like, reload your original Web page file and incorporate the effect into it.

NOTE Many of these extra options use features that were covered in the Intermediate HTML Tutorial (Saturday Afternoon). If you haven't done that tutorial, or you're just running short on time, you might want to skip ahead to the discussion of creating the middle section of your Web page that relates to the Web page example you are using, and then come back and experiment with some of the suggested extra options later.

Option #1: Set the Width and Height Dimensions of Your Banner Graphic

It is a good idea to set the WIDTH and HEIGHT attributes for any inline images other than small bullet icons. That way, surrounding text will appear on the screen without waiting for your image to finish downloading. To set these dimensions, you need to know the actual dimensions of your image. If you have created your own custom banner graphic, you can find out its size in Paint Shop Pro by clicking on View and Image Information. If you are using WEBPAGE.GIF, the sample banner graphic provided with the example Web pages, you should set WIDTH="400" and HEIGHT="100" in the IMG tag. If you are using DUMMY.GIF, the dummy banner graphic displayed in the figure illustrations, you should set WIDTH="500" and HEIGHT="100" in the IMG tag, as shown here:

```
<P><IMG SRC="dummy.gif" WIDTH="500" HEIGHT="100">
```

To find out more about setting dimensions for inline images, see "Setting Image Height and Width" in the Saturday Afternoon session.

Option #2: Center Your Banner Graphic and Level-One Heading

Most current Web browsers support centering of headings and paragraphs. The most commonly supported centering method involves setting the ALIGN attribute in a heading or paragraph tag. To center your banner graphic and your level-one heading, insert an ALIGN="center" attribute value in the P and H1 tags, like this:

```
<P ALIGN="center"><IMG SRC="The file name of your banner graphic">

<H1 ALIGN="center">Your Level-One Heading</H1>
```

Figure 6.4 shows what this would look like in a Web browser that supports horizontally aligning paragraphs and headings.

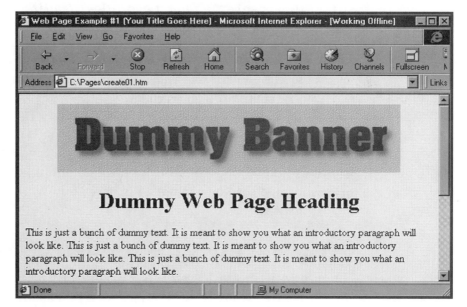

Figure 6.4

You can center-align both your banner graphic and your level-one heading.

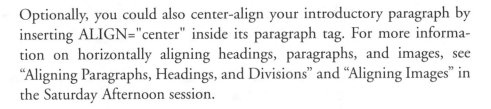

Optionally, you could also center-align your introductory paragraph by inserting ALIGN="center" inside its paragraph tag. For more information on horizontally aligning headings, paragraphs, and images, see "Aligning Paragraphs, Headings, and Divisions" and "Aligning Images" in the Saturday Afternoon session.

Option #3: Add a Custom Horizontal Rule

An additional touch to your Web page is a horizontal rule between your level-one heading and your introductory paragraph. Center-alignment is the default alignment for horizontal rules, so if you want to set a percentage width for a horizontal rule, you should do it here in conjunction with a center-aligned level-one heading. To insert an unshaded horizontal rule that has a size of 10 pixels and extends across 66 percent of the browser window below a center-aligned level-one heading, you would do this:

```
<P ALIGN="center"><IMG SRC="The file name of your
banner graphic">
<H1 ALIGN="center">Your Level-One Heading</H1>
<HR SIZE="10" WIDTH="66%" NOSHADE>
```

NOTE You can also set the width of your horizontal rule in pixels by leaving off the percent sign (%) at the end of the WIDTH attribute value.

Figure 6.5 shows how this looks in a browser that supports changing the size and width of a horizontal rule. For more information on setting the size, width, and shading of a horizontal rule, see "Working with Rules" in the Saturday Afternoon session.

Option #4: Use a Graphic Rule

For an even nicer touch, you can use a graphic rule rather than a horizontal rule. By setting the HEIGHT and WIDTH attributes in the IMG

tag, along with placing it in a center-aligned paragraph, you can get an effect similar to what you could achieve using the horizontal rule, except that you get to add some extra color to your page. If you want, you can experiment with RAIN_LIN.GIF, the sample graphic rule that was used in the Intermediate HTML Tutorial. I've included it with the Web page example files you installed this morning. For instance, you might substitute RAIN_LIN.GIF for the horizontal rule that was used in the previous exercise like this (see figure 6.6):

```
<P ALIGN="center"><IMG SRC="The name of your banner graphic">
```

```
<H1 ALIGN="center">Your Level-One Heading</H1>
```

```
<P ALIGN="center"><IMG SRC="rain_lin.gif" WIDTH="65%" HEIGHT="10">
```

For more information on using graphic rules in your Web pages, see "Using Graphic Rules" in the Saturday Afternoon session.

Custom horizontal rule

Figure 6.5

A strategically placed horizontal rule can add a nice touch.

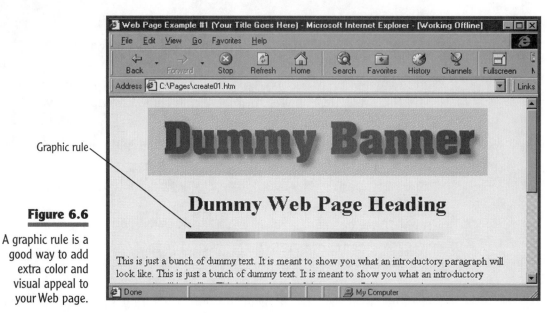

Graphic rule

Figure 6.6

A graphic rule is a good way to add extra color and visual appeal to your Web page.

ON THE

CD

The CD-ROM has a Web art library that includes an assortment of graphic rules. Just select "Book Examples" and "Web Art," then follow the instructions for reviewing or installing these files. Or use Paint Shop Pro's browse feature (Open, Browse) to preview all the images in a folder on the CD-ROM, so you can easily pick out just the ones you want to use. Also, check Appendix A, "The Web Resources Directory," for references to where you can find graphic rules and other Web art on the Web.

Option #5: Wrap Your Heading around a Logo Graphic

You don't have to settle for a plain banner graphic and level-one heading, centered and stacked on top of each other. If your company has a logo, you can wrap your level-one heading around it to get a side-by-side look. For an extra touch, right-align your level-one heading. Since I don't expect you to have a logo graphic all ready and handy (and in GIF format to boot), I've included a sample logo graphic, LOGO.GIF, with the example Web page files that you can use just to see how this works. If you want to create your own customized logo graphic, just create a GIF file

that is about 150 pixels wide by 100 pixels high. Try out the following example to see how this works (I changed the percentage width of the graphic rule from the previous option to 100%, just for a final touch):

```
<P><IMG SRC="logo.gif" ALIGN="left"><BR>
<H1 ALIGN="right">A Web Page<BR> Using a Link List<BR
CLEAR="left"></H1>
<P ALIGN="center"><IMG SRC="rain_lin.gif" WIDTH="100%"
HEIGHT="10">
```

Figure 6.7 shows what this will look like in a Web browser that supports wrapping text around images.

You'll notice in the code example that the ALIGN="left" attribute value in the IMG tag causes the following level-one heading to flow around the right side of the image, rather than being displayed beneath it. Notice also that a BR tag has been inserted following the image to move the heading down and align it more closely with the middle, rather than the top, of the image. (Remember, you can't set both left- and middle-alignment of an image, only one or the other.) Depending on the size of the logo graphic you use, you may need to add one or more additional BR tags here to move the heading down to a position that suits you (yes, I know

Figure 6.7

Instead of a centered banner and heading, you can wrap your heading around a logo graphic.

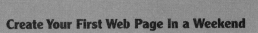

that earlier I said not to use multiple BR tags, but this is a case where nothing else can really do the trick). Also, at the end of the heading, another BR tag with the CLEAR="left" attribute set has been inserted to ensure that any following elements, such as your introductory paragraph, don't also try to wrap around your logo graphic. For an added touch, the level-one heading that is wrapping around the image has been set to right-alignment.

You can wrap your heading around the left side of a right-aligned graphic by reversing the relative positions of the image and the heading, while inserting ALIGN="right" inside the heading tag. At the end of the heading, you should use CLEAR="right" in place of the CLEAR="left" attribute.

For more information on wrapping text around left- or right-aligned images, see "Wrapping Text around Images" in the Saturday Afternoon session.

Option #6: Set Your Headings in a Monospaced Font

It would be nice to think that you could just tag your headings with the TT (Teletype) tag to display them in a monospaced font. This used to be a dependable trick, but you can't count on it now. The latest version of Internet Explorer noticeably shrinks a level-one heading when the TT tag is nested inside it. I'm sure this is a bug, so hopefully it will be fixed in future versions. You can make Internet Explorer treat this properly if you nest the H1 tag inside the TT tag, but then Navigator will entirely ignore the TT tag. So what to do? One answer is to use the FACE attribute of the FONT tag to specify Courier New or Courier as the font face.

Here's an example of using the FACE attribute to set the level-one heading to a monospaced font:

```
<H1 ALIGN="center"><FONT FACE="courier new,
courier">Dummy Web Page Heading</FONT></H1>
```

To display your level-two headings (H2) in a monospaced font, you would need to tag each one individually. See Figure 6.8 for how this looks in Internet Explorer.

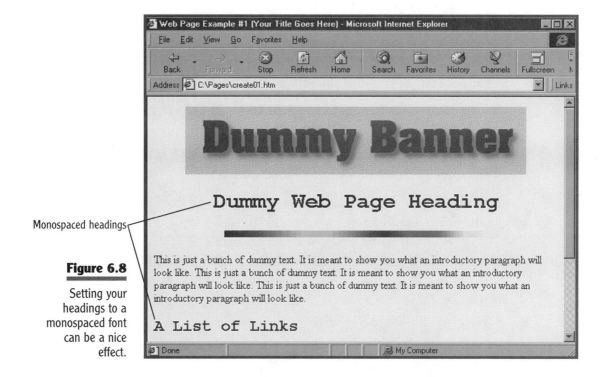

Monospaced headings

Figure 6.8

Setting your
headings to a
monospaced font
can be a nice
effect.

You can assign font faces other than monospace fonts using the FACE attribute of the FONT tag. To set a sans serif font, list "verdana, helvetica, arial" as the font faces. For more information on using the FACE attribute of the FONT tag, see "Changing Font Faces" in the Saturday Afternoon session.

The only problem with this solution is that it will only work in browsers that support the FONT tag and its FACE attribute. The older TT tag trick was a lot more universal, but unfortunately how the latest version of Internet Explorer handles this pretty much precludes its use.

Option #7: Use a Drop Cap Image

There is no tag for creating a drop cap, but you can create a graphic of the first letter of your paragraph and then insert it in place of that letter.

Set left-alignment in the IMG tag and following text wraps around the graphic. I've included a sample drop cap graphic, DROP-T.GIF, with the example Web page files, that can be used to insert a drop cap "T" at the start of the introductory paragraph:

```
<P><IMG SRC="drop-t.gif" ALIGN="left">This is your
introductory paragraph text.
```

See Figure 6.9 to see what this looks like in a Web browser that supports wrapping text around a left-aligned image.

You can easily use a graphics program such as Paint Shop Pro to create drop cap graphics and save them as GIF-format graphic files. (Note: DROP-T.GIF is 52 pixels wide by 55 pixels high.) For an added touch, set the background color to transparent (see the Graphics Tutorial scheduled for tonight for instructions on how to create transparent GIF images).

Drop cap

Figure 6.9

Adding a drop cap graphic is a good way to spice up the first paragraph in your Web page.

Take a Break

You can see how this is starting to work, and you may want to rush right on to the guts of the page. But it might be a good idea to stop and stretch, touch your toes, and get your energy level up for the next section. Scratch your cat, if you've got one. Water your plants. See you in a few minutes!

Middle Section (First Example Web Page)

If you have selected the first example Web page (a Web page with a list of external links) as your guide or template, you should proceed with this section—skip to the next section if you're using the second example. The middle section of the Web page example file you've chosen, BASIC-1.HTM, includes the following list of links:

```
<H2>A List of Links</H2>
<UL>
<LI><A HREF="http://www.callihan.com/create2/index.htm">
Create Your First Web Page in a Weekend (2nd
Edition)</A>: HTML is for everyone!
<LI><A HREF="http://www.w3.org/">World Wide Web Consor-
tium</A>: Find out the latest about the Web and HTML.
<LI><A HREF="http://www.infohiway.com/faster/homebcs.htm">
The Bandwidth Conservation Society</A>: Save bytes—
don't be a bandwidth hog.
</UL>
```

Adding a Subheading

The example includes a level-two heading (H2). Right now, the text simply indicates that a list of links follows the heading. You can exclude this or you can insert the specific subheading that you want. If you're creating a Web page focused on your favorite hobby, such as stamp collecting, then the subheading here might read "Philatelist Links," or something like that. If you're including a level-two heading, insert it like this:

```
<H2>Insert Your Level-Two Heading</H2>
```

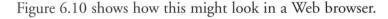
Figure 6.10 shows how this might look in a Web browser.

Creating a List of External Links

The example template uses a list of hypertext links to other pages on the Web. For instance, you might want to create a list of your favorite links, or a list of links related to an interest, hobby, or personal expertise.

Actually, you don't have to include a list of any kind—you can completely eliminate it. Nothing says your Web page can't include just a banner graphic, a level-one heading, one or more paragraphs of text, and your address block. Nothing says you can't insert your links, in context, within your paragraph text. You might just want to include a list without links, or you might want to list the links without explanatory or descriptive text. Or you might want to include explanations for some links but eliminate them from others that you feel are largely self-explanatory. Feel free to eliminate the descriptions, the links, or the entire list.

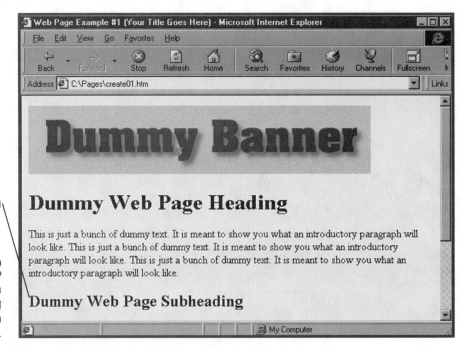

Dummy subheading

Figure 6.10

You can use a level-two heading to further identify a list of links.

The following is an example for creating a link list with descriptions. (If you only want to create a list here, eliminate the links and link text. If you want to create a link list without descriptions, eliminate the link descriptions.) Follow this example to create a link list with descriptions:

```
<UL>

<LI><A HREF="Insert the URL of your first link">Insert
the link text</A>: Insert the link description.

<LI><A HREF="Insert the URL of your second link">Insert
the link text</A>: Insert the link description.

</UL>
```

Most link lists include more than two items. To add items to your link list, just duplicate either of the item examples shown here as many times as necessary to create your full link list, inserting the specific URLs, link text, and descriptive text for each additional link list item. Figure 6.11 shows what the example link list looks like in a Web browser.

For additional information on creating hypertext links and link lists, see "Creating Hypertext Links" and "Creating Link Lists" in the Saturday Morning session.

Sample link list

Figure 6.11

A link list, preferably with descriptions, is a good way to connect your visitors to your favorite destinations on the Web.

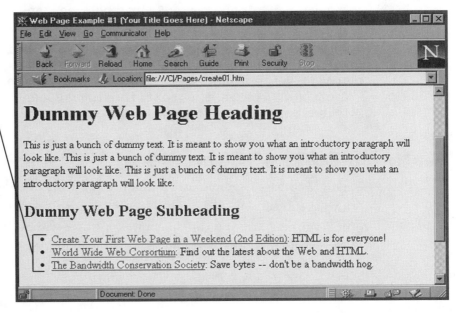

Middle Section (Second Example Web Page)

If you have selected the second example Web page (a Web page using sub-sections) as your guide or template for creating your Web page, you should proceed with this section. The example Web page file you've chosen, BASIC-2.HTM, includes the following list of internal links, which acts as a table of contents for the following subsections:

```
<UL>

<LI><A HREF="#sub1">First Subsection</A>: This link
jumps to the first subsection.

<LI><A HREF="#sub2">Second Subsection</A>: This link
jumps to the second subsection.

</UL>

<H2><A NAME="sub1"></A>First Subsection</H2>

<P>This is the text for the first subsection. This is
the text for the first subsection. This is the text
for the first subsection. This is the text for the
first subsection. This is the text for the first sub-
section. This is the text for the first subsection.
This is the text for the first subsection.

<H2><A NAME="sub2"></A>Second Subsection</H2>

<P>This is the text for the second subsection. This is
the text for the second subsection. This is the text
for the second subsection. This is the text for the
second subsection. This is the text for the second sub-
section. This is the text for the second subsection.
This is the text for the second subsection.
```

Creating a Table of Contents

This Web page example uses a link list as a table of contents for the fol-lowing subsections. Although the example includes descriptions for each link, nothing says you can't use a link list here without descriptions. Feel free to eliminate the descriptions or to include descriptions only where

you feel they are necessary. Use the following HTML code list as a guide in creating a link list to serve as a table of contents for the following subsections:

```
<UL>
<LI><A HREF="#sub1">Insert the link text</A>: Insert
the link description.
<LI><A HREF="#sub2">Insert the link text</A>: Insert
the link description.
</UL>
```

Although the example contains only two items, you should include as many link list items as you have subsections to which you want to link. Just duplicate either of the list items for as many additional links as you need to add, then edit them to add new anchor names, link text, and link descriptions. Note also the "sub1" and "sub2" anchor names correspond to the same anchor names that are used to create the "target" links in the subheadings for the subsections. When creating additional list items in your table of contents, you should be sure that each hypertext anchor has a unique anchor name ("sub3," "sub4," and so on).

Creating the Subsections

Next, you need to create the subheadings and subsections that correspond to the list items in your table of contents:

```
<H2><A NAME="sub1"></A>Insert first subheading</H2>
<P>Insert text for the first subsection . . .
<H2><A NAME="sub2"></A>Insert second subheading</H2>
<P>Insert text for the second subsection . . .
```

See Figure 6.12 to see what your table of contents and subsections might look like in a Web browser.

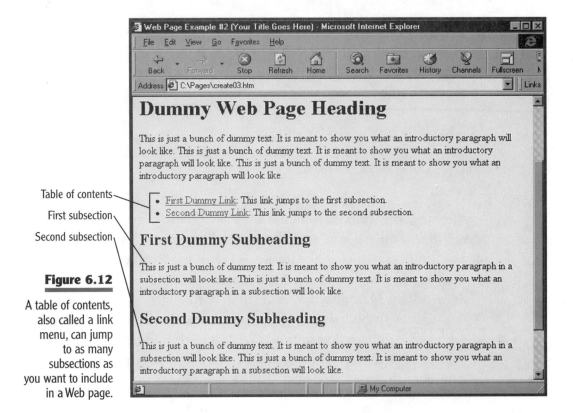

Table of contents

First subsection

Second subsection

Figure 6.12

A table of contents, also called a link menu, can jump to as many subsections as you want to include in a Web page.

To create additional subsections, just duplicate the second subsection example as many times as you need. For additional information on creating hypertext links and link lists, see "Creating Hypertext Links" and "Creating Link Lists" in the Saturday Morning session.

Extra Options

The following extra options apply specifically to the second basic Web page example. Later in the session, I'll give you an additional option that allows you to create an icon link list rather than a regular link list when you're using any of the three Web page examples.

Option #1: Use a Definition List to Format Your Subsections

You can give your subsections a slightly different look by using a definition list (DL), also called a glossary list. Using a definition list indents your subsection paragraph text instead of displaying it flush to the left margin. Just insert your subheading on the definition term (DT) line, and use definition data (DD) tags for any following paragraph tags, like this:

```
<DL>
<DT><H2><A NAME="sub1"></A>Your first subheading</H2>
<DD><P>The text for the first subsection . . .
<DT><H2><A NAME="sub2"></A>Your second subheading</H2>
<DD><P>The text for the second subsection . . .
</DL>
```

To include additional subsections, just duplicate either of the preceding subsection examples, then plug in the relevant text. Also, you can include additional indented paragraphs in each subsection by beginning each paragraph with a DT tag rather than a P tag. Figure 6.13 shows what a Web page using definition list subsections might look like in a Web browser.

Effect of DT (Definition Term) tag

Effect of DD (Definition Data) tag

Figure 6.13

You can use a definition list to give your subheadings and subsections a different look.

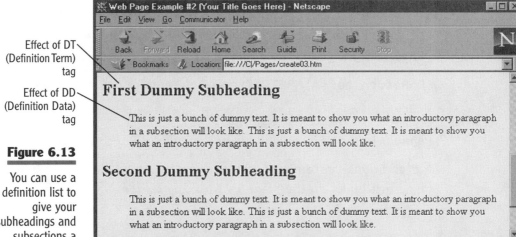

Alternatively, you could nest your paragraph text within BLOCK-QUOTE tags to get a similar look. For more information on using definition lists or block quotes, see "Creating Definition Lists" and "Using Block Quotes" in the Saturday Morning session.

Option #2: Add Loop-Back Links

If you're using more than just a few subsections or if your subsections are fairly long, you may want to include loop-back links that let viewers jump back to your menu list, without having to scroll all the way back up to the top of your page, after they finish reading a subsection.

```
<UL><A HREF="toc"></A>

<LI><A HREF="#sub1">The link text</A>: The link
description.

<LI><A HREF="#sub2">The link text</A>: The link
description.

</UL>

<DL>

<DT><H2><A NAME="sub1"></A>Your first subheading</H2>

<DD><P>The text for the first subsection . . .

<P>Return to <A HREF="#toc">Table of Contents</A>.

<DT><H2><A NAME="sub2"></A>Your second subheading</H2>

<DD><P>The text for the second subsection . . .

<P>Return to <A HREF="#toc">Table of Contents</A>.

</DL>
```

Figure 6.14 shows what this might look like in a Web browser.

For additional information on creating hypertext links, see "Creating Hypertext Links" in the Saturday Morning session.

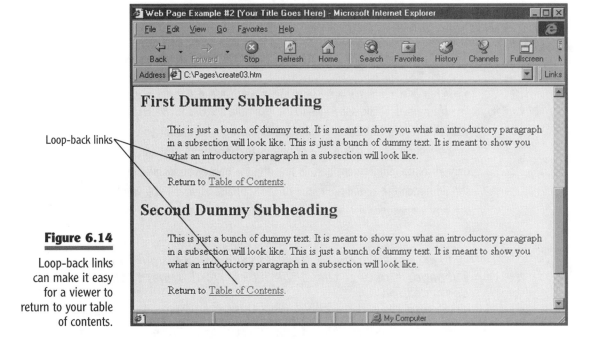

Loop-back links

Figure 6.14

Loop-back links
can make it easy
for a viewer to
return to your table
of contents.

Middle Section (Third Example Web Page)

If you have selected the third example Web page (a Web page with sub-pages) as your guide or template for creating your Web page, you should proceed with this section. The middle section of the Web page example file you've chosen, BASIC-3.HTM, includes a table of contents that links to two example subpages (BASIC-3A.HTM and BASIC-3B.HTM).

This is the middle section of the third Web page example (BASIC-3.HTM):

```
<H2>Table of Contents</H2>
<UL>
<LI><A HREF="basic-3a.htm">First Subpage</A>: This
links to the first subpage.
<LI><A HREF="basic-3b.htm">Second Subpage</A>: This
links to the second subpage.
</UL>
```

Creating a Table of Contents

Edit the table of contents of the third example Web page, inserting the file name, link text, and description text for each subpage you are linking to:

 NOTE

The file names for the subpages in the example are BASIC-3A.HTM and BASIC-3B.HTM. You need to substitute the actual names you want to use for your subpages, either variants of your main page's name or names that are more descriptive of the subpages. The only absolute requirement here is that the file name you include in the link menu below should match the actual file name of the subpage to which you want to link.

```
<UL>

<LI><A HREF="Insert the file name of your first
subpage">Insert the link text</A>: Insert the link
description.

<LI><A HREF="Insert the file name of the second
subpage">Insert the link text</A>: Insert the link
description.

</UL>
```

Figure 6.15 shows what this might look like in a Web browser.

 NOTE

If the file for your subpage is in the same directory as your main page, you only need to insert its file name. Otherwise, if your subpage is in the same directory structure, or even on the same server, I recommend that you insert a relative URL, rather than an absolute URL (see the sidebar titled "Using Relative URLs" in the Saturday Morning session). For now, you should store all files, including subpages, graphics, and icons, that you want to use in your working directory. After you get a better feel for how HTML works, you'll probably want to start organizing different Web page projects in their own subdirectories, while still sharing common files—and you'll want to use relative URLs to link files across directories. But for now, as long as you just put everything in your working directory, you don't have to worry about that.

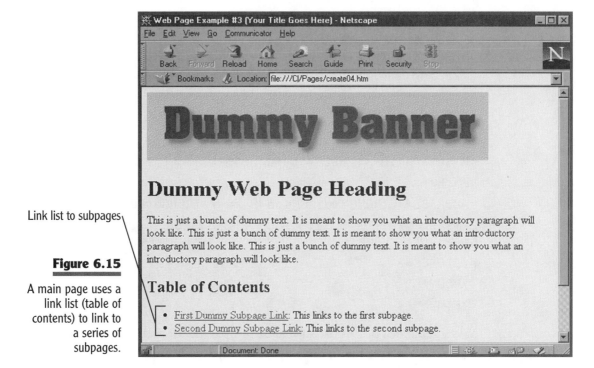

Link list to subpages

Figure 6.15

A main page uses a
link list (table of
contents) to link to
a series of
subpages.

For additional information on hypertext links, see "Creating Hypertext
Links" in the Saturday Morning session. For more information on link
lists, see "Creating Link Lists" in the Saturday Morning session.

Creating Your Subpages

I've provided two example subpages, BASIC-3A.HTM and BASIC-3B.HTM,
but other than their file names, they are almost the same.

The following is the example subpage, BASIC-3A.HTM, linked from the
example home page.

```
<HTML>
<HEAD>
<TITLE>Web Page Example #3a (Your Title Goes Here)</TITLE>
</HEAD>
```

```
<BODY>

<H1>First Subpage</H1>

<P>This is the text for the first subpage. This is the
text for the first subpage. This is the text for the
first subpage. This is the text for the first subpage.
This is the text for the first subpage. This is the
text for the first subpage. This is the text for the
first subpage.

<P>Return to <A HREF="basic-3.htm">Home Page</A>.

<P><HR>

<ADDRESS><STRONG>Your Name Here</STRONG><BR>

E-mail: <A HREF="mailto:your@address.com">your@address.com
</A>

</ADDRESS>

</BODY>

</HTML>
```

Save a separate copy of the subpage example file for each subpage you want
to create. You can name them sequentially (SUB-1.HTM, SUB-2.HTM,
and so on). Or you can use file names that are more descriptive
(ABOUT.HTM, PRICES.HTM, CONTACT.HTM, and so on) and
more closely fit the actual subpages you want to create. The only
requirement is that the file names match what you use in your table of
contents on your main page (or vice versa).

Go ahead and edit your subpage, inserting a title, level-one heading,
introductory paragraph, and loop-back link to your main page:

```
<HEAD>

<TITLE>Insert a title for your subpage</TITLE>

</HEAD>

<BODY>

<H1>Insert your subpage level-one heading</H1>

<P>Insert an introductory paragraph . . .

<P><A HREF="Insert the file name of your main
page">Return to Home Page.</A>
```

Figure 6.16 shows what this might look like in a Web browser.

A subpage doesn't have to be this simple, of course. It can be a complete Web page, including a list of external links, as in the first Web page example, or a table of contents linking to internal subsections, as in the second Web page example. It could even link to subpages of its own! In creating your subpages, feel free to use any of the example Web pages as models.

For suggestions and directions for creating the bottom section (containing the address block) of your subpage, see "Bottom Section (All Three Example Web Pages)."

Extra Options for Subpages

You have several options for tying your subpages more closely to the main page.

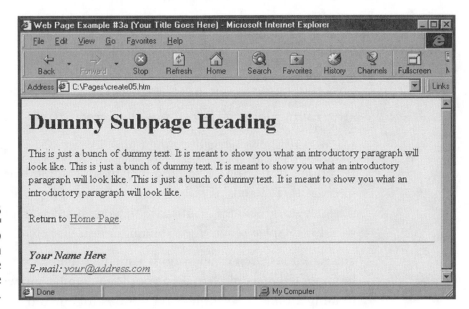

Figure 6.16

A subpage is a Web page linked from the home page of a multi-page Web site.

Option #1: Add a Banner or Logo Graphic to Your Subpage

The example subpage doesn't have a banner or logo graphic. Using a banner or logo graphic for your subpages can help tie them together, however. A handy trick is to resize your banner graphic for display as a logo on your subpages. Normally, you wouldn't want to resize an image downward, because you want images downloaded with your pages from the Web to be as small as possible. In this case, however, you only run into a bandwidth penalty if you end up getting a lot of visitors to your subpage who aren't coming to it by way of your main page. If that happens, you should probably use a second, smaller version of your banner graphic instead of resizing the original. Also, if there is a significant size difference between your full-size banner graphic and your resized logo graphic, it will probably take longer for your image to load into memory and be displayed than would be the case if you pulled it into your paint program to resize it.

The example shown here inserts and resizes DUMMY.GIF, the dummy banner graphic that is included with the example Web page files. (If you are using WEBPAGE.GIF, set the WIDTH to 200 instead of 250.)

```
<P><IMG SRC="dummy.gif" WIDTH="250" HEIGHT="50">
```

```
<H1>Your subpage level-one heading</H1>
```

Figure 6.17 shows what this might look like in a Web browser.

If you are using your own custom banner graphic here, you'll need to insert WIDTH and HEIGHT values that are proportional to the actual size of your graphic. For instance, if your banner graphic is 550 pixels wide by 150 pixels high, then you might resize it here to 225 by 75 pixels.

You could also center-align both your logo graphic and your level-one heading, or you could left-align your logo graphic and wrap the level-one heading around it. See the extra options for the top section of all three example Web pages for more information on how to apply those features.

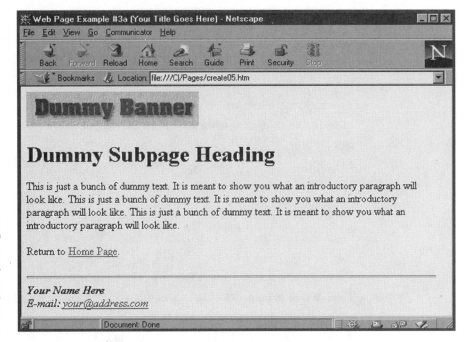

Figure 6.17

You can resize the banner graphic from your main page and use it as a logo graphic on your subpages.

NOTE The subpage example includes a loop-back link at the bottom of the page. This is a navigational device that lets the user get from the subpage to the home page. Including a loop-back link on subpages is important because you don't know how somebody is going to end up at a subpage—he doesn't have to go through your home page to get to it, but can jump in from anywhere as long as he has its URL. If someone comes to your subpage via a search engine, for example, pressing the Web browser Back button returns him to the search engine list, not to your home page.

Option #2: Use a Navigational Icon

Navigational icons are a way to visually indicate a link without having to spell it out. Generally, an arrow or hand pointing up indicates that a link will return to the home page. An image of a house is also often used to

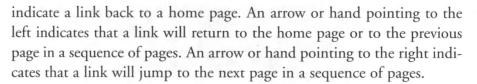
indicate a link back to a home page. An arrow or hand pointing to the left indicates that a link will return to the home page or to the previous page in a sequence of pages. An arrow or hand pointing to the right indicates that a link will jump to the next page in a sequence of pages.

The following example uses an arrow pointing left as a navigational icon to indicate that the link returns to the home page:

```
<P><A HREF="The file name of your main page"><IMG
SRC="arr-left.gif" HEIGHT="50" WIDTH="50" ALT="Home"
BORDER="0"></A>

<P><HR>
```

Figure 6.18 shows what this might look like in a Web browser.

TIP

If you're creating a series of subpages that visitors should view in sequence, you could use a right-pointing arrow or hand to indicate a link to the next subpage in the series. In that context, a left-pointing arrow would indicate a link back to the previous page. An up-pointing arrow could then indicate a link to the home page. A common navigational icon on the Web is the image of a house, indicating a link back to the home page. Besides the left-pointing arrow you've already seen (ARR-LEFT.GIF), a right-pointing arrow (ARR-RGHT.GIF) and an up-pointing arrow (ARR-UP.GIF) have been included with the example Web page files. For even more images that work great as navigational icons, see the Web Art Library on the CD-ROM.

The example uses the ALT attribute in the IMG tag to identify the navigational icon for people who can't see the image itself. You should always use an ALT attribute with navigational icons, because a navigational icon offers no other indication of the graphic's purpose. For more information on using navigational icons, see "Creating Navigational Icons" in the Saturday Afternoon session.

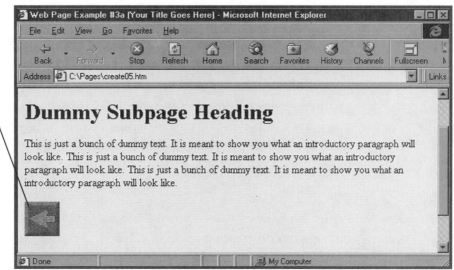

Navigational Icon

Figure 6.18

You can use a navigational icon as a loop-back link.

Bottom Section (All Three Example Web Pages)

The bottom section of the example Web pages contains the address block and is the same for all three example Web pages (as well as for the example subpages included with the third Web page example:

```
<HR>
<ADDRESS>
<STRONG>Your Name Here</STRONG><BR>
E-mail: <A HREF="mailto:your@address.com">your@address.com</A>
<BR>
Last Modified: Current date here
</ADDRESS>
</BODY>
</HTML>
```

Creating Your Address Block

Edit the address block, inserting your name, your e-mail address, and the current date:

```
<ADDRESS>
<STRONG>Insert your name here</STRONG><BR>
E-mail: <A HREF="mailto:Insert your e-mail
address">Insert your e-mail address again</A><BR>
Last Modified: Insert the current date
</ADDRESS>
```

Figure 6.19 shows what this might look like in a Web browser. For more information on creating an address block, see "Signing Your Work" in the Saturday Morning session.

Extra Options for the Bottom Section

The following are some extra options you can use to dress up your address block in the bottom section of your Web page.

Option #1: Vary the Height and Shading of the Horizontal Rule

You can change the height and shading of the horizontal rule. For instance, to use a 10-pixel unshaded rule as a separator between the rest of your Web page and your address block, do the following:

```
<HR SIZE="10" NOSHADE>
<ADDRESS>
```

Figure 6.20 shows what this might look like in a Web browser.

Option #2: Use a Graphic Rule in Place of a Horizontal Rule

You can add more color and pizazz to your page by using a graphic line rather than a horizontal rule as a separator. The example here uses RAIN_LIN.GIF, the same graphic rule image you saw in the extra option for inserting a

graphic rule between the level-one heading and the introductory paragraph. The graphic rule is set in the following example at a width of 100% and a height of 10 pixels:

```
<P><IMG SRC="rain_lin.gif" WIDTH="100%" HEIGHT="10">
<ADDRESS>
```

Figure 6.21 shows what this might look like in a Web browser.

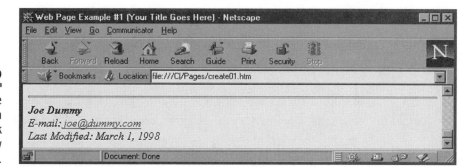

Figure 6.19

Every Web page should have an address block telling a visitor how to contact you.

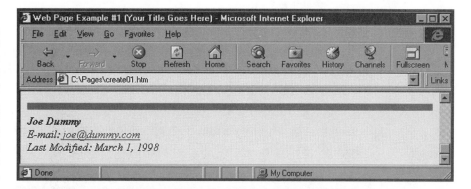

Figure 6.20

To more emphatically separate your address block, increase the size of the horizontal rule and turn the shading off so you get a solid rule.

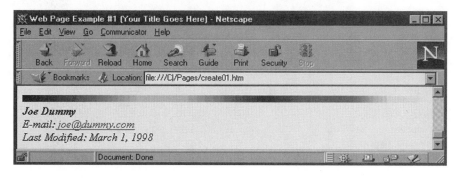

Figure 6.21

To even more emphatically separate your address block, use a multicolor graphic rule.

Option #3: Center Your Address Block

You don't have to use a left-flush address block. You can center it for Web browsers that can read the <CENTER> and </CENTER> tags. For instance:

<ADDRESS>

<CENTER><STRONG>*Your name*</STRONG>

E-mail: <A HREF="mailto:*Your e-mail address*">*Your e-mail address again*</A>

Last Modified: *The current date***</CENTER>**

</ADDRESS>

Figure 6.22 shows what this might look like in a Web browser.

NOTE   You could also insert a center-aligned paragraph at the start of the address block, but this has the effect of moving the address text further down from the horizontal rule.

If you're creating a home page with subpages, you should create an address block for each page. Signing and dating all your pages is a good idea. Remember, you don't know how somebody is going to get to a particular page—he doesn't have to go through your home page to get to one of your subpages. Some search engines use robot agents (sometimes called *worms* or *spiders*) to scan and index the Web. These agents can pick up your subpages even when you don't list them—and direct people to the depths of your site who have no idea where it is or what else might be on it.

Figure 6.22

Address blocks are often centered to make them stand out.

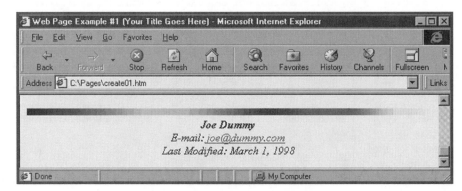

Extra Options for the Whole Page

This section contains a series of extra options that you can use to adjust the overall look and feel of your Web page. This section applies to all three example Web pages. The options include creating an icon link list, changing the background and text colors, setting font sizes and colors, and using a background image.

Option #1: Create an Icon Link List

Using an icon link list (instead of a plain unordered (bulleted) link list) is a good way to add color and visual appeal to your Web page. Because an icon link list doesn't use an unordered list, you need to first delete the UL start and end tags, and all the LI tags, so that the text for your link list looks like this:

 NOTE

In the following, URL refers to the first basic Web page example, anchor name refers to the second basic Web page example, and subpage file name refers to the third basic Web page example.

```
<A HREF="The URL, anchor name, or subpage file name for
your first link">The link text</A>: The link description.
```

```
<A HREF="The URL, anchor name, or subpage file name for
your second link">The link text</A>: The link description.
```

Now, to create an icon link list, you need to add three bits of code: a paragraph tag at the start of the list, a graphic icon bullet at the start of each list line, and a BR tag with the CLEAR="left" attribute value set. To do this, edit the text for your link list like this:

```
<P><IMG SRC="icon.gif" ALIGN="left" HSPACE="5" VSPACE="5">
```

```
<A HREF="The URL of your first link">The link text</A>:
The link description.<BR CLEAR="left">
```

```
<IMG SRC="icon.gif" ALIGN="left" HSPACE="5" VSPACE="5">
```

```
<A HREF="The URL of your second link">The link
text</A>: The link description.<BR CLEAR="left">
<IMG SRC="icon.gif" ALIGN="left" HSPACE="5" VSPACE="5">
<A HREF="The URL of your third link">The link text</A>:
The link description.<BR CLEAR="left">
```

ON THE

CD

The example that follows uses ICON.GIF, an icon bullet I've included with the example Web page files. The CD-ROM includes quite a few additional icon bullets that you can try using as well. Just select "Book Examples" and "Web Art," then follow the instructions for reviewing or installing these files. Or use Paint Shop Pro's browse feature (Open, Browse) to preview all the images in a folder on the CD-ROM, so you can easily pick out the ones you want to use.

Figure 6.23 shows how an icon link list might look applied to the first basic Web page example.

For more information on creating icon link lists, see "Creating Icon Link Lists" in the Saturday Afternoon session. For a variation on creating an icon link list that allows as many indented lines as you want, try creating an icon link list using a table. For information on creating icon link lists using tables, see "Creating Icon Bullet Link Lists" in the Tables Tutorial.

ICON.GIF

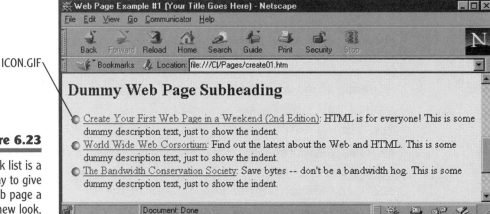

Figure 6.23

An icon link list is a good way to give your Web page a whole new look.

Option #2: Set Background, Text, and Link Colors

You can add significant impact to your Web page just by changing the background and text colors. The text colors here include not just the text color (TEXT), but the color of links (LINK), visited links (VLINK), and activated links (ALINK), which are links where you have pressed but not released the mouse button. To change the colors for your background and text, you have to add some color attributes to the <BODY> tag. Here's an example that looks pretty good:

```
<HTML>

<HEAD>

<TITLE>Your title</TITLE>

</HEAD>

<BODY BGCOLOR="#004080" TEXT="#ffff00" LINK="#00ff00"
VLINK="#a4c8f0" ALINK="#ff8000">
```

Figure 6.24 gives some idea of what this might look like in a Web browser (to see the actual colors, you need to hop over to your Web browser).

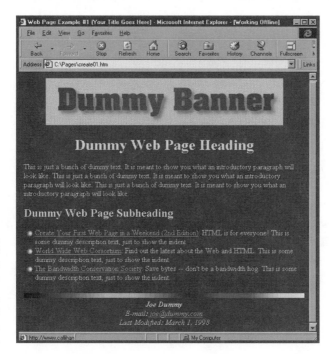

Figure 6.24

To give your Web page a completely different look, assign colors to the background, text, and links.

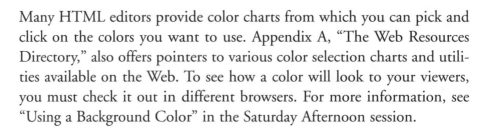

Many HTML editors provide color charts from which you can pick and click on the colors you want to use. Appendix A, "The Web Resources Directory," also offers pointers to various color selection charts and utilities available on the Web. To see how a color will look to your viewers, you must check it out in different browsers. For more information, see "Using a Background Color" in the Saturday Afternoon session.

Option #3: Set Font Sizes and Colors

Besides setting the overall background, text, and link colors, you can radically alter the look of your Web page by changing the size and color of sections of your text. You can use the BASEFONT, FONT, BIG, and SMALL tags to change the size of a section of text. You can use the FONT tag to change the color of a section of text. This example uses the BASEFONT to change the overall size of the text font to "4" (the regular default font size is "3") and uses the FONT tags to change the size of the level-one and level-two headings to "7" and "6" and their colors to "aqua" (one of the 16 color names that you can use to specify a color). The code illustration shows the first basic Web page example, but if you're using one of the other two examples, you should have no trouble adapting the code to the example you're using.

```
<BODY BGCOLOR="#004080" TEXT="#ffff00" LINK="#00ff00"
VLINK="#a4c8f0" ALINK="#ff8000">
```

```
<BASEFONT SIZE="4">
```

```
<P ALIGN="center"><IMG SRC="Your banner graphic">
```

```
<H1 ALIGN="center"><FONT SIZE="7" COLOR="aqua">Your
level-one heading</FONT></H1>
```

```
<P>Your introductory paragraph. Your introductory para-
graph. Your introductory paragraph. Your introductory
paragraph.
```

```
<H2><FONT SIZE="6" COLOR="#FF8000">Your level-two sub-
heading</FONT></H2>
```

The hex code, #FF8000, is actually for the color "orange." Orange is not included in the 16 standard color names. Both of the latest versions of Internet Explorer and Navigator recognize "orange" as a color name, but there's no guarantee that other browsers will do the same. Figure 6.25 shows what this might look like in a Web browser.

For more information on changing font sizes and colors, see "Working with Fonts" in the Saturday Afternoon session.

Option #4: Use a Background Image

You can add a background image to your Web page by using the BACK-GROUND attribute in the BODY tag. In the following example, comment out your previous BODY tag and insert the new BODY tag with MOTTLE.GIF (included with the example Web page files) set as a background image, and change the colors of the two headings to blue and green, respectively:

```
<HTML>
<HEAD>
<TITLE>Your title</TITLE>
</HEAD>
<!—<BODY BGCOLOR="#004080" TEXT="#ffff00"
LINK="#00ff00" VLINK="#a4c8f0" ALINK="#ff8000">—>
<BODY BACKGROUND="mottle.gif">
<BASEFONT SIZE="4">
<P ALIGN="center"><IMG SRC="dummy.gif">
<H1 ALIGN="center"><FONT SIZE="7" COLOR="blue">Dummy
Web Page Heading</FONT></H1>
<P>This is just a bunch of dummy text. It is meant to
show you what an introductory paragraph will look like.
This is just a bunch of dummy text. It is meant to
show you what an introductory paragraph will look like.
This is just a bunch of dummy text. It is meant to
show you what an introductory paragraph will look like.
<H2><FONT SIZE="6" COLOR="green">Dummy Web Page Subheading
</FONT></H2>
```

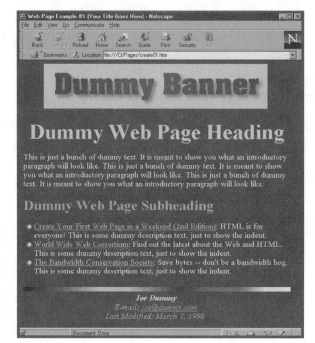

Figure 6.25

You can add even
more emphasis and
color to your Web
page by assigning
font sizes and
colors.

Figure 6.26 gives some idea of what this might look like in a Web browser (since this includes some color, you need to hop over to your Web browser to see what it really looks like).

For more information on using background images, see "Using a Background Image" in the Saturday Afternoon session.

Option #5: Use a Transparent Banner Graphic Against a Background Image

One way to give your Web page a three-dimensional look is to use a banner graphic with its background color set to transparent against a background image. The text in your banner graphic will appear to float on top of the background image.

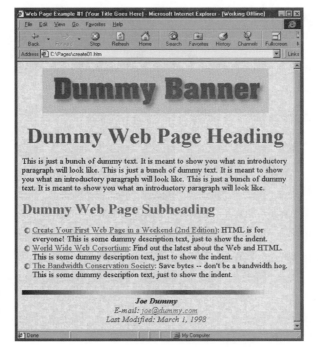

Figure 6.26

For a dramatic effect, use a background image.

Since I haven't yet shown you how to create transparent GIF images, I've included an example banner graphic with its background color set to transparent, DUMMY_TR.GIF, that you can use to see exactly what this looks like. Figure 6.27 shows what using a transparent banner graphic might look like in a Web browser.

```
<BODY BACKGROUND="mottle.gif">
<BASEFONT SIZE="4">
<P ALIGN="center"><IMG SRC="dummy_tr.gif">
```

Option #6: Pulling Out All the Stops

This option combines many of the extra options that have been presented here, including using a background image, assigning text and link colors, setting the base font size, using a transparent banner graphic, center-aligning

headings, setting the font size and color of headings, creating centered graphic rules with custom widths and heights, and creating an icon link list. The example that follows uses the first basic Web page example as the base. The italics indicate text you have already inserted, or must insert, in place of the example text.

```
<HTML>

<HEAD>

<TITLE>Your title</TITLE>

</HEAD>

<BODY BACKGROUND="mottle.gif" TEXT="#804040" LINK="green">

<BASEFONT SIZE="4">

<P ALIGN="center"><IMG SRC="dummy_tr.gif">

<H1 ALIGN="center"><FONT SIZE="7" COLOR="#205AB3">Your
level-one heading</H1></FONT>

<P ALIGN="center"><IMG SRC="rain_lin.gif" WIDTH="85%"
HEIGHT="10">

<P>Your introductory paragraph text . . .

<H2 ALIGN="center"><FONT SIZE="6" COLOR="#205AB3">Your
level-two heading</H2></FONT>

<P><IMG SRC="icon.gif" ALIGN="left" HSPACE="5" VSPACE="5">
<A HREF="http://www.callihan.com/create2/index.htm">
Create Your First Web Page in a Weekend (2nd Edition)</A>:
HTML is for everyone!<BR CLEAR="left">

<IMG SRC="icon.gif" ALIGN="left" HSPACE="5" VSPACE="5">
<A HREF="http://www.w3.org/">World Wide Web Corsortium
</A>: Find out the latest about the Web and HTML.<BR
CLEAR="left">

<IMG SRC="icon.gif" ALIGN="left" HSPACE="5" VSPACE="5">
<A HREF="http://www.infohiway.com/faster/homebcs.htm">
The Bandwidth Conservation Society</A>: Save bytes—
don't be a bandwidth hog.<BR CLEAR="left">

<P ALIGN="center"><IMG SRC="rain_lin.gif" WIDTH="75%"
HEIGHT="10">

<ADDRESS>
```

```
<CENTER><FONT SIZE="5" COLOR="red"><STRONG>Your name here
</STRONG></FONT><BR>

E-mail: <A HREF="mailto:Your e-mail address">Your e-mail
address again</A><BR>

Last Modified: Current date here</CENTER>

</ADDRESS>

</BODY>

</HTML>
```

Figure 6.28 shows how this might appear in a Web browser.

Option #7: Define a Style Sheet

I include some examples of using styles in the Saturday Afternoon and Evening sessions. There is not enough time or space to devote to styles, but you don't have to be an expert in using Cascading Style Sheets to add some

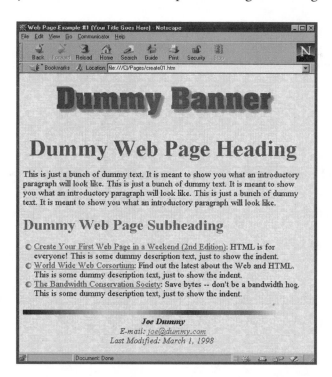

Figure 6.27

A transparent banner graphic can give your page a 3-D look.

nice touches to your Web page. Take a look at STYLE.HTM, an example Web page that uses a style sheet. (You'll find it with the other example Web page files.) Here's what's in it:

```
<HTML>

<HEAD>

<TITLE>Web Page Example #1 (Your Title Goes
Here)</TITLE>

<STYLE type="text/css">

<!--

BODY {background: url(mottle.gif); background-attach-
ment: fixed}

DIV.head {font-family: sans-serif; font-weight: bold;
font-size: 175%; text-align: center; color: #FF8000;
margin-top: -5; margin-bottom: -15}

DIV.top {border: solid red; border-style: ridge; back-
ground: #000080; padding: 10}
```

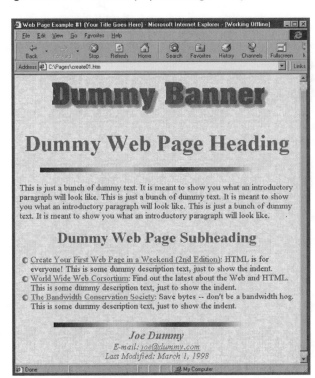

Figure 6.28

Nothing says you can't pull out all the stops and use all the extra options at once.

```
H2 {font-family: sans-serif; font-weight: 900; text-
align: center; color: green; margin-left: 1em; margin-
right: 1em; background: #FF9D6F; margin-top: 1em}

H3, H4, H5 {font-family: Verdana, Helvetica, sans-serif;
color: #FF8000}

P {font-size: 105%; color: maroon}

P.top {font-size: 105%; color: yellow; font-weight: 600}

DIV.middle {font-family: sans-serif}

UL {color: navy; list-style: url(redball.gif)}

LI {color: navy; font-size: 85%}

A {color: red; font-weight: bold; font-family: sans-serif}

HR {color: red}

DIV.bottom {color: green}

SPAN.name {color: fuchsia; font-size: 150%}

—>

</STYLE>

</HEAD>

<BODY>

<P ALIGN="center"><IMG SRC="dummy_tr.gif">

<DIV CLASS="top">

<DIV CLASS="head"<P>Dummy Web Page Heading</DIV>

<P CLASS="top">This is just a bunch of dummy text. It
is meant to show you what an introductory paragraph
will look like. This is just a bunch of dummy text. It
is meant to show you what an introductory paragraph
will look like. This is just a bunch of dummy text. It
is meant to show you what an introductory paragraph
will look like.

</DIV>

<H2>Dummy Web Page Subheading</H2>

<UL>

<LI><A
HREF="http://www.callihan.com/create2/index.htm">Create
Your First Web Page in a Weekend (2nd Edition)</A>: HTML
is for everyone!
```

```
<LI><A HREF="http://www.w3.org/">World Wide Web Consor-
tium</A>: Find out the latest about the Web and HTML.
<LI><A
HREF="http://www.infohiway.com/faster/homebcs.htm">The
Bandwidth Conservation Society</A>: Save bytes—don't
be a bandwidth hog.
</UL>
<DIV CLASS="bottom">
<HR SIZE=5 WIDTH="95%" NOSHADE>
<ADDRESS>
<CENTER><SPAN CLASS="name">Joe Dummy</SPAN><BR>
E-mail: <A
HREF="mailto:joe@dummy.com">joe@dummy.com</A><BR>
Last Modified: March 1, 1998
</CENTER>
</ADDRESS>
</DIV>
</BODY>
</HTML>
```

The #FF8000 hex codes included in the example specify an "orange" color. Figure 6.29 shows what STYLE.HTM looks like in Internet Explorer.

The current versions of Internet Explorer and Netscape Navigator differ fairly significantly in how they display this file. Internet Explorer offers superior support for style sheets, which are the wave of the future.

If you want to find out more about style sheets, you can find the W3C's full specification for Cascading Style Sheets, level 1, at `http://www.w3.org/TR/REC-CSS1-961217`. You can also find a list of links to style sheet resources on the Web in Appendix A, "The Web Resources Directory." I've also included in Appendix B, "The Web Tools Directory," a list of links to software tools that automate creating style sheets.

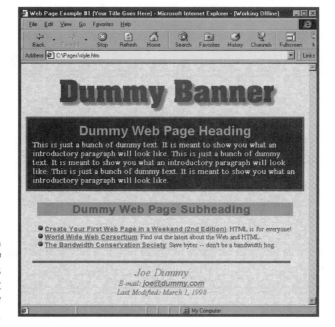

Figure 6.29

You can do things with styles that you can't do any other way.

What's Next?

You should now have created your first Web page. Hooray! True, you may have stuck to creating a very basic Web page, which uses only tags and features from the Basic HTML Tutorial. Or you may have incorporated a number of the suggested extra options to snazz and jazz it up, most of which are based on tags and features from the Intermediate HTML Tutorial. You may also have used one of the example banner graphics or the example link list I provided as placeholders until you get the time to create your own. A Web page tends to be a work in progress—never, ever finished, in other words. And one page tends to lead to another, and to another, and so on.

If you have managed to do everything I've put before you up until now, all in a single weekend, that's fantastic. Even if you've stuck to doing the Basic HTML Tutorial, skipped all the extra options when creating your first Web page, and used my sample banner and links, you've still accomplished a lot!

So what will you do now? If you haven't yet done all the HTML tutorials, you should do those first, before trying to go on and do the Graphics Tutorial that I've scheduled for tonight. If you haven't completed the Intermediate HTML Tutorial or the Tables Tutorial yet, you might want to do one of them for your Sunday evening session.

For those of you who have managed to finish everything so far, and who still have some time and energy left, I've got the Graphics Tutorial scheduled for you this evening. If you want to give it a try, take a break, have some dinner, and come back to learn how to use Web graphics to create some really neat special effects for your pages.

On the other hand, you may be ready to call it a day! Feel free to come back and do the Graphics Tutorial—or any of the other tutorials that you've skipped—on another day, or another weekend.

The Graphics Tutorial

(BONUS SESSION)

- ✪ Creating Special Effects with Paint Shop Pro
- ✪ Creating Interlaced GIFs
- ✪ Using Fill Effects
- ✪ Creating 3-D Buttons

It's Sunday evening! If you are on schedule, you planned your first Web page this morning and created it this afternoon. This evening, I'll show you how to use Paint Shop Pro, a great shareware paint program, to add different special effects to your Web graphics.

NOTE If you are using the Windows 3.1 version of Paint Shop Pro, you should find the sections on creating interlaced and transparent GIFs easy to follow—the Windows 3.1 procedures match the steps I'll be providing for the Windows 95 version pretty closely. Unfortunately, the Windows 3.1 version cannot do any of the special effects (drop shadows, 3-D buttons and bullets) that the remainder of this tutorial focuses on. In the section on creating drop shadows, however, I've included a tip on how you can create a very similar effect in the Windows 3.1 version of Paint Shop Pro.

Creating an Image Folder

You'll be using a couple of example background images in this tutorial that were included with the rest of the example Web page files when you copied them to your working folder for planning and creating your first Web page. This morning, I suggested that you create a new working folder, C:\PAGES, for planning and creating your first Web page, but you also had the option of continuing to use C:\HTML as your working folder. In this tutorial, I'll be referring to your working folder as C:\PAGES— if you are using C:\HTML or anything else, you'll need to substitute the name you're using whenever I refer to C:\PAGES.

Create a folder called C:\PAGES\IMAGES inside your working folder to hold the images you'll be creating in this session.

Installing and Running Paint Shop Pro

You can install Paint Shop Pro directly from Prima's interface for the CD-ROM. To install either the Windows 95 or the Windows 3.1 version of Paint Shop Pro, do the following:

1. Insert the CD-ROM in your CD-ROM drive.

2. For Windows 3.1 only:

    A. Run File Manager, then select File, Run to open the Run window.

    B. In the Command Line text box, type **D:\primacd.exe** (where D:\ is the CD-ROM drive)

3. At the opening screen of Prima's CD-ROM interface:

    A. Click on Multimedia.

    B. Click on Paint Shop Pro.

    C. The Install radio button should already be selected. Just click on OK to install Paint Shop Pro.

4. To install the Windows 95 version of Paint Shop Pro, select the 32 Bit radio button; to install the Windows 3.1 version of Paint Shop Pro, select the 16 Bit radio button. Click on OK.

To run Paint Shop Pro in Windows 95, click on the Start button, then select Programs, Paint Shop Pro, and Paint Shop Pro 4; in Windows 3.1, double-click on its icon in the program group that has been created for it.

Creating Special Effects with Paint Shop Pro

In this section, you'll sample some of the many different special effects that you can create easily with Paint Shop Pro. Because the graphics capabilities of Paint Shop Pro are so rich, you'll just be scratching the surface, but it will be a deep scratch. This tutorial will cover the following ground:

- ✪ Screen Layout
- ✪ Interlaced GIFs
- ✪ Transparent GIFs
- ✪ Drop Shadows
- ✪ Transparent Drop Shadows
- ✪ Fill Effects
- ✪ 3-D Buttons

Screen Layout

Pause for a moment and go over the Paint Shop Pro screen layout. This is important because throughout this section, I'll refer to different parts of Paint Shop Pro's screen by name instead of describing them in detail. As you go through the following exercises, you can use Figure 7.1 as a quick reference to what is what on the screen.

 NOTE The screen layout presented here is for the Windows 95 version of Paint Shop Pro. If you are using the Windows 3.1 version, you'll need to extrapolate a bit, as the layout and appearance of the 3.1 version's screen is somewhat different from that of the Windows 95 version.

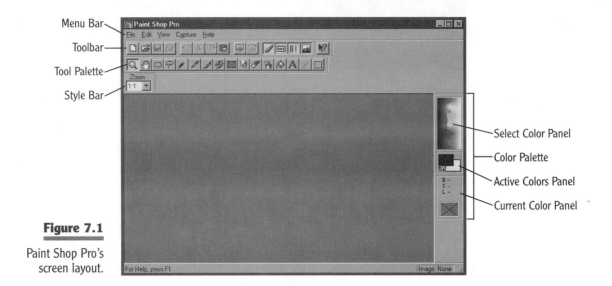

Menu Bar
Toolbar
Tool Palette
Style Bar

Select Color Panel
Color Palette
Active Colors Panel
Current Color Panel

Figure 7.1

Paint Shop Pro's
screen layout.

The following list describes the items labeled on Figure 7.1:

- **Menu Bar**. This is the set of pull-down menus (File, Edit, View, and so on) that you see at the top of almost any Windows program screen.

- **Toolbar**. This is the top row of buttons, which are primarily shortcuts for operations that can be carried out using the menu bar. For instance, instead of selecting File, New to create a new image, you can just click on the first toolbar button (New). The toolbar also includes four icons grouped at the right that you can use to toggle the display of the tool palette, style bar, and color palette. You can also toggle the display of the Histogram window (but we won't be dealing with this feature). In this tutorial, for the sake of clarity, I'll refer to the menu bar equivalents for these buttons, rather than to the buttons them- selves. As you become more familiar with the operations involved, feel free to use the toolbar buttons in place of their menu bar equivalents. (This is roughly the same as what is in the Windows 3.1 version.)

- **Tool Palette**. This is the second row of buttons. These buttons will get a lot of use as you manipulate your image. They allow you to zoom in or out, move your image in the image window, select part of the image, paint, erase, fill, add text, and so on. (In the Windows 3.1 version, this is the Paint Toolbox. The tool icons are roughly the same as on the Tool Palette in the Windows 95 version, except the Text tool is a capital T rather than a capital A.)

✿ **Style Bar.** This is located under the tool palette. The contents of the style bar can change depending on which tool is selected on the tool palette. For instance, when you first start Paint Shop Pro, the Zoom tool is selected on the tool palette and the Zoom Control box (which allows you to set the zoom factor for an image) is displayed on the style bar. (In the Windows 3.1 version, this is called the Tool Control Panel.)

✿ **Color Palette.** This is located on the right side of Paint Shop Pro's screen. There are three parts to the Color Palette: the Select Color panel, the Active Colors panel, and the Current Color panel:

- **Select Color Panel.** You can use this panel to quickly select and apply a color. When you move the mouse pointer into the Select Color panel, the pointer turns into the Dropper tool. As you move the pointer around in the panel, you'll see the color underlying the dropper displayed in the Current Color panel. To assign the current color as the foreground color, click on the left mouse button. To assign the current color as the background color, right-click. (This doesn't work in the Windows 3.1 version.)

- **Active Colors Panel.** This panel contains two overlapped rectangles that display the currently selected foreground and background colors. In addition to the method described previously, you can also assign foreground and background colors by clicking on either of the rectangles. The Color dialog box appears, allowing you to select the specific color you want to assign. (In the Windows 3.1 version, the foreground color and background color rectangles are on the Select Toolbox.)

- **Current Color Panel.** This panel displays the current color when you select a color from the Select Color panel (as described earlier) or when you use the Dropper tool to pick a color from the image window. The palette settings for the color are also displayed here—depending on the preference you've set, either as the HSL (hue, saturation, and luminance) or as the RGB (red, green, and blue) palette values. (This is not present in the Windows 3.1 version, although if the Eye Dropper tool is selected from the Select Toolbox, the RGB values of any colors under the Eye Dropper are shown on the Status Bar at the bottom of the Paint Shop Pro window.)

✿ **Image Window.** This is the window that contains the actual graphic you are creating. Note that you can have more than one image window open at a time, but only one of them will be the active image window. (This is the same in the Windows 3.1 version.)

Creating Interlaced GIFs

An interlaced GIF works by using multiple passes to scan all the lines in an image. This allows the full image, although not all the lines in an image, to appear before the file has been entirely downloaded from the Internet. The advantage of this is that it allows a viewer to see what the full image is before every line in the image is available. The disadvantage is that an interlaced GIF image file is a bit larger than a corresponding noninterlaced GIF image file, and thus takes a bit longer to download entirely. For this reason, some people don't like interlaced GIF images, but the benefit of a viewer being able to get a quicker look at the full image before it has completely downloaded outweighs the disadvantage of a slightly longer overall download time.

Creating an Image

You'll be starting out with a fairly simple image here, but you'll add to it as I demonstrate more of the special effects that follow. To create your starting image, follow these steps:

1. Select File, New.

2. In the New Image dialog box, set the Width to 450 and the Height to 150.

3. The remaining settings should be: Background color: White (this option is not present in the Windows 3.1 version), and Image Type: 16.7 Million Colors (24 Bit) (see Figure 7.2).

4. Click on OK.

Selecting a Foreground Color

1. Click on the foreground color rectangle in the color palette. The Color dialog box appears, as shown in Figure 7.3. The Color dialog box allows you to select from 48 colors (44 colors, 2 grays, and black and white). On the right is the color matrix that enables you to select from many more color gradations. You can also create a selection of custom colors.

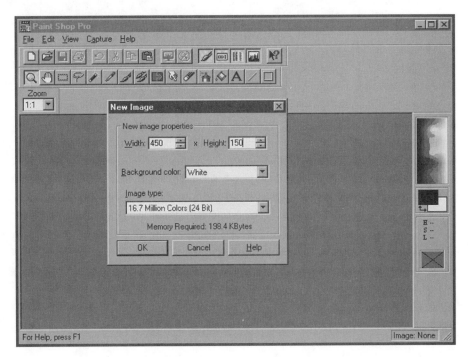

Figure 7.2

The New Image dialog box defines the dimensions, background color, and color depth of a new image.

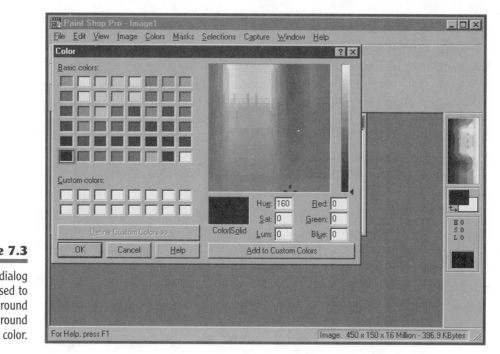

Figure 7.3

The Color dialog box is used to select a foreground or background color.

2. Click on the color red (the second color down in the first column). You'll see your selection reflected on the right in the color matrix and the Color/Solid rectangle.

3. Click on OK. The foreground color rectangle has changed to red.

NOTE   If you've used this copy of Paint Shop Pro previously, you might have set the background color rectangle to some color other than white. If you have, to reset this rectangle back to white, click on the background color rectangle, select the color white (bottom-right corner), and then click on OK.

Inserting Text

1. Click on the Text tool (the "A" icon) on the tool palette and then click in the middle of your image's window. (In the Windows 3.1 version, the Text tool is the "T" icon.)

2. In the Add Text dialog box, select Arial as the Name of your font, Bold as the Style, and 72 (points) as the Size. Check the AntiAlias check box. Make sure the Floating check box is checked. Leave any other settings as they are. (The Floating check box is not present in the Windows 3.1 version.)

◄ ◄

Anti-aliasing smooths out the edges of a font by fuzzing the pixels around the edge and alternating different shades of the font's color to give the appearance of a smoother contour. This can help to get rid of some of the "jaggies" that can be seen in a font's rounded contours or diagonal edges. This option is only available for images that have either a 256-color gray-scale or a color depth that is greater than 256 colors.

◄ ◄

3. In the text box (Enter text here:) at the bottom of the window, type **Headline**. (See Figure 7.4.)

4. Click on OK. Position the mouse pointer on top of the "Headline" text, then hold down the left mouse button and drag the text to reposition it as close as you can to the center of the image window. When you get it positioned where you want it, release the mouse button. (This works a little differently in the Windows 3.1 version. Once you click on OK to insert your text, you can move the mouse cursor to freely reposition your text in the image window, but once you click on the mouse button, your text will be glued in place.)

As shown in Figure 7.5, you'll notice that the letters are surrounded by a dashed line, meaning that the text is selected. You'll also notice that the letters of "Headline" have been filled with red, the selected foreground color.

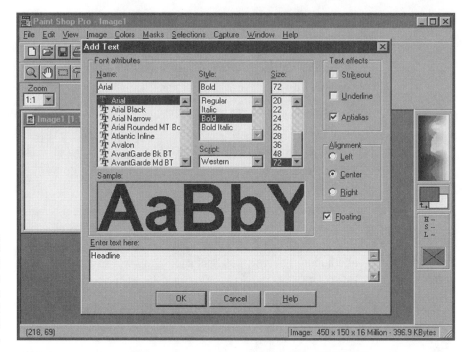

Figure 7.4

In the Add Text
dialog box, the
word Headline
has been set
as a 72-point
bold Arial font.

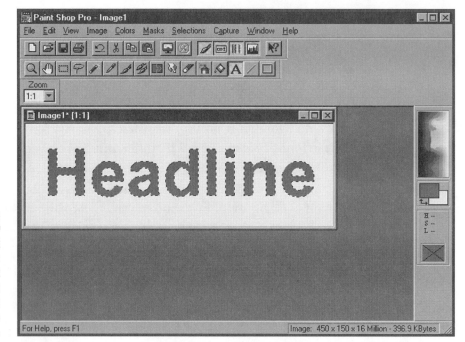

Figure 7.5

When you add text
to an image
window, the text
appears in the
current foreground
color and is
selected.

Saving an Interlaced GIF

Now that you have created a simple image, you can save it as an interlaced GIF image. To save your current image as an interlaced GIF, follow these steps:

1. Select File, Save (or Save As). The Save As dialog box appears.

2. In the Save in list box at the top, change the folder to your \IMAGES folder (C:\PAGES\IMAGES).

3. In the File name box, type **headline.gif**. In the Save as type box, select "GIF—CompuServe" as the file type. In the Sub type box, make sure "Version 89a—Interlaced" is selected. (See Figure 7.6.)

NOTE There are two types of GIF files, Version 87a and Version 89a. Both versions can be saved as either interlaced or noninterlaced, but only Version 89a can be saved as transparent. I always save my GIFs as Version 89a GIFs. Another difference between the two versions is that Version 89a allows the creation of animated GIFs (for information on resources and tools for creating animated GIFs, see Appendix A, "The Web Resources Directory," and Appendix B, "The Web Tools Directory."

4. Click on Options, then select the Do not save any transparency information radio button. Click on OK.

5. Click on Save. Click on Yes to allow Paint Shop Pro to reduce the number of colors to 256 (GIFs can only have up to 256 colors). You'll notice that "Image1" has been replaced in the title bar of the image window with the name of your image file.

NOTE You may wonder why you started out creating an image using 16.7 million colors, only to reduce the number to 256 colors. First, GIF images can have up to 256 colors. Second, many of the special effects covered in this tutorial require the color depth to be set to 16.7 million colors. If you started at 256 colors, you'd be out of luck; these special effects just won't work.

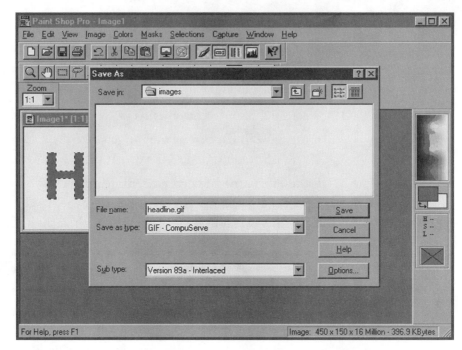

Figure 7.6

HEADLINE.GIF is saved here as a "Version 89a-Interlaced" GIF.

Creating Transparent GIFs

The second kind of GIF file you can create is a transparent GIF image. A transparent GIF image is created by setting one of the colors in the image to be displayed as transparent.

NOTE Don't expect a transparent GIF to look different from any other GIF image when viewed with Paint Shop Pro or another paint program or graphics viewer. The image will only appear transparent when viewed with a Web browser.

There are two ways to create a transparent GIF image in Paint Shop Pro. The first is to designate the current background color for the image as transparent, while the second is to designate a palette entry number. In this tutorial, you'll use the first method, mainly because it is easier than doing it the other way.

Saving Your Image with a Transparent Background

Saving an image with a transparent background is a two-stage process. First, select the color in the background color rectangle that matches the color of the part of your image that you want to be transparent. Then save your work as a GIF image with the background color (the color selected in the background color rectangle) designated as transparent.

◄ ◄

Background color is the color selected in the background rectangle, which isn't necessarily the color that is in the background of your image. Paint Shop Pro can't see your image; it'll take whatever color you pick in the background rectangle and treat it as the background. So if you want the color in the background of your image to be saved as transparent, it has to match the color you select in the background color rectangle.

◄ ◄

Follow these steps to save your image with the background color set to transparent:

1. If the background color rectangle is still white, skip to the next step. If the background color rectangle is a color other than white, click in the background color rectangle, then select white as the background and click on OK.

2. Select File and Save As. The file information should be unchanged from when you saved your interlaced image, so leave all the file information as it is.

3. Click on Options, then select the Set the transparency value to the background color radio button. (See Figure 7.7.)

4. Click on OK and then click on Save. (Since you already did so when you saved your image earlier, you won't be prompted to reduce the color depth here to 256 colors.)

5. When prompted to replace the existing file, click on Yes. That's it. You've just created a transparent GIF image.

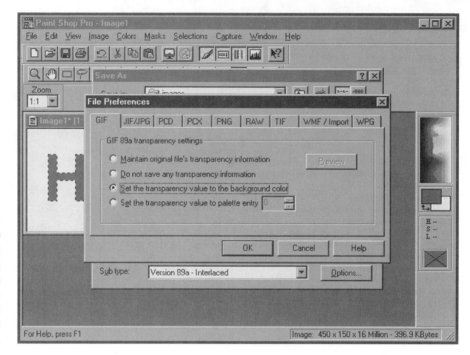

Figure 7.7

For your background color to be saved as transparent, the correct radio button has to be selected in the File Preferences dialog box.

Viewing Your Transparent Image

To view your transparent image, you need to do two things:

1. Create an HTML file that uses your transparent image and a background image to help show it off.
2. View the HTML file in your Web browser.

Creating the HTML File

Run Notepad and type in the following:

```
<HTML>
<HEAD><TITLE>Headline HTML File</TITLE>
</HEAD>
<BODY BACKGROUND="backgrnd.gif">
```

```
<P ALIGN="center"><IMG SRC="images/headline.gif"
WIDTH="450" HEIGHT="150">
</BODY>
</HTML>
```

Save this file in the working folder for your HTML files, C:\PAGES, as HEADLINE.HTM.

NOTE BACKGROUND="backgrnd.gif" displays a background image that is in the same folder as the HTML file (C:\PAGES). The IMG tag uses a relative URL (SRC="images/headline.gif") to display your GIF image, which has been saved in the C:\PAGES\IMAGES folder). If you are confused about how relative URLs work, review "Using Relative URLs" in the Saturday Morning session.

FILE, OPEN

Viewing Your HTML File in Your Web Browser

Run your Web browser and open HEADLINE.HTM from your working folder. You'll see the text, "Headline," displayed transparently against the background image. (See Figure 7.8.)

Figure 7.8

The transparent image floats in front of the background image.

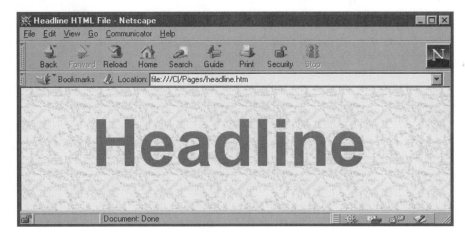

And that's it. Pretty easy. You just have to remember to make sure that the color displayed in the background color rectangle matches the one in your image that you want to be transparent, and that your save options specify setting the background color as transparent.

There is one added complication that I haven't covered yet. In the previous example, the background color of your image and the predominant color of the background image that is being used are the same: white. When these two colors do not match fairly closely (they don't have to be identical), problems can sometimes arise when using anti-aliased fonts and blurred drop shadows.

For instance, in the HTML file that you created for the previous example, if you substitute BGCOLOR="#FF8000" (the hex code for "orange") for BACKGROUND="backgrnd.gif", and save the file and pull it up in your browser, you'll be able to see the anti-aliasing around the edges of the letters. And the problem is even worse if you want to use a blurred drop shadow in a transparent GIF—if the background color of your image does not closely match the predominant color of your background image (or match a background color almost perfectly), your drop shadow will not blur into the background when it is displayed in a browser. Instead, it will have a very noticeable cookie-cutter effect. But have no fear—later in this tutorial, in the "Creating Effective Transparent Drop Shadows" section, I'll be showing you how to create drop shadows that will meld seamlessly into any background image or color.

Creating Drop Shadows

One of the easiest and most effective special effects you can add to your graphic is a drop shadow. This gives a 3-D effect to your image, with the drop shadow looking like a shadow cast upon the background of the image.

NOTE

Drop shadows are a Windows 95 special effect, but I've included a subsection at the end of this section, "Creating Drop Shadows in Windows 3.1," that'll show you how to fudge a blurred drop shadow without Windows 95. If you are using the Windows 3.1 version, go ahead and skip ahead to that subsection now.

Because the drop shadow special effect requires that your image have more than 256 colors, you first need to increase the number of colors. Select Colors, Increase Color Depth, and 16 Million Colors (24 bit). Next, do the following steps to add a drop shadow effect to your image:

1. Click on the foreground color rectangle in the Color Palette. Choose any color (other than red; you've used that one) that you think might look good (for instance, try selecting the blue-green—the third color down in the fourth column). Click on OK.

2. Select Image, Special Effects, and Add Drop Shadow.

3. In the Drop Shadow dialog box, select Foreground Color for the Color, 255 for the Opacity, 36 for the Blur, and 6 for both the Vertical and Horizontal Offset. (See Figure 7.9.)

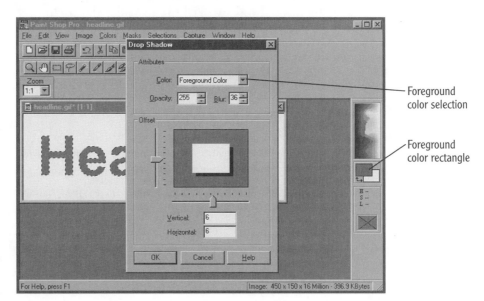

Foreground color selection

Foreground color rectangle

Figure 7.9

The Drop Shadow dialog box

The Opacity setting determines how opaque or transparent the drop shadow will be, with a value of "0" being totally transparent and a value of "255" being completely opaque. The Blur setting determines how much the edges of the drop shadow are blurred against the background, with a higher number setting a higher degree of blur.

4. Click on OK. The drop shadow is added to your text.

5. To get a better look at your image without the dashed selection lines around the text, select Selections, Select None. (See Figure 7.10.)

Reduce the Color Depth to 256 Colors:

Because a GIF file can have only 256 colors, reduce the number of colors to 256 again before saving your new image:

1. Select Colors, Decrease Color Depth, and 256 colors (8 bit).

2. In the Decrease Color Depth dialog box, since you're using a blur effect here, I recommend that you select Optimized as the Palette, and Error diffusion as the Reduction method. Selecting the Standard palette will result in a noticeable banding effect in your drop shadow. Also, it won't hurt to select the Include Windows colors and the Reduce color bleeding check boxes, as well. Click on OK.

3. Select File, Save, to save your image (as HEADLINE.GIF in C:\PAGES\IMAGES).

It is a good idea, unless your image already has very few colors (or gradations of colors), to decrease the colors to 256 *before* saving your file. If you wait until Paint Shop Pro prompts you to do this as part of the Save routine (as happened when you saved the file earlier), you won't be able to undo the changes that might occur in your image. However, if you do it yourself before saving, you can always select Edit and Undo to undo the color reduction. You can then manipulate your graphic to try to get a better result or save it as a JPG file instead.

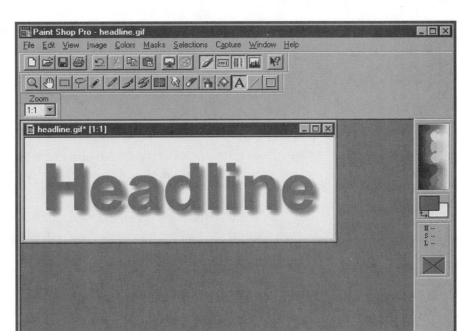

Figure 7.10

A drop shadow
has been added
to the text.

Viewing Your HTML File in Your Web Browser

Hop back over to your Web browser, where HEADLINE.HTM should
still be displayed. Reload the page to display your new transparent image
using the drop shadow effect (press Ctrl+R in either Navigator or Internet
Explorer). Assuming you left the background rectangle set to white and
the background color of the image both white and transparent, the text in
your image and the drop shadow will appear to be floating transparently
against the background image in your Web browser. (See Figure 7.11.)

Creating Drop Shadows in Windows 3.1

There is a way in the Windows 3.1 version of Paint Shop Pro to fudge
something that looks like a blurred drop shadow, even though that effect
is not specifically available. Here's how you do it:

1. Select the color for your drop shadow in the foreground color rectangle (for instance, select bright blue, the fourth color down in the fifth column). Then click on the Text tool inside your image window to add some text.

2. In the Add Text dialog box, select a 72-point bold Arial font and type your text ("Headline," for instance) in the Text box. Check the AntiAlias check box. Click on OK. Move your mouse to position the text in the middle of your image window, and then left-click to insert it.

3. Apply the Wind deformation to your text: select Image, Deformations, and Wind. In the Wind dialog box, select the From Left radio button. Set the Strength to 10, for instance. Click on OK.

4. Select another color in the foreground color rectangle (for instance, select bright orange, the fourth color down in the second column), then click on the Text tool inside your image window again to add the top layer of your text effect.

5. Don't change any of the settings in the Add Text dialog box. Click on OK. Move your mouse to position your new text so that it is positioned slightly up and to the left of the text you previously blurred using the Wind effect. When it is positioned to your satisfaction, left-click to insert the text. (See Figure 7.12.)

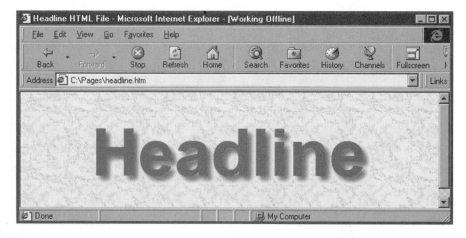

Figure 7.11

Both the text and the drop shadow seem to float on top of the background image.

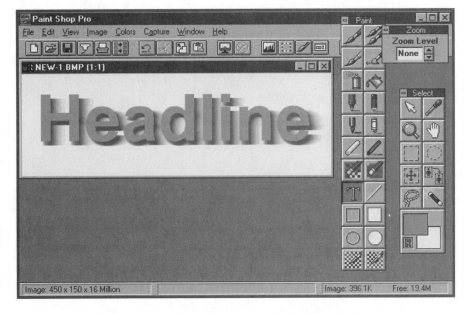

Figure 7.12

You can fudge a blurred drop shadow in the Windows 3.1 version of Paint Shop Pro by applying the Wind deformation to the underlying text.

That's it. Just reduce the color depth to 256 colors and save your image as a GIF 89a image with the background color (white) set to transparent. If you need to display your image against a background image with a predominant color other than white, or against a background color other than white, see the following section, "Effective Transparent Drop Shadows," for some techniques that can also be used in the Windows 3.1 version of Paint Shop Pro.

Effective Transparent Drop Shadows

The image you just created has a transparent drop shadow, but it will only work if it is displayed against a background image in which the primary color is white. If you want to display a drop shadow against a background image in which the color is not white, you need to set the color of your transparent background to match the predominant color in the background image as closely as possible.

In this section I'll be showing you a technique that you can use to match a transparent drop shadow to virtually any background image. This can be very effective on a Web page and go a long way toward making your Web page really stand out—in fact, if you check around the Web, you have to look a long time to find a page that uses a drop shadow effect against anything other than a white background or a background image in which the predominant color is white.

The Cookie-Cutter Effect

What I call the "cookie-cutter" effect occurs when a blur effect is created, and none of the blurred colors can be set to transparent. Only the non-blurred background color can be set to transparent. As long as your image's transparent background color and the primary color of the background image are the same or very similar, you won't notice that the blurred colors are not actually transparent. Display your image against a background color with a different primary color (black instead of white, for instance), and the non-transparent blurred colors will jump out at you like they've been cut out with a cookie-cutter.

Seeing is believing, however. If you want to see this cookie-cutter effect firsthand, retrieve the background image that is being displayed, then create and save a negative image of it:

1. Select File, Open. In the Open dialog box, go to C:\PAGES; then double-click on the file name of the background image (BACK-GRND.GIF) to open it.

2. Select Colors, Negative Image.

3. Next, select File, Save As. Rename the image to BACKGRN2.GIF and save it in C:\PAGES).

4. You don't want to save this file as a transparent GIF, so click on Options and then select Do not save any transparency information. Click on OK.

Editing Your HTML File

Next, edit your HTML file so that it will display the new background image:

1. Hop back over to Notepad and edit HEADLINE.HTM so that it matches what is shown here:

```
<HTML>
<HEAD><TITLE>Transparent Headline</TITLE>
</HEAD>
<BODY BACKGROUND="backgrn2.gif">
<P ALIGN="center"><IMG SRC="images/headline.gif"
WIDTH="450" HEIGHT="150">
</BODY>
</HTML>
```

2. Resave this file (HEADLINE.HTM in C:\PAGES).

Viewing Your HTML File in Your Web Browser

Hop back over to your Web browser and load HEADLINE.HTM. As shown in Figure 7.13, you should see a rather pronounced cookie-cutter effect at the edges of your drop shadow.

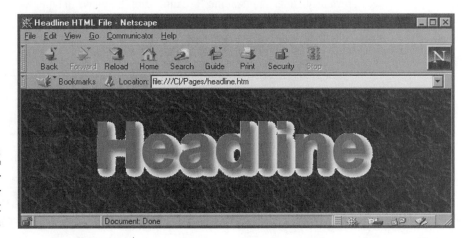

Figure 7.13

A cookie-cutter effect around your drop shadow is not what you want.

NOTE You'll run into the same problem when applying special effects other than drop shadows, such as blurs, wind effects, and even anti-aliasing, where the effect is blended with the background. The methods I'll be showing here for matching a transparent background to a background image or background color apply equally to any effect that uses a blur.

In the following sections, I'll show you how to create a transparent drop shadow effect against a background image in which black is the predominant color. Then I'll show you how to take a colored background image, select its predominant color, and assign this color as the transparent color for your image.

Creating a Transparent Drop Shadow for a Black Background

To fix the cookie-cutter effect problem in the previous image, you'll need to create a new transparent image from scratch, substituting black as the background color.

 NOTE If you are using the Windows 3.1 version of Paint Shop Pro, follow the instructions given previously under the heading "Creating Drop Shadows in Windows 3.1" to create a new image here, rather than the steps given in this section.

1. Clear all your images by selecting Window, Close All.

2. Start a new image in Paint Shop Pro by selecting File, New. In the New Image dialog box, select black (instead of white) as the Background color. Leave the Width set to 450 and the Height set to 150, and the Image type to 16.7 million colors. Click on OK.

3. Click in the middle of your image window with the Text tool. Leave all the settings in the Add Text dialog box as they are (72-point bold Arial font with "Headline" as the text). Click on OK.

(You'll notice that the text is now blue-green, the foreground color you selected previously when you created the drop shadow. If you want your text to be a different color, you should select the color you want as your foreground color before creating your text.)

4. To more precisely position the text, drag it to where you want it in the image window.

5. Select a new color in the foreground color rectangle. This is the new color for your drop shadow. Because you are creating an image against a black background, choose a lighter color (for instance, try selecting light yellow, which is the first color in the second column).

6. Select Image, Special Effects, and Add Drop Shadow. Leave all the settings in the Drop Shadow dialog box as they are (Foreground Color as the Color, 255 as the Opacity, 36 as the Blur, 6 as the Vertical and Horizontal Offsets). Click on OK.

7. To get a better look at your image, select Selections and Select None. (See Figure 7.14.)

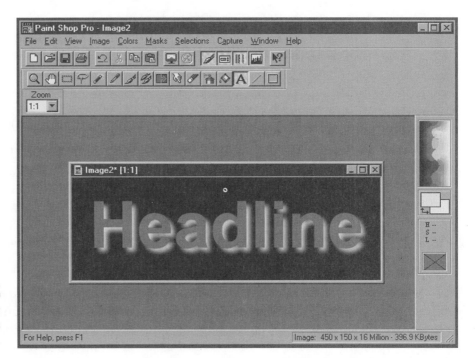

Figure 7.14

A light yellow drop shadow has been added.

8. Click on the background color rectangle and select black as the color (bottom-left corner). Click on OK.

9. Reduce the number of colors to 256 by selecting Colors, Decrease Color Depth, and 256 Colors. Leave all the settings as they are. Click on OK.

10. Select File and Save As. Select Options and the Set the transparency value to the background color radio button. Save your file as HEADLIN2.GIF in C:\PAGES\IMAGES.

Editing and Viewing Your HTML File

Next, edit your HTML file so that it will display the new background image:

1. Hop back over to Notepad and edit HEADLINE.HTM so that it matches what is shown here:

```
<HTML>
<HEAD><TITLE>Transparent Headline</TITLE>
</HEAD>
<BODY BACKGROUND="backgrn2.gif">
<P ALIGN="center"><IMG SRC="images/headlin2.gif"
WIDTH="450" HEIGHT="150">
</BODY>
</HTML>
```

2. Resave this file (HEADLINE.HTM in C:\PAGES).

Hop back over to your Web browser and reload (Ctrl+R) HEAD-LINE.HTM. As shown in Figure 7.15, your drop shadow should now meld seamlessly into the largely black background image.

Creating a Drop Shadow Against a Colored Background Image

It's no problem to tell if the predominant color of a background image is white or black, and then to assign the corresponding transparent color in your image, but what if it's some other color? Or what if your background image has several colors? The following technique will enable you to match the predominant color of most background images. The process has two main stages. First, you load a colored background image, use the Dropper tool to lift the predominant color (or pretty close) and assign it to the background color rectangle. Then you create your transparent image with the background of your image filled with the assigned background color, add the text and the drop shadow, set your background color to transparent, then save it. Voilà! It will meld seamlessly with the background image. No cookie-cutter effect.

NOTE This technique works equally well in the Windows 3.1 version of Paint Shop Pro.

Using the Dropper Tool to Pick Up and Assign a Background Color

1. Clear all the image windows you currently have open in Paint Shop Pro. (Hint: select Window, Close All).

2. I've included a sample background image, 3DGREEN1.GIF, with the example Web page files that you'll be using in this example. Just choose File, Open and then go to C:\PAGES and open 3DGREEN1.GIF in Paint Shop Pro.

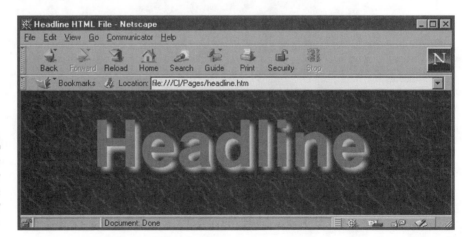

Figure 7.15

The drop shadow now seamlessly melds into the predominantly black background.

3. To make it easier to pick out the color you want, increase the zoom factor to 4:1. Select View, Zoom In, and 4:1.

4. Click on the Dropper tool from the Tool Palette (sixth button from the left) and then move the pointer inside the zoomed-in background image. Move the cursor over the image until it is positioned over what looks like the predominant color in the image—this a bit of a subjective process, so you'll just have to make your best try here. You can see the color beneath the cursor displayed in the Current Color panel. If you don't get a close enough match the first time, you'll just have to try again. (See Figure 7.16.)

5. Right-click to assign the color that is beneath the Dropper cursor to the background color rectangle.

6. Clear the 3DGREEN1.GIF image window by clicking on the "X" button in the upper-right corner (all you needed from it was the background color).

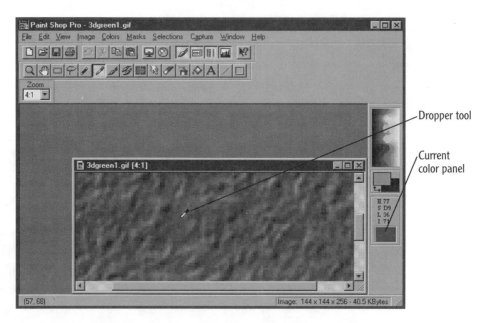

Figure 7.16

The Dropper tool can be used to pick up a color and assign it to either of the color rectangles.

Creating a New Transparent Image Using the New Background Color

If you are using the Windows 3.1 version of Paint Shop Pro, follow the steps previously described under "Creating Drop Shadows in Windows 3.1" to create a new drop-shadowed image. (When you open your new image window, the background of your image will automatically be filled with the green background color that you just assigned to the background color rectangle.)

1. Start a new image by selecting File, New. Make sure you select Background Color from the Background color list box. The other settings, unless you have changed them since the last example, should be left as they are (450 and 150 as the Width and Height, 16.7 Million Colors (24 Bit) as the Image type.

2. Leave the foreground rectangle color as it is (light yellow should still be there) and use it for your text. Click on the Text button on the tool palette and then click on the pointer in the middle of your image window. In the Add Text dialog box, click on OK to accept the previous settings (72-point bold Arial font with "Headline" as the text). You'll notice that the text is now light yellow, the color that was previously set for the foreground color.

3. To more precisely position the text in the center of the image window, hold down the mouse button on the text and drag it to exactly where you want it in the image window.

4. Click on the foreground color rectangle to select a new color for your foreground. This will be the color of your drop shadow. Because you are creating an image against a colored background, choose a color that will contrast with your text as well as with the background color (for instance, try selecting brick red—the fourth color down in the first column). Click on OK.

5. Select Image, Special Effects, and Add Drop Shadow. Leave the settings as they are and click on OK. To get a better look at your image, select Selections and Select None. (See Figure 7.17.)

6. Reduce the number of colors to 256 by selecting Colors, Decrease Color Depth, and 256 Colors. Instead of Error diffusion, select Nearest color as the reduction method. Leave the other settings as they are. Click on OK.

NOTE Nearest color was selected as the reduction method here in order to avoid the possibility of having the background color dithered, which can result in a speckled instead of a solid-color background, which will not be transparent.

7. Select File and Save As. Save your image as HEADLIN3.GIF in C:\PAGES\IMAGES. Since you reset the Save options on your last save, setting the background color to be transparent, you don't need to reset this option now (unless you've changed it in the meantime).

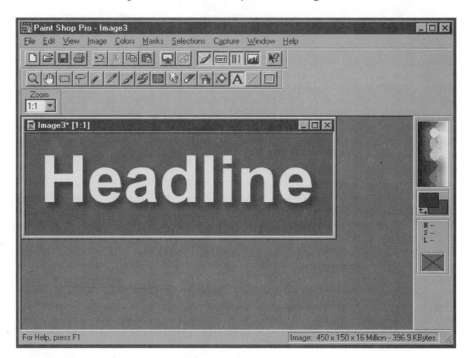

Figure 7.17

A brick red drop shadow has been added.

Editing and Viewing Your HTML File

Hop back over to Notepad and edit HEADLINE.HTM, adding the background image, 3DGREEN1.GIF, you are using and the new banner graphic you just saved, so that it matches what is shown here:

```
<HTML>
<HEAD><TITLE>Transparent Headline</TITLE>
</HEAD>
<BODY BACKGROUND="3dgreen1.gif">
<P ALIGN="center"><IMG SRC="images/headlin3.gif"
WIDTH="450" HEIGHT="150">
</BODY>
</HTML>
```

Resave HEADLINE.HTM in C:\PAGES (File, Save).

Hop back over to your Web browser and reload the page (Ctrl+R). The text and the drop shadow in your image should appear to float on top of the background image, as shown in Figure 7.18.

Creating a Drop Shadow Against a Background Color

Displaying a drop shadow transparently against a background color set in your HTML can actually be a little tricky. The main problem is matching the transparent background color of your image to the background color in your HTML file. You've got to make a very close match of the colors. The method I detail here for doing this involves either using additional software tools (which you may not have installed on your computer) or using the Web to access a color-picking resource. You may not want to take the time for that now, so I'm only going to provide the general steps you need to follow rather than have you go through the step-by-step procedures during this particular session.

Figure 7.18

If you know the trick, you can seamlessly float a transparent drop shadow on top of a colored background image.

In Appendix A, "The Web Resources Directory," and Appendix B, "The Web Tools Directory," I've included links to online color-picking utilities that are available on the Web, as well as to software tools that you can download and use on your own computer.

NOTE The instructions provided here should work equally well for the Windows 3.1 version of Paint Shop Pro.

The process you need to follow to do this involves using an HTML Editor that includes a color picker tool that will both insert the hex codes for a color into your HTML file and tell you what the RGB (Red/Green/Blue) values are for the color.

ON THE

CD

Agile 1-4-All, an HTML editor for Windows 95, is available on the CD-ROM. It has a color-picking utility you can use to include a background color in your page and find out what the RGB codes are for it. Many other HTML editors, such as HTML Notepad, use the very same color picker (it's part of Windows) and are available for download from the Web—see Appendix B, "The Web Tools Directory," for links.

First, you need to run your HTML editor and create or open an HTML file, and position your cursor where you want the hex code to be inserted (inside the BODY tag, if you are adding a background color). In Agile 1-4-All, to access the Color Picker, you click on the diamond button (at the end of the second row of buttons), click on the "..." button in the Color Selection dialog box, then click on Define Custom Colors. Use the cursor and the slider to select the color you want. Make note of the Red/Green/Blue values (you'll need to use them later) in the lower-left corner of the window. Click on OK to insert the hex codes for the color into your HTML file (if you haven't already typed it, you'll need to provide the "BGCOLOR=" part of the attribute).

NOTE HTML editors, even if they use the same color picker, may differ somewhat in how they insert the hex code for a color into your HTML file: Agile 1-4-All just inserts the hex codes (you need to provide the BGCOLOR attribute in the BODY tag), while others, such as HTML Notepad, will insert the whole attribute, both BGCOLOR and the hex codes, into the BODY tag.

Once you've inserted a background color into your HTML file and made note of its RGB values, you need to hop back over to Paint Shop Pro and start a new blank image. Click on the background color rectangle, then in the Color dialog box, type in the same Red/Green/Blue values you made note of before, and click on OK. Finally, with the Flood Fill ("Paint Bucket") tool selected, and Solid Color selected as the Fill style, right-click with the mouse inside your blank image window. Your image should match the color in the background color rectangle. Add some text, then apply a drop shadow effect to it, as shown earlier in this session.

Now, this is where it gets even trickier. That's because you need to reduce the number of colors in your image without altering the color of the background. This is more difficult than it sounds. Select Colors, Decrease Color

Depth, and 256 Colors. Select Optimized as the Palette and Nearest color as the Reduction method. Leave the Include Windows colors check box checked. Click on OK.

You may see a slight change in the background color, as the color-depth reduction tries to match it to the 256-color palette. That shouldn't be a problem (the background colors in your HTML file and your image don't have to be a perfect match, just pretty close). The main thing you are trying to avoid here is any dithering or error diffusion when making the reduction, which could break up the solidity of your background color and render it less than transparent (it would look speckled in your browser).

Finally, save your image file as a GIF image with the background color set to transparent. Then edit your HTML file with the matching background color set so that it will display your image. When you pull up the HTML file in your browser, the drop shadow effect should meld into the background color. See Figure 7.19 for an example of what this might look like.

Using Fill Effects

You can also use a variety of different *fill effects*—effects you can create using the Flood Fill tool (the Paint Bucket button) on the tool palette. You'll be using the same image here that you created in the "Creating a Drop Shadow Against a Colored Background Image" section (if you don't have the image from that example currently in Paint Shop Pro, you should go back and recreate it before proceeding with the following examples). I'll be showing you how to do three different fill effects: a solid fill, a radial fill, and a pattern fill.

NOTE You can create solid color fills using the Windows 3.1 version of Paint Shop Pro. You won't be able to do the sections on creating pattern or gradient fills, since those effects are not included in the Windows 3.1 version and I don't have a handy work-around for you.

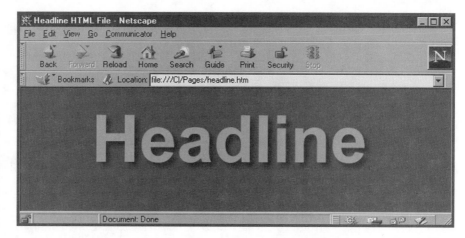

Figure 7.19

If you know the trick, you can seamlessly float a transparent drop shadow on top of a background color.

Using a Solid Fill

Assign a color in the foreground color rectangle, then click on the Flood Fill tool (the Paint Bucket button) with the pointer inside what you want to fill. Try filling the letter H with a solid yellow fill:

1. Increase the number of colors to 16.7 million: Select Colors, Increase Color Depth, and 16 Million Colors.

2. Click on the foreground color rectangle and then select a color with which to fill the letter H (try the salmon pink—the third color down in the last column). Click on OK.

3. Click on the Flood Fill tool (the Paint Bucket button) on the tool palette. In the Fill style control on the style bar, select Solid Color. The Match mode should have RGB Value selected. Increase the Tolerance setting to 80.

4. Position the pointer inside the letter H and then click on the left mouse button. The letter H will be filled with the foreground color you selected, as shown in Figure 7.20.

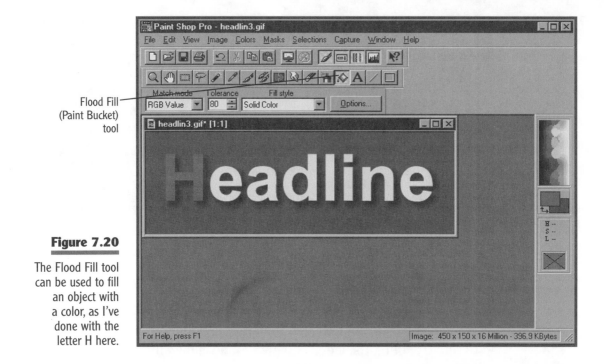

Flood Fill
(Paint Bucket)
tool

Figure 7.20

The Flood Fill tool
can be used to fill
an object with
a color, as I've
done with the
letter H here.

Using a Pattern Fill

Another neat effect is to fill an object with a pattern. You can use any image currently loaded in Paint Shop Pro as a pattern. The best images are background images that contain a pattern or texture. Any image that you want to use as a pattern, however, must first be opened in Paint Shop Pro. To open a background image to use as a fill pattern, follow these steps:

1. Select File, Open. Then open BACKGRND.GIF from C:\PAGES. (See Figure 7.21.)

2. Click on the title bar of the HEADLINE.GIF image window to bring it to the front.

3. The Flood Fill tool (the Paint Bucket button) should still be selected (if not, reselect it). In the Fill style control on the style bar, select Pattern.

Background image

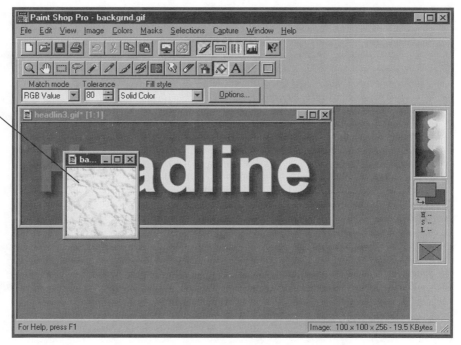

Figure 7.21

BACKGRND.GIF
has been opened in
Paint Shop Pro
so you can use it
to define a pattern
fill effect.

4. Click on the Options button on the Style Bar to display the Define New Pattern dialog box. In the New pattern source drop-down list, select Backgrnd.gif. (See Figure 7.22.)

5. Click on OK.

6. With the Flood Fill tool still selected (the Paint Bucket button), position the pointer inside the H in "Headline" and left-click. As shown in Figure 7.23, the letter H in "Headline" is filled with the selected pattern.

 TIP   If you accidentally fill the wrong thing (the background, for example), just select Edit, Undo.

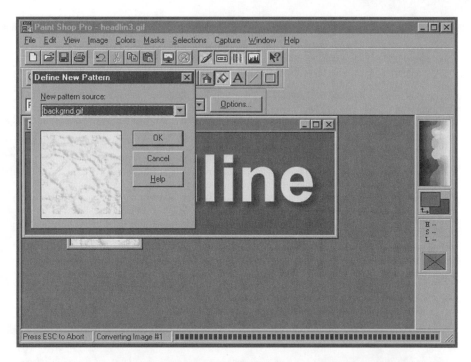

Figure 7.22

You can define a fill pattern based on any file, such as a background image, open in Paint Shop Pro.

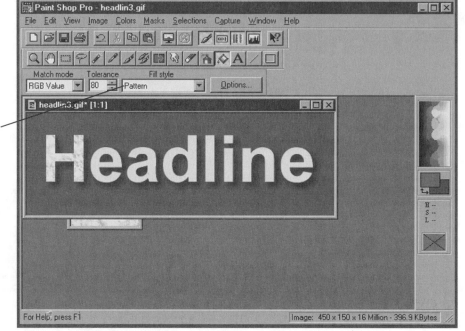

Fill style selection

Figure 7.23

The letter H has been filled with the defined pattern.

Using a Gradient Fill

Another neat effect you can use to really spiff up your Web graphics is a gradient fill. Paint Shop Pro has four different gradient fills that you can use: linear, rectangular, sunburst, and radial. In the following example, I'll be showing you how to apply a linear gradient fill to your Web graphics:

CAUTION If you are using an earlier version of Paint Shop Pro than the version (4.14) included on the CD-ROM, you should be aware that Version 4.12 has a bug that may crash Paint Shop Pro if you try to create a linear gradient fill effect. If you are using Version 4.12, you should skip this section, or install Version 4.14 from the CD-ROM. Alternatively, you could substitute one of the other gradient fill effects.

1. A gradient fill utilizes both the foreground color and the background color to create the fill. Leave the salmon pink selected in the foreground color rectangle. Click in the background color rectangle and select the other color for the fill: for this example, select the bright orange (fourth down in the second row). Click on OK.

2. Although you can fill a letter, as you did previously, without selecting it, linear gradient fills look best when you select the letters you want to fill. Select the Magic Wand tool (the fifth from the left on the Tool Palette (the second row of buttons). Click inside the first e to select it. To select the remainder of the letters (a, d, l, i, n, and e), press and hold Shift and click in each letter in turn.

3. Select the Flood Fill tool (the Paint Bucket button). In the Fill style drop-down list on the Style Bar, select Linear Gradient.

4. Click on Options and set the Direction to 180 degrees. (See Figure 7.24.) Click on OK.

5. Click inside the first e. Click in each of the remaining letters (a, d, l, i, n, and e). Last, click in the dot on the i. The last seven letters should be filled with the linear gradient fill. To get a better look at your image, select Selections and Select None. (See Figure 7.25.)

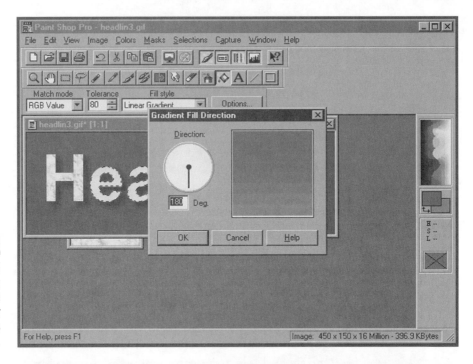

Figure 7.24

In the Gradient Fill
Direction dialog
box, you can see
what a linear
gradient fill is
going to look like.

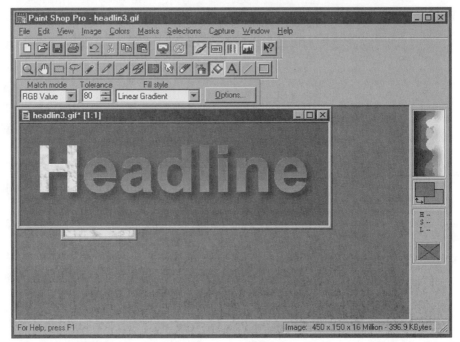

Figure 7.25

Both a pattern and
a linear gradient fill
have been used
here to get a
different look.

6. Select the Dropper tool. Position it over the green background of your image and right-click to reselect it as the color in the background color rectangle. (This is important to do here, because otherwise your background will not be saved as transparent.)

7. Reduce the number of colors to 256.

8. Select File and Save As, and save your file as HEADLIN4.GIF in C:\PAGES\IMAGES.

Editing and Viewing Your HTML File

Hop back over to Notepad and edit HEADLINE.HTM, adding the background image, so that it matches what is shown here:

```
<HTML>
<HEAD><TITLE>Transparent Headline</TITLE>
</HEAD>
<BODY BACKGROUND="3dgreen1.gif">
<P ALIGN="center"><IMG SRC="images/headlin4.gif"
WIDTH="450" HEIGHT="150">
</BODY>
</HTML>
```

Resave HEADLINE.HTM in C:\PAGES (File, Save). Hop back over to your Web browser and reload HEADLINE.HTM (Ctrl+R) to see what your image looks like. (See Figure 7.26.)

Creating 3-D Buttons

Paint Shop Pro has a really neat special effect that you can use to create 3-D buttons. This feature can easily be used to create very effective and attractive image links and navigational icons.

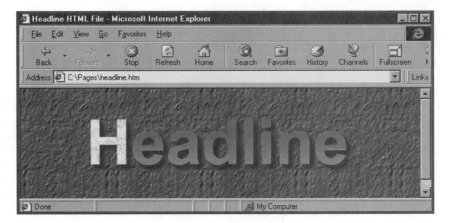

Figure 7.26

Here a pattern and linear gradient fill as well as a drop shadow are transparently set off against a background image.

NOTE 3-D buttons are a Windows 95-only special effect. You won't be able to do this section if you are using the Windows 3.1 version of Paint Shop Pro. You should skip ahead to the "Program Details" at the end of this session.

For this example, you'll buttonize your "Headline" graphic. Here's how to turn your "Headline" graphic into a 3-D button:

1. Increase your colors again: Colors, Increase Color Depth, and 16 Million Colors.

2. The color of the 3-D relief for the button is controlled by the selection for the background color. Select a new color in the background color rectangle. Try the slate blue that is the third color down in the fifth column.

3. Select Image, Special Effects, and Buttonize. Select 8 as the Edge Size. Select the Transparent Edge radio button. (To preview what your button is going to look like, click on Preview, then adjust the edge size up or down to suit—you can move the Buttonize dialog box out of the way to get a better look at your image.) Click on OK. (See Figure 2.27.)

4. Reduce the number of colors to 256.

5. Select File and Save As, and save your file as HEADLIN5.GIF in C:\PAGES\IMAGES.

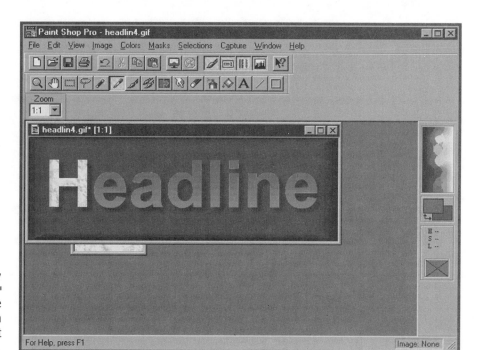

Figure 7.27

You can buttonize
any image you can
create in Paint
Shop Pro.

Editing and Viewing Your HTML File

Hop back over to Notepad and edit HEADLINE.HTM, adding the
background image, so that it matches what is shown here:

```
<HTML>
<HEAD><TITLE>Transparent Headline</TITLE>
</HEAD>
<BODY BACKGROUND="3dgreen1.gif">
<P ALIGN="center"><IMG SRC="images/headlin5.gif"
WIDTH="450" HEIGHT="150">
</BODY>
</HTML>
```

Resave HEADLINE.HTM in C:\PAGES (File, Save). Hop back over to
your Web browser and reload HEADLINE.HTM (Ctrl+R) to see what
your image looks like. (See Figure 7.28.)

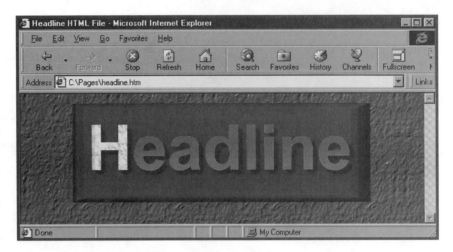

Figure 7.28

Here a pattern and linear gradient fill, as well as a drop shadow, are transparently set off against a background image.

Although you didn't do it in this tutorial, some very nice effects can be created by combining pattern fills—using wood or stone textures, for instance, with the buttonizing effect. Try using contrasting wood texture pattern fills (any background image you can load into Paint Shop Pro can be used as a pattern fill) for the text and the button body, and throw in a drop shadow while you're at it. Or get really colorful, trying out different color combinations. Your imagination is your only limit.

PROGRAM DETAILS

Paint Shop Pro by JASC, Inc.
The Paint Shop Pro program included on the CD-ROM is an evaluation version that will cease working after 90 days. If you would like to register the software (highly recommended), here are the details:

Registration: $69   **Phone: 1-800-622-2793**
http://www.jasc.com/   **FAX: 1-612-930-9172**
E-Mail: order@jasc.com

Other Software by JASC, Inc.: ImageCommander (image manager), Pixel 3D (3-D rendering), Media Center (file manager and slide show program), and Image Robot (batch image processor).

What's Next?

Many other effects can be achieved in Paint Shop Pro. The few that I've shown here are just some of the ones I consider to be particularly effective for creating graphics for the Web. At the very least, you should now have a solid foundation on which to expand your use of Paint Shop Pro in the future.

Apply as many of the techniques covered in this session as you want as you create your own customized banner graphic for your Web page. You should know enough now to put together something really super-duper. Experiment, be creative. Don't just stick to the examples that were shown in this session—strike out on your own and see what you can come up with. Use a transparent drop shadow against a colored background. Use the buttonize feature to create any buttons or navigation icons you want to use. Play around with different color and pattern combinations. You never know what you can come up with until you try it.

Also, check out some of the graphics resources and tools that are listed in Appendixes A and B. You'll find links to graphics tutorials and information, as well as links to 3-D modeling, GIF animation, and image map programs.

If you've learned Basic HTML, planned and created your first Web page, and completed this session's optional Graphics Tutorial, you've laid down a very solid foundation for your future Web publishing efforts! Feel free to come back at another time to do any of the optional tutorials that you may have missed this time around. You've come a long way!

If you've managed to complete everything this weekend, then you are well on your way to becoming a certified Web publishing whiz! Check out Appendixes A and B for many links to resources and tools that will allow you to add many advanced HTML features into your Web pages, such as frames, forms, scripts, applets, cascading style sheets, and the newest Dynamic HTML features.

Once you've got your Web page finalized and ready to go, check out Appendix D, "Putting It Up on the Web," for instructions on how to use WS-FTP, a great FTP program that is included on the CD-ROM, to transfer your Web page to a server on the Web. For information on finding an affordable Web host for your pages, see Appendix A. Also, I've set up a Web site to provide you assistance and guidance in finding an affordable Web host, including an extensive listing of Web hosts and their services and prices. You'll find a link to it at the Web site for this book, at `http://www.callihan.com/create2/`.

APPENDIX A

The Web Resources Directory

Look in this directory for links to all manner of Web publishing resources, including references, tutorials, and other information. You should assume that all Web addresses (URLs) listed here are "http://" addresses, unless otherwise indicated (by "ftp://" or "gopher://"). Later versions of Navigator and Internet Explorer will add "http://" for you automatically, so there is no need to actually type it in the Location/ Address box. Other browsers, however, may require you to type it in. If it is the exclusive protocol, Navigator and Internet Explorer will also automatically add the "ftp://" and "gopher://" for you, but will default to "http://" if it isn't.

General Web Publishing Resources

HTML Guides, Tutorials, and References

The Bare Bones Guide to HTML by Kevin Werbach
`werbach.com/barebones/`

A Beginner's Guide to HTML by NCSA
`www.ncsa.uiuc.edu/General/Internet/WWW/HTMLPrimer.html`
Excellent guide to HTML from the creators of Mosaic. Updated to include HTML 4.0.

Introduction to HTML by Peter Flynn
`www.ucc.ie/~pflynn/books/ch7-8.html`
Excerpt from Peter Flynn's book, *The World Wide Web Handbook*. Ins and outs of HTML specifications, DTDs, and so on, as well as an introduction to HTML markup.

Introduction to HTML by Eric A. Meyer and Case Western Reserve University
`www.cwru.edu/help/introHTML/toc.html`
The most novel aspect of this site is the interactive quizzes that follow after each chapter. Now includes two sequels, one on HTML 2.0 Forms, the other on HTML 3.2.

Introduction to HTML by Ian Graham
`www.utoronto.ca/webdocs/HTMLdocs/NewHTML/htmlindex.html`
Excellent A-to-Z reference.

HTML Reference by Microsoft
`www.microsoft.com/workshop/author/newhtml/htmlr020.htm`
This is Microsoft's rundown on the current state of HTML, including use of its own extensions.

HTML 3.2

HTML 3.2 Reference Specification by W3C
`www.w3.org/TR/REC-html32.html`
The official specification for HTML 3.2.

Wilbur—HTML 3.2 by the Web Design Group
`www.htmlhelp.com/reference/wilbur/`
A rundown on HTML 3.2, with the layman in mind.

HTML 3.2 and Netscape 4.0: How to tame the wild Mozilla by Andrew B. King
webreference.com/html3andns/
Covers HTML 3.2 and Netscape extensions (NHTML).

HTML 4.0

HTML 4.0 Specification by W3C
www.w3.org/TR/REC-html40/
www.w3.org/TR/REC-html40/appendix/changes.html

Dynamic HTML

Dynamic HTML in Netscape Communicator by Netscape
developer.netscape.com/library/documentation/communicator/dynhtml
    /index.htm

Dynamic HTML by Microsoft
www.microsoft.com/workshop/author/dhtml/

Dynamic HTML Index
www.all-links.com/dynamic/

HTML Style Guides

HTML references can tell you what HTML is and what it's supposed to do, but they can't necessarily tell you how to use it to the best effect.

What is good hypertext writing? by Jutta Degener
www.cs.tu-berlin.de/~jutta/ht/writing.html

How to Make Great WWW Pages! by Carlos L. McEvilly
www.c3.lanl.gov/~cim/webgreat/first.html

The Ten Commandments of HTML by Sean Howard of Visionary Designs
www.visdesigns.com/design/commandments.html

The Hall of Shame by FLUX
www.meat.com/netscape_hos.html

Style Guide for online hypertext by Tim Berners-Lee
www.w3.org/pub/WWW/Provider/Style/Overview.html
Wise words from the inventor of the Web.

HTML Resources: **Style** by the HTML Writers Guild
`www.hwg.org/resources/html/style.html`
This is another list of style guides.

Web Page Templates

Netscape Web Page Templates by Netscape
`home.netscape.com/assist/net_sites/starter/samples/templates/`
`    index.html`

Web Page Templates by the Web Diner
`www.webdiner.com/templates/index.htm`

Omnibus Web Publishing Web Sites

The HTML Writers Guild List of HTML Resources
`www.hwg.org/resources/html/`

The Web Developer's Virtual Library
`www.Stars.com/`

DevEdge Online by Netscape
`developer.netscape.com/index.html`
Netscape's omnibus Web authoring site.

Site Builder Workshop by Microsoft
`www.microsoft.com/workshop/default.asp`
Microsoft's omnibus Web authoring site.

The HTML Goodies Domain by Joe Burns
`www.htmlgoodies.com/`
Great collection of tutorials on all manner of things HTML.

The HTML Guru by Chuck Musciano
`members.aol.com/htmlguru/`
From the author of *HTML: The Definitive Guide*. Q & A's, hints and tricks, and pages
on transparent images, access counts, Web art and sound, and lots more.

Web Publishing Webzines

Web Developer Magazine
`www.webdeveloper.com/`

The Web Developer's Journal
nctweb.com/nct/software/eleclea.html

Internet World Daily
www.internetworld.com/

TechWeb: The Technology Information Source
techweb.cmp.com/

WebTechniques: Solutions for Internet and Web Developers
www.webtechniques.com/

InternetUser by ZDNet
www.zdnet.com/products/internetuser.html

World Wide Web Journal
www.w3j.com/
The journal of the World Wide Web Consortium.

Web Review
webreview.com/

HTML Features

These are links to resources and information on specific HTML features
and functions that are available on the Web.

Tables

HTML Table Tutorial by Urban A. LeJeune
www.charm.net/~lejeune/tables.html
Excellent tutorial on creating tables, focused on Netscape Navigator.

TableMaker by Sam Choukri
www.bagism.com/tablemaker/
A neat online utility that allows you to enter your table data into a form, then creates
the HTML table for you.

So You Want A Table, Huh? by Joe Burns
www.htmlgoodies.com/table.html

Setting Colors

Colors by InfiNet
www.infi.net/wwwimages/colorindex.html

The Hex Color Guide
www.cranfield.ac.uk/docs/hex/

ColorMaker by Sam Choukri
www.bagism.com/colormaker/
Point and click to specify colors for the background, text, and links—then specify a Web page and see the new colors applied to the page.

Victor Engel's No Dither Netscape Color Palette
www.onr.com/user/lights/netcol.html

The Joy of Hex (Get Hexed!) by Pequod
www.stardot.com/%7Elukeseem/hexed.html

Forms

So, You Want A Form, Huh? by Joe Burns
www.htmlgoodies.com/forms.html

Image Maps

Clickable Image Maps by Russ Jones
www.ora.com/oracom/inet/miis/

So You Want An Image Map, Huh? by Joe Burns
www.htmlgoodies.com/imagemap.html
Excellent tutorial aimed at the non-techie.

Frames

Frames: An Introduction by Netscape
home.netscape.com/assist/net_sites/frames.html

Sharky's Netscape Frames Tutorial by Charlton Rose
www.newbie.net/sharky/frames/menu.html
Great page on using frames.

FrameShop! by Sam Choukri
www.bagism.com/frameshop/
Specify the dimensions of your main frame and subframes and this online utility will create them for you.

Introduction to Frames by Webspinners
www.spunwebs.com/frmtutor.html
An excellent tutorial on creating frames.

Special Characters

The extended, or special, characters that can be used in Web pages are defined by the ISO-8859-1 character set, also sometimes called the ISO-Latin1 character set.

ISO-8859 briefing and resources by A. J. Flavell
ppewww.ph.gla.ac.uk/~flavell/iso8859/iso8859-pointers.html

Character code coverage—browser report by A. J. Flavell
ppewww.ph.gla.ac.uk/~flavell/iso8859/browser-report.html
Reports on support among browsers for ISO 8859-1 characters.

8 bit ASCII codes (for ISO-Latin1 character set) by W3C
www.w3.org/pub/WWW/MarkUp/Wilbur/latin1.gif

Cascading Style Sheets

Cascading Style Sheets, level 1 by W3C
www.w3.org/TR/REC-CSS1-961217
The official specification for Cascading Style Sheets, level 1.

Cascading Style Sheets, level 2 by W3C
www.w3.org/TR/WD-CSS2/
The official specification for Cascading Style Sheets, level 2.

WebDeveloper.com's Guide to Cascading Style Sheets by Scott Clark
www.webdeveloper.com/categories/html/html_css_1.html

Creating Your First Style Sheet by Eric Meyer
webreview.com/97/10/10/style/index.html

Programming

JavaScript, JScript, and ECMAScript

Documentation: JavaScript by Netscape
developer.netscape.com/library/documentation/javascript.html

JScript Start Page by Microsoft
`www.microsoft.com/jscript/`
Find out about Microsoft's implementation of JavaScript.

Introduction to JavaScript by Stefan Koch
`rummelplatz.uni-mannheim.de/%7Eskoch/js/script.htm`

VBScript Product Documentation by Microsoft
`www.microsoft.com/vbscript/us/techinfo/vbsdocs.htm`
Everything about VBScript, including a tutorial, reference, and complete documentation.

CGI and Perl

The Perl Language Home Page
`language.perl.com/`

CGI Resources by Sanford Morton
`www.halcyon.com/sanford/cgi/index.html`
Includes a forms tutorial, CGI tips and tricks, a Perl workshop, and more.

perlWWW
`www.oac.uci.edu/indiv/ehood/perlWWW/`
Omnibus Perl site.

Selena Sol's Public Domain CGI Script Archive and Resource Library
`www.extropia.com/Scripts/`

Matt's Script Archive by Matt Wright
`worldwidemart.com/scripts/`
A big repository of CGI scripts that are free for non-commercial use.

Java

Gamelan: The Official Directory for Java by developer.com
`www.developer.com/directories/pages/dir.java.html`

Brewing Java: A Tutorial by Elliotte Rusty Harold
`sunsite.unc.edu/javafaq/javatutorial.html`

The Java Tutorial by Sun Microsystems
`java.sun.com/docs/books/tutorial/`
Tutorial by the inventors of Java.

The Java Development Kit by Sun Microsystems
`java.sun.com/products/jdk/`
Develop your own Java applets. Free for download.

The Java Boutique
`javaboutique.internet.com/`
Download Java applets that you can include in your Web pages.

ActiveX

ActiveX Controls Overviews by Microsoft
`www.microsoft.com/workshop/prog/controls/controls-f.htm`

ActiveX Directory by developer.com
`activex.developer.com/`
A directory of ActiveX controls that you can download and use.

Graphics Resources

These are links to graphics information and resources available on the Web
that can assist you in graphically enhancing a Web page or Web site.

General Graphics Resources

Graphics FAQ by The Aldridge Company
`www.aldridge.com/faq_gra.html`

DiP: A Guide to Digital Pictures & More
`www.algonet.se/~dip/index.html`
Links, tips, and tricks for Painter, PhotoShop, and Kai's Power Tools.

The Pixel Foundry by Tom Karlo and Josh Hartmann
`the-tech.mit.edu/KPT/`
Adobe Photoshop and Kai's Power Tools tips and tricks.

Creating graphics for the Web by .designer
`www.widearea.co.uk/designer/`
Includes info on using JavaScript mouse events, an anti-aliasing guide, and tips for optimizing Photoshop for the Web.

The Bandwidth Conservation Society
`www.infohiway.com/faster/index.html`
Reduce color depth, increase loading speeds.

Paint Shop Pro Resources and Tutorials

Web Graphics on a Budget: Paint Shop Pro Tips and Tricks
http://wctravel.com/web/

The Original PSP Tips and Tricks by Webweaver
http://www.webweaverxxi.com/psp40/index.html

Backgrounds

So You Want A Background, Huh? by Joe Burns
www.htmlgoodies.com/backgrnd.html

Web Art

AOLpress Clip Art Gallery
www.aolpress.com/gallery/index.html
Excellent selection of backgrounds, sidebars, and icons.

Barry's Clip Art Server
www.barrysclipart.com/

Rose's Backgrounds
www.wanderers2.com/rose/backgrounds.html

Laurie McCanna's Free Art Website
www.mccannas.com/

Ender Design: Realm Graphics
www.ender-design.com/rg/

Icon 'n Stuff by Arjen van Mierlo
www.xs4all.nl/~arjenvm/pics/index_gb.html

Netscape Background Sampler
home.netscape.com/assist/net_sites/bg/backgrounds.html

Animation

The 1st Internet Gallery of GIF Animation
www6.uniovi.es/gifanim/galframe.htm

Gif Animations
www.mcm.acu.edu/~surdilot/animations.html

Get Animated! by the Web Diner
www.webdiner.com/annexe/gif89/snowstp1.htm

Fonts

Typography
www.transmission23.com/fonts/index.html
A collection of strange, unusual, and unique freeware/shareware fonts.

Font Kingdom
homepages.tig.com.au/~muzzle/fontk/index.html

FONTZ v2.0
indigo.simplenet.com/fontz/main.shtml
Bills itself as the Net's premier freeware, shareware, and public domain font archive.

Putting It Up on the Web

Placing Your Web Page

The following are resources you can use to locate a free or affordable presence provider for your Web pages:

Budget Web Index by Alex Chapman
budgetweb.com/budgetweb/index.html

Low cost web hosting services by theblade
www.theblade.org/

The Free Webpage Provider Review by Maximillian Lee
www.digiweb.com/~maxlee/FWPReview/

Free WWWeb Space Providers by Barry B. Floyd
www.geocities.com/SiliconValley/7331/freespac.html

The Free Pages Page by Peter da Silva
starbase.neosoft.com/~peter/freepages.html

Web Host Directory
www.webhostdir.com/

Top Hosts
www.tophosts.com/

thedirectory of Internet Service Providers
www.thedirectory.org/
A worldwide list of providers. Touts itself as the biggest on the Web.

FrontPage 98 Web Presence Providers List by Microsoft
microsoft.saltmine.com/frontpage/wpp/list/

Promoting Your Web Page

Submit It!
www.submit-it.com/
Submit your Web page to 15 different search engines and indexes while filling out only one form.

AddURL by the HOME TEAM
www.addurl.com/

1 2 3 Promote by Nancy Bargine
www.123promote.com/
Check the links at the bottom of the page for loads of Web site promotion information.

The Internet Link Exchange
www.linkexchange.com/
Free banner exchange program.

Validating Your Web Page

Doctor HTML by Thomas Tongue and Imagiware
imagiware.com/RxHTML.cgi
Check your page for spelling errors, image bandwidth and syntax, document, table, form structure, dead links, and command hierarchy.

Dr. Watson by Addy and Associates
watson.addy.com/
This is a free service that understands HTML 3.2, and Netscape and Microsoft extensions up to version 4.0. It also can check your links and your spelling.

HTML Validation Resources by the Web Developer's Virtual Library
stars.com/Authoring/HTML/Validation/Resources.html
A compendium of validation information and resources.

W3C HTML Validation Service
http://validator.w3.org/
An HTML 4.0 validator from the World Wide Web Consortium.

APPENDIX B

The Web Tools Directory

You can find links in this directory to a wide range of software tools that can assist or enhance your Web publishing efforts. I've excluded mention of the Windows version where both Windows 3.1 and Windows 95 versions are available, mentioning it where a tool is available only in one or the other version. Windows 3.1 versions will almost always run under Windows 95 (or Windows NT) without a problem. Windows 95 versions, however, will not run under Windows 3.1. There are 32-bit versions that will run under Windows 3.1 with the installation of Win32s, available with any software that requires it. I try to mention whenever that is the case.

The majority of tools listed are inexpensive to register (less than $100). I've included the cost of registration only if it might be considered expensive (more than $100) or to highlight a bargain.

Web Browsing Tools

Included in this section is any software that is related to Web browsing, which includes multilingual and offline Web browsers, Web automation agents, and any other miscellaneous Web browsing utilities I have found.

General Information on Web Browsers

Want to know about browsers? Follow these links to find out the latest.

BrowserCaps
`objarts.com/bc/`
A catalog of the HTML support provided by different Web browsers, by David Ornstein. Survey results on how different browsers handle HTML. Add your browser to the results.

BrowserWatch
`www.browserwatch.com/`
Breaking news on the browser front.

Web Browsers

There's more to the world of Web browsing than just Navigator and Internet Explorer. Here are links to those programs.

Netscape Navigator/Communicator
`home.netscape.com/`
Navigator is still the name of the browser, while Communicator is the name of the suite. A must-have for any serious Web publisher, even if only to preview how your pages are going to look. Free.

Microsoft Internet Explorer
`http://www.microsoft.com/ie/download/`
The other major Web browser that no serious Web publisher can afford to ignore, if only to preview how your pages are going to look. Free.

Opera by Opera Software
`traviata.nta.no/index.html`
My favorite runner-up browser. Less than a tenth the heft of the N and M behemoths (can fit unzipped on a single 1.4MB floppy), while still providing a full-featured browsing environment, including mail and news readers, plug-in support and more. Optimized for keyboard browsing. Supports HTML 3.2, including frames, tables, text wrap around images, background sound, inline video, and more. Evaluation version is available.

HotJava by Sun Microsystems

`java.sun.com/products/hotjava/`

The only browser written completely in Java. Worth a look. Free for individual non-commercial use.

NCSA Mosaic

`www.ncsa.uiuc.edu/SDG/Software/WinMosaic/HomePage.html`

Of historical interest, at least, as the browser that established the paradigm and directly spawned both Navigator and Internet Explorer. NCSA has stopped development of this browser, the last version of which is Version 3.0. Supports most of HTML 3.2. Windows 95/NT only. Version 2.11 for Windows 3.1 is still available, but only supports HTML 2.0, with a smattering of HTML 3.0 tags thrown in. Free.

Lynx for Win32

`www.fdisk.com/doslynx/lynxport.htm`

A port of Lynx that runs under Windows 95 (but not Windows 3.1, even with Win32s). Worth checking out, just so you can preview what your pages will look like in Lynx.

Multilingual Web Browsers

Although English is pretty much the *lingua franca* (that's a switch) of the Web, it isn't the only language being used on the Web. Here are some Web browsers with multilingual capabilities, so, you can cruise the Web in a native or adopted language other than English.

Video On Line Internet Browser

`www.vol.it/VOLB/browser.html`

Surf in Czech, Egyptian, Finnish, French, German, Greek, English, Italian, Maltese, Norwegian, Polish, Spanish, Swedish, Turkish. Earlier versions are available in Arabic, Danish, Hungarian, Dutch, Portuguese, and Russian. Windows 3.1. Two Macintosh versions are available, but languages not specified. Free.

Accent Multilingual Mosaic

`www.accentsoft.com/Main/moseng.html`

Supports 30 different languages, including Russian, Arabic, Greek, or Japanese, even while using the U.S. version of Windows. Designed to work under any language version of Windows 95 or Windows 3.1 (requires Win32s, available at site). 30-day evaluation version.

HMView by Bersoft Hypertext Systems

`traviata.nta.no/index.html`

Supports Dutch, Spanish, French, German, Italian, and English. Supports frames, and is an offline browser as well. Registered users can redistribute freely (as CD-ROM front-end or whatever).

Offline Web Browsers

These browsers let you browse Web pages on your local hard drive without having to go online first. They also come in handy for CD-ROM front-ends when you're publishing hypertext content. Besides, many of them are small enough to run from a floppy, which makes them very useful on some systems. Unfortunately, the software that automates downloading content from the Web for offline viewing—an entirely different category of product—is often advertised under this term. I've chosen to stick to *offline browser* here, as these tools used the term first, while listing the other tools under the next heading, "Pre-Fetching Agents."

Webview Offline Web Browser by South Pacific Information Services, Ltd.
`www.spis.co.nz/webcentr/webview.htm`
An offline Web browser from New Zealand that supports frames, tables, font size changes. Shareware (with nag screens).

AOLpress by AOL
`www.aolpress.com/`
Works out of the box as an offline browser, as well as being a regular browser and a pretty good HTML editor. Free.

NavRoad Offline Browser by FAICO Information Solutions
`home.netvigator.com/~godfreyk/netroad/`
Supports tables, forms, frames, client-side image maps, and so on.

HMView by Bersoft Hypertext Systems
`bersoft.com/hmview/`
Offline multilingual browser. Supports local CGI scripts.

Pre-Fetching Agents

These programs automate your online sessions, downloading Web pages (and their graphics) while you sleep, so you can then browse them offline on your local hard drive. They're often called offline browsers, but (as noted in the previous section) that term is already in use for something else. To avoid confusion, and just because I think it better describes what these programs actually do, I've chosen here to refer to these programs by another term that has been used to describe them—*pre-fetching agents.*

Auto WinNet
www.webcom.com/autownet/
Evaluation version allows you to download files from FTP sites by the truckload, hammering at busy sites until they open, or scheduling downloads for late at night, and so on. Registered version also includes WWW, e-mail, and mail list and newsgroup automation.

Web Whacker by Forefront
www.ffg.com/whacker/
Automatic downloading (or *whacking*) of Web pages, complete Web sites, including text and images, for offline browsing. Evaluation version expires after whacking 15 URLs.

HTML Editing Tools

Included in this section is anything related to HTML editing, which includes not only HTML editors but word processor add-ons, converters, templates, authoring suites, wizards, strippers, and validation tools.

HTML Editors

HoTMetaL by SoftQuad
www.sq.com/products/hotmetal/hm-ftp.htm
Free version.

HotDog by Sausage Software
www.sausage.com/
14-day and 30-day evaluation versions are available. You can, however, extend the trial period one time via e-mail.

HTMLed by Internet Software Technologies
www.ist.ca/htmled.html

HTML Assistant Pro by Brooklyn North Software Works
www.brooknorth.com/products/products.html

Web Weaver by McWeb Software
www.mcwebsoftware.com/webweav.html
Latest version features global search and replace, frame wizard, floating frames, and more. Evaluation version is available.

Webber32 by Cerebral Systems Development Corporation
www.expertelligence.com/webber32/
Includes frames assistant, generates META info. Shareware.

HTML NotePad by Cranial Software
www.cranial.com/software/htmlnote/
One of my favorite editors. A cross between Windows Notepad and a full-feature HTML editor. Shareware.

Aardvark Pro by Functional Business Systems of Australia
www.tmgnet.com/aardvark/
Shareware.

AOLpress by AOL
www.aolpress.com/
Was GNNpress (before that NaviPress). Not just a browser, but a pretty good HTML editor as well. Free.

Gomer HTML Editor by Stoopid Software
stoopidsoftware.com/
30-day trial version is available.

WebEdit by Luckman Software
www.ditr.com/software/webedit/
Includes FTP upload, home page, and frame wizards. 30-day trial version is available.

WebPen by Informatik Inc.
www.informatik.com/webpen.html
Supports frames, tables, forms, spell check, search and replace. Also works as an offline browser. Pro version supports image maps, transparent GIF creation.

HTML Builder by FLFSoft
www.flfsoft.com/HTMLBuilder.html
32-bit version for both Windows 3.1 and 95. Windows 3.1 requires Win32s. Freeware.

WinHTML by Gulf Coast Software
www.gcsoftware.com/winhtml.html
Demo version available.

InContext Spider
www.incontext.com/products/spider1.html
30-day evaluation version is available. Windows 3.1.

Web Ed for Windows
www.ozemail.com.au/~kread/webed.html
Windows 3.1. Free.

The Web Media Publisher
www.wbmedia.com/publisher/
32-bit HTML editor that includes FTP upload and internal Web browser. Evaluation version.

Splash! by Beam Software
www.gosplash.com/
WYSIWYG HTML editor with a few extra bells and whistles, including inserting and customizing Java applets, drag-and-define table creation, FTP upload facility. 21-day evaluation version is available.

TextPad by Helios Software Solutions
www.textpad.com/
Notepad on steroids. Not really an HTML editor, but just right for the diehard hand-coder who wants complete and total control over the HTML coding process. Features: no file size limit, spell checker, auto word wrap, keystroke macro recorder, sorting, search and replace, multiple windows. Interfaces with CSE 3310 HTML Validator. Shareware.

Word Processor Add-Ons

Internet Assistant for Microsoft Word
www.microsoft.com/word/internet/ia/
Freeware add-on for Microsoft Word.

HTML Author for Microsoft Word
www.salford.ac.uk/iti/gsc/htmlauth/summary.html
Shareware. Versions are available for both Word 6 (Windows 3.1) and Word 7 (Windows 95).

The Ant
telacommunications.com/ant/antdesc.htm
HTML conversion macro for Word for Windows 6, Word for Macintosh, NT, and Windows 95. Demo version.

Wp2Html for WordPerfect
www.res.bbsrc.ac.uk/wp2html/
Converts WordPerfect files to HTML. Runs stand-alone and is designed for the batch conversion of multiple existing WP documents. Can convert tables, text, styles, and most formatting codes. Can handle equations and figures, subject to the limitations of HTML (Netscape). Evaluation kit, which is an earlier version of the software and works with WordPerfect 5.1 or 5.2 files.

HTML Convertors

These can be handy if you have a large amount of data or documents that you don't want to take the time to hand-code. Results may need a little polishing, though.

DBF to HTML Convertor by Ronald A. "Andy" Hoskinson

`members.aol.com/andyhosk/software.html`

Converts dBase/XBase files into HTML. Rated one of the "TOP 200 WEB TOOLS" by *PC/Computing Magazine* (August 1996). Shareware.

ForeHTML.Pro by ForeFront

`www.ff.com/Products/ForeHTMLPro/index.html`

A universal authoring environment for HTML Help, NetHelp, and WinHelp. Can convert WinHelp to HTML. Windows 95 demo version is available.

KeyView Pro by Verity

`www.keyview.com/`

Works as a file viewer and converter. Can convert many different formats to HTML. Can function as a Netscape or Internet Explorer plug-in or as stand-alone application. Windows 95/NT evaluation version. Windows 3.1 version is only available with CD-ROM version.

RTFtoHTML 3.0 by Chris Hector

`www.w3.org/Tools/rtftohtml-3.0.html`

The latest version of RTFtoHTML, incorporating features from RTFtoWEB. Converts between RTF (Rich Text Format) and HTML. Supports tables, Netscape and Microsoft extensions, splitting long documents into smaller files. Supports coversion from RTF export from Microsoft Word, WordPerfect, Next, Claris Works, Framemaker, and any other word processor capable of exporting RTF files. Versions are available for Windows 3.1/DOS, Windows 95/NT, Mac 68xx/PowerPC, OS/2, and multiple Unix variations. Shareware.

WebMaker by Harlequin

`www.harlequin.com/webmaker/`

Converts between Framemaker and HTML. Offers customizable conversion of text, graphics, tables, and equations. Available for Windows 3.1, Macintosh, and Power Mac. Windows 95 version promised. Demoware, but the feature limitation is that you can only create up to five separate HTML pages from any one FrameMaker document. Registration is only $99 (which beats $495 for WebWorks Publisher by a mile).

Web Publisher by SkiSoft

`www.skisoft.com/`

Bills itself as an automated Web page production tool that can convert and enhance documents from Word, WordPerfect, Ami-Pro, and FrameMaker into Web pages. Converts images, tables, tables of contents (with links to headings), and numbered or bulleted lists. Places signatures, mailto URLs, and corporate images and logos into your documents. 30-day trial version. Windows 3.1.

Web Authoring Suites

QuickSite

www.sitetech.com/

Project- and database-oriented Web site development and management system that requires no HTML coding. Automatically establishes all links to your pages. Supports embedding of forms. Transfers finished files to your site via FTP. A 30-day evaluation version is available.

Internet Creator: The Web Site Builder by Forman Interactive

www.formaninteractive.com/ic4.htm

Build and maintain unlimited number of Web sites, including online stores, with no need to learn HTML. 15-day evaluation version. Windows 3.1.

Snaglet Pack by Sausage Software

http://www.sausage.com/snaglets/snaglets.html

Bundle of ten utilities previously available separately, including Java animation, image map, frame, 3-D button, scrolling marquee, and background image utilities. Registration $69 (previously $389).

Wizards

Web Wizard: The Duke of URL by ARTA Software Group

www.halcyon.com/artamedia/webwizard/

WorldDoc by SPI Inc.

www.dispi.com/spi/

Allows point-and-click creation of Web pages without having to learn HTML. 15-day trial version is available.

Dr. Web's Internet ListKeeper

www.drweb.com/

Designed for the user who knows absolutely nothing about the Internet but wishes to maintain a frequently changing Web page. Automatically generates Web pages and FTPs them to your server. Provides default styles or can be customized for custom Web pages. 30-day evaluation version.

Link Testers and Validation Tools

CyberSpyder Link Test by Aphrodite's Software

www.cyberspyder.com/cslnkts1.html

Checks your links. Shareware.

Linkbot by Tetranet Software
`www.tetranetsoftware.com/linkbot-info.htm`
Checks your links. 30-day evaluation version is available.

CSE 3310 HTML Validator
`www.htmlvalidator.com/csesetup.exe`
Run an HTML validator from your own desktop rather than using an online validator.
Windows 95/NT shareware.

SiteMan by GreyScale Systems
`www.morning.asn.au/siteman/index.html`
An offline site management tool that checks links, analyzes HTML files, does global
search and replace, and finds orphans in multiple-directory Web sites. Available in three
versions, SiteMan 2 for Windows 3.1 (for single-directory Web sites), and SiteMan 3-
16 for Windows 3.1 and SiteMan 3-32 for Windows 95/NT (both for multiple-directory
Web sites). Evaluation version.

Graphics Tools

Look here for links to graphic programs and utilities that you can use to
create and enhance Web art, including graphics editors, viewers, converters,
utilities, and 3-D modeling and animation tools.

Graphics Editors

LView Pro by MMedia Research Corporation
`www.lview.com/`
Available in two versions, Version 1.D2 and Version 2.0. Think of the difference as similar to that between "Classic Coke" and "New Coke." Version 1.D2 is really more of a
graphics viewer, with some graphic editing capabilities added in. It also makes it a breeze
to assign any color as transparent. Version 2.0 is really a gussied-up version that is more
directly trying to compete with Paint Shop Pro as a graphics editor. One thing Version
2.0 can't do that Version 1.D2 can, is open multiple images and dump them to your
printer. Shareware.

Paint Shop Pro by JASC, Inc.
`www.jasc.com/pspdl.html`
Full-feature photo-paint program that supports over 30 image formats, as well as Adobe
Photoshop plug-ins. Was previously shareware, but latest versions stop working after 90
days. Registration is $69.

MagicViewer
www.crayonsoft.com/

This program does image editing, including fills and special effects, as well as batch conversions and animated GIFs. Evaluation version. Windows 95/NT.

Photo Line
www.ciebv.com/

Image processing and painting software with lots of goodies (rated 5 cows by TuCows). From Germany. Evaluation version is available for Windows 95/NT. Registration is only $69.

QFX Image Editing Software
www.qfx.com/

Full-featured image editing, painting, and composition program. Demo version is available (Windows 3.1, requires Win32s). Registration of full version is $399 (50 percent off retail).

Dragon Draw for Windows by Cognitronix
www.cognitronix.com/dragdraw.htm

Easy-to-use drawing package that draws lines, boxes, and circles with seven fill patterns and all the standard Windows colors, plus irregular polygons, Bezier curves, pie charts, and TrueType fonts. Demo version. Windows 95/NT.

Micrografx Picture Publisher 7
www.micrografx.com/PicturePublisher/prodinfo.asp

Photo-editing program with lots of special effects. Demo version is available. Registration is just $99.95. Windows 95/NT.

Viewers and Converters

Graphic Workshop for Windows by Alchemy Mindworks
www.mindworkshop.com/alchemy/gww.html

Converts files from wide range of file formats, and also lets you reverse, rotate, flip, crop, and scale images, manipulate and adjust color, contrast, brightness, dithering, and so on, reduce color depth, and convert multiple files. Can be run in batch mode. Available in 16-bit and 32-bit versions.

WebImage by Group42
www.group42.com/webimage.htm

Does transparent and animated GIFs, client-side or server-side image maps, color reduction and image scaling, plus graphic format conversions. 10-day evaluation version is available.

GraphX Viewer by Group42
www.group42.com/graphx.htm

Image viewing and conversion program. Windows 3.1. Freeware.

VuePrint by Hamrick Software
www.hamrick.com/
A JPEG/GIF viewer.

PolyView by Polybytes
www.polybytes.com/
Multithreading graphics viewing, conversion, and printing utility for Windows 95/NT. Shareware.

VuGrafix by Informatik, Inc.
www.informatik.com/vugrafix.html
Views 10 different image formats, does thumbnails and slide shows, as well as the usual array of image manipulations. Evaluation version is available.

Dr. Jack's HTMLView
www.drjack.com/htmlview/welcome.htm
An image browser that allows you to batch view graphic files, even in different directories. Only a 9-day evaluation period, but registration is just $10.

ThumbsPlus by Cerious Software
www.cerious.com/
Graphic file viewer and converter. You can use it to browse, view, edit, crop, launch external editors, and copy images to the Clipboard. Can convert to several formats, either one at a time or in batch mode. Evaluation version.

ACDSee and **PicaView** by ACD Systems
www.acdvictoria.com/
ACDSee is an image viewer and thumbnail browser that can also view animated GIFs. Evaluation version. PicaView is an add-on for Windows Explorer. Evaluation version available for Windows 95/NT.

3-D Modelers and Ray Tracers

Want to create your own 3-D bullets, buttons, and other objects? Check out these programs:

Genesis 3D by Silicon Dream Ltd.
www.silicond.demon.co.uk/
A fully functional and free 3-D editor.

Behemot Graphics Editor
www.geocities.com/SiliconValley/3526/
The new name for RT Editor, now a true Windows 95/NT program. RT Editor for Windows 3.1 (requires Win32s) is still available. Both Behemot Graphics Editor and RT Editor are freeware.

3DEnvMap by Thanassis Tsiodras

`manolito.image.ece.ntua.gr/~ttsiod/3denvmap.html`

3-D renderer from Greece. Requires WinG, which is available from site.

Pixel 3D by Jasc Software

`www.jasc.com/p3d.html`

From the maker of Paint Shop Pro. 15-use evaluation version is available. Registration is only $69.

POV-Ray

`www.povray.org/`

Freeware raytracing program. Supposedly without the most intuitive user interface and a bit difficult to learn, but a powerhouse once you've figured it out. Windows 3.1/95 (Windows 3.1 requires Win32s). MS-DOS, Mac, and Amiga versions also available.

Ray Dream 3D by Fractal Design

`www.metacreations.com/products/rd3d/`

From the maker of Painter. Does 3-D images and animations. Demo versions are available for Windows 95 and Mac. Registration is $149.

Animation

GIF Construction Set for Windows by Alchemy Mindworks

`www.mindworkshop.com/alchemy/gifcon.html`

Creates transparent and animated GIFs. Shareware.

GIF Animator Lite by ULead

`www.ulead.com/webutilities/gale/gale_main.htm`

Creates transparent and animated GIFs. Windows 95. Freeware.

Animagic GIF Animator

`rtlsoft.com/animagic/`

30-day evaluation version is available.

Audio and Video Tools

Look here for links to multimedia programs and utilities that you can use to add animation, sound, and video to your Web pages.

Audio

Cool Edit by Syntrillium Software
www.syntrillium.com/
Digital audio recorder, editor, and mixer. Shareware and demo versions are available.

RealAudio by Progressive Networks
www.realaudio.com/
Has two products, RealAudio Player and Real AudioServer, which enable playing and delivering of streaming audio. Requires that your server license Real AudioServer. RealAudio Player can be downloaded for free.

TrueSpeech by DSP Group
www.dspg.com/player/main.htm
Create and serve up streaming audio without the need for server software. Use Cool Edit to create PCM-encoded WAV files, then use Sound System for Windows 95/NT to create TrueSpeech WAV files. The player is available free for download.

ToolVox Encoder and Player by Voxware
www.voxware.com/low/toolvox.htm
Enables streaming audio encoding and playing. 53:1 compression ratio. Both encoder and player are available for free.

Internet Wave Player by VocalTec
www.vocaltec.com/iwave.htm
A free streaming audio player from the creators of Internet Phone.

Crescendo by LiveUpdate
www.liveupdate.com/proddes.html
This is a free MIDI player. Available as a Netscape plug-in for Windows 3.1/95 and Macintosh. Also available as an ActiveX plug-in for Internet Explorer. Crescendo Plus is a streaming MIDI player, available for $19.95.

MidiGate by PRS Corp
www.prs.net/midigate.html
Another MIDI player.

WinAmp
www.winamp.com/main.html
MPEG audio player. It plays all Layer 2 and Layer 3 MPEG audio streams. 14-day evaluation version is available. Windows 95/NT. Registration only $10.

Audioactive by Telos Systems
www.audioactive.com/
MPEG3 encoder and player. Free player can play Audioactive or Shockwave encoded audio.

Video

Video for Windows by Microsoft
`ftp://ftp.microsoft.com/Softlib/MSLFILES/WV1160.exe`
Windows 3.1.

QuickTime by Apple
`www.apple.com/quicktime/`
Plays MOV format.

NET TOOB by Duplexx Software
`www.duplexx.com/`
Plays MPEG-1, AVI, MOV, and FLI files, in addition to WAV, MIDI, and SND sound files.

VMPEG
`tucows.phx.cox.com/reviews/win3x/softmult/html/vmpeg.html`
A Windows 3.1 MPEG player.

PowerFLiC 32bit
`tucows.phx.cox.com/mult95.html`
Shareware Windows 95 player that handles FLIC and FLI files.

VivoActive VideoNow
`www.vivo.com/products/videonow/vidnowjp.htm`
Stream video and audio from any Web site. Registration only $49. Player is free.

Multimedia Xplorer by Moon Software
`www.moonsoftware.ee/mxplorer.html`
Plays MPEG, AVI, MOV files, in addition to many sound formats. Also functions as an image viewer, icon extractor, and animated cursor viewer. 30-day Windows 95 evaluation version is available.

MPEGPlay
`ftp://papa.indstate.edu/winsock-l/Windows95/Graphics/mpegw32h.zip`
An easy-to-use Windows 95 MPEG viewer.

HTML Utilities

Look here for links to HTML utilities that can assist you in implementing image maps, forms, tables, frames, colors, Java applets, and JavaScripts in your Web pages.

Image Map Utilities

Mapedit by Boutell.Com, Inc.
`www.boutell.com/mapedit/`
Supports client-side image maps. Evaluation period is 30 days, plus 10 days grace period.

Map This
`www.spocom.com/download/`
A 32-bit freeware image map utility (Windows 3.1 requires Win32s, which is available from the site). Supports client-side image maps.

LiveImage by My Software Company
`www.mediatec.com/`
Client-side image map utility. 14-day evaluation version. Windows 95/NT.

Forms Utilities

WebForms by Q&D Software Development
`www.q-d.com/`
Automates the creation of both Mailto and CGI forms, and will even write the CGI script for you. In addition, WebForms can import and maintain your form responses, which it stores in an MS Access database. Shareware.

mailto: Formatter by Robert Fries
`homepage.interaccess.com/~rpfries/mailtoFormatter.html`
If you decide to hand-code your own Mailto forms, one of the problems is how to decode the form responses into a human-readable format. This, and the following program, provides an answer. Freeware.

Form Reader by Ridgeley House Software
`ftp://oak.oakland.edu/pub/simtelnet/win95/html/frrd9521.zip`
    (Windows 95)
`ftp://oak.oakland.edu/pub/simtelnet/win3/html/frrd21w. zip`
    (Windows 3.1)
Another form response reader and formatter. Download from the OAK Software Repository (http://oak.oakland.edu/) at either of the above addresses.

Tables Utilities

XL2HTML.XLS by Jordan Evans
`rs712b.gsfc.nasa.gov/704/dgd/xl2html.html`
Converts Excel spreadsheets (ranges) to HTML tables. Works with Excel 5.0 for Windows 3.1 and Excel 7.0 for Windows 95. Freeware.

hcTableToHtml by Yuri M. Lesiuk
www.w3.org/hypertext/WWW/Tools/hcTableToHtml.html
A freeware WinWord 6.0 table-to-HTML converter.

Tbl2HTML by John Dirkman
www.cadd.nps.usace.army.mil/tbl2html.htm
This is another freeware WinWord 6 table-to-HTML converter.

Frames Utilities

Frame-It by GME Systems
www.iinet.net.au/~bwh/frame-it1.html
Point-and-click interface for generating frames.
14-day evaluation version.

FrameTool by Infomatik.
www.informatik.com/framex.html

Color Utilities

Color Machine
w3.one.net/~hamilte/webworkshop/colors.html
Small utility that automates insertion of hex color codes. Free.

Color Browser by Maximized Software
www.maximized.com/shareware/colorbrowser/
Another utility for inserting color hex codes. Shareware.

Style Sheet Utilities

CSSize by Electricite de France
lara0.exp.edf.fr/glazman/CSSize/cssize.en.htm
Reads an HTML document and transforms selected elements or attributes into styles.
Windows 95 beta-test version currently available.

CoffeeCup StyleSheet Maker++
www.coffeecup.com/style/
Select style properties from menus and apply them to HTML elements. Windows
95/NT shareware.

StyleMaker by Danere Group
danere.com/StyleMaker/
Supports applying the new Filter properties—blurs, drop shadows, glows, waves and
much more. (Filters supported only by IE 4.0, so far.) This software is described as
shareware, but a 15-day evaluation period is also mentioned. Windows 95/NT.

Programming and Dynamic HTML Utilities

Perl for Win32

www.ActiveState.com/

This is a Windows 95/NT port of the Perl programming language, which is the most commonly used language for writing CGI scripts.

Astound WebMotion

www.astound.com/products2/webmotion/webmotion.html

Add Java-based multimedia and interactivity without need for programming. 30-day trial version is available. Windows 95/NT and Mac. Registration is only $69.

Astound Dynamite

www.astound.com/products2/dynamite/index.html

Dynamic HTML authoring environment. 30-day trial version is available. Windows 95/NT and Mac.

BannerShow by WebGenie Software

www.webgenie.com/Software/Banner/

Create Java-based rotating banners without CGI, including text or graphic banners, text scrolling special effects, seamless rotation of graphics, frames support, and more. Can be used to display rotating banners or to link to other pages or frames at your site. Windows 95 shareware. $29 to register.

Miscellaneous Software

Look here for links to miscellaneous software tools and resources that are useful to Web publishers—software collections, FTP and Telnet software, Internet tools, anti-virus scanners, and file compression utilities.

Software Collections

TUCOWS: The Ultmate Collection of Winsock Software by Scott A. Swedorski

tucows.phx.cox.com/

Stroud's CWSApps List

www.stroud.com/

Tudogs: The Ultimate Directory of Gratis Software

www.dockside.co.za/egben/tudogs/begin.html

This one focuses on free software.

The WinSite Archive
www.winsite.com/

ZDNet Software Library
www.hotfiles.com/

www.32bit.com
www.32bit.com/software/index.phtml
Windows 95/NT software collection.

WinFiles.com
www.winfiles.com/
Windows 95/NT/98/CE software collection.

Beverly Hills Software: The Windows NT Resource Center
www.bhs.com/
Features the best 32-bit shareware, freeware, trialware, and drivers with a focus on Windows NT.

Icon Shareware
www.iconshareware.com/software/net.html
A guide to the latest and greatest shareware software on the Net.

SHAREWARE.COM by C/NET
www.shareware.com/
Great source for shareware software on the Net.

FTP Programs

WS_FTP by Ipswitch, Inc.
www.ipswitch.com/
My favorite FTP program.

CuteFTP by Alex Kunadze
www.cuteftp.com/
Another FTP client.

Integrated Internet FTP by Kent D. Behrens
www.aquila.com/kent.behrens/
Still another FTP client.

Anti-Virus Scanners

Thunderbyte Anti-Virus
`www.thunderbyte.com`

VirusScan by Network Associates (previously McAfee).
`www.nai.com/products/antivirus/virusscan/default.asp`

File Compression/Decompression Utilities

WinZip by Nico Mak Computing, Inc.
`www.winzip.com/`
Uncompress zip, tar, or virtually any other compressed file from the Web. Shareware.

Drag and Zip by Canyon Software
`www.canyonsw.com/dnz.htm`
Zips and unzips .ZIP, .LZH, .GZ, TAR files and works with Uuencoded, Xxencoded, MIME and Bin/Hex files. Makes Win 16 and Win 32 self-extracting files with no additional purchase, as well as auto launch and password-protected self-extracting zips. Also scans zip files for viruses. Evaluation version is available.

Stuffit Expander for Windows
`tucows.phx.cox.com/comp.html`
Freeware compression and decompression utility that can handle "stuffed" SIT files (which WinZip can't). Windows 3.1.

APPENDIX C

Special Characters

The ISO 8859-1 character set uses 8 bits, allowing for 256 code positions. Numbers 0 through 31 and 127 are control characters. Numbers 32 through 126 correspond to the US-ASCII characters that you can type at the keyboard. Numbers 128 through 159 are designated as unused in ISO 8859-1, but both Windows and the Macintosh assign characters to many of these positions. Numbers 160 through 255 designate extended (or special) characters included in ISO 8859-1 that should be displayable on all computer systems supporting this character set.

Reserved Characters

These are the numerical and named characters that are reserved for formatting HTML tags and codes.

TABLE C.1 RESERVED CHARACTERS

Number	Name	Description	Character
"	"	Double quotation	"
&	&	Ampersand	&
<	<	Left angle bracket	<
>	>	Right angle bracket	>

Unused Characters

Both Windows and the Macintosh assign characters to many of the code positions the ISO 8859-1 character set designates as unused, and 12 of these extra characters are dissimilar on the two systems. Below I've listed all the characters that are displayable in Windows, of which three are not available on the Macintosh. *There is no guarantee that any of these characters will display on other platforms.* Therefore my recommendation is that you avoid using these characters—even the ones that have been assigned HTML character names.

TABLE C.2 UNUSED CHARACTERS

Number	Name	Description	Character
€		Unused	
		Unused	
‚		Single quote (low)	,
ƒ		Small Latin f	ƒ
„		Double quote (low)	„
…		Ellipsis	...
†		Dagger	† (not on Mac)
‡		Double dagger	‡

TABLE C.2 UNUSED CHARACTERS

Number	Name	Description	Character
ˆ		Circumflex	ˆ
‰		Per mile sign	‰
Š		S-caron	Š (not on Mac)
‹		Left angle quote	‹
Œ		OE ligature	Œ
		Unused	
Ž		Unused	
		Unused	
		Unused	
‘		Left single quote	'
’		Right single quote	'
“		Left double quote	"
”		Right double quote	"
•		Bullet	•
–	–	En dash	–
—	—	Em dash	—
˜		Small tilde	~
™	™	Trademark	™
š		s-caron	š (not on Mac)
›		Right angle quote	›
œ		oe ligature	œ
		Unused	
ž		Unused	
Ÿ		Y-umlaut	Ÿ

Special Characters

The following characters, 160 through 255, are all part of the ISO 8859-1 character set. These characters should generally be available on any operating system that uses the ISO-8859-1 character set, which is most of them. However, the 14 marked below are not available on the Macintosh and should be avoided.

	TABLE C.3 SPECIAL CHARACTERS		
Number	**Name**	**Description**	**Character**
		Non-breakable space	[ ] (brackets added)
&#161;	&iexcl;	Inverted exclamation	¡
&#162;	&cent;	Cent sign	¢
&#163;	&pound;	Pound sign	£
&#164;	&curren;	Currency sign	¤
&#165;	&yen;	Yen sign	¥
&#166;	&brvbar;	Broken vertical bar	¦ (not on Mac)[1]
&#167;	&sect;	Section sign	§
&#168;	&uml;	Umlaut	¨
&#169;	&copy;	Copyright	©
&#170;	&ordf;	Feminine ordinal	ª
&#171;	&laquo;	Left guillemet	«
&#172;	&not;	Not sign	¬
&#173;	&shy;	Soft hyphen	–
&#174;	&reg;	Registration	®
&#175;	&hibar;	Macron	¯
&#176;	&deg;	Degree	°
&#177;	&plusmn;	Plus/minus sign	±
&#178;	&sup2;	Superscripted 2	² (not on Mac)

TABLE C.3 SPECIAL CHARACTERS

Number	Name	Description	Character
³	³	Superscripted 3	³ (not on Mac)
´	´	Acute accent	´
µ	µ	Micro sign	µ
¶	¶	Paragraph sign	¶
·	·	Middle dot	·
¸	¸	Cedilla	¸
¹	¹	Superscripted 1	¹ (not on Mac)
º	º	Masculine ordinal	º
»	»	Right guillemet	»
¼	¼	1/4 fraction	¼ (not on Mac)
½	½	1/2 fraction	½ (not on Mac)
¾	¾	3/4 fraction	¾ (not on Mac)
¿	¿	Inverted question mark	¿
À	À	A-grave	À
Á	Á	A-acute	Á
Â	Â	A-circumflex	Â
Ã	Ã	A-tilde	Ã
Ä	Ä	A-umlaut	Ä
Å	Å	A-ring	Å
Æ	Æ	AE diphthong	Æ
Ç	Ç	C-cedilla	Ç
È	È	E-grave	È
É	É	E-acute	É
Ê	Ê	E-circumflex	Ê
Ë	Ë	E-umlaut	Ë

TABLE C.3 SPECIAL CHARACTERS

Number	Name	Description	Character
Ì	Ì	I-grave	Ì
Í	Í	I-acute	Í
Î	Î	I-circumflex	Î
Ï	Ï	I-umlaut	Ï
Ð	Ð	Uppercase Eth	Ð (not on Mac)
Ñ	Ñ	N-tilde	Ñ
Ò	Ò	O-grave	Ò
Ó	Ó	O-acute	Ó
Ô	Ô	O-circumflex	Ô
Õ	Õ	O-tilde	Õ
Ö	Ö	O-umlaut	Ö
×	×	Multiplication sign	x (not on Mac)[2]
Ø	Ø	O-slash	Ø
Ù	Ù	U-grave	Ù
Ú	Ú	U-acute	Ú
Û	Û	U-circumflex	Û
Ü	Ü	U-umlaut	Ü
Ý	Ý	Y-acute	Y (not on Mac)
Þ	Þ	Uppercase Thorn	Þ (not on Mac)
ß	ß	Sharp s (German)	ß
à	à	a-grave	à
á	á	a-acute	á
â	â	a-circumflex	â
ã	ã	a-tilde	ã

TABLE C.3 SPECIAL CHARACTERS

Number	Name	Description	Character
ä	ä	a-umlaut	ä
å	å	a-ring	å
æ	æ	ae diphthong	æ
ç	ç	c-cedilla	ç
è	è	e-grave	è
é	é	e-acute	é
ê	ê	e-circumflex	ê
ë	ë	e-umlaut	ë
ì	ì	i-grave	ì
í	í	i-acute	í
î	î	i-circumflex	î
ï	ï	i-umlaut	ï
ð	ð	Lowercase Eth	ð (not on Mac)
ñ	ñ	n-tilde	ñ
ò	ò	o-grave	ò
ó	ó	o-acute	ó
ô	ô	o-circumflex	ô
õ	õ	o-tilde	õ
ö	ö	o-umlaut	ö
÷	÷	Division sign	÷
ø	ø	o-slash	ø
ù	ù	u-grave	ù
ú	ú	u-acute	ú
û	û	u-circumflex	û

TABLE C.3 SPECIAL CHARACTERS

Number	Name	Description	Character
ü	ü	u-umlaut	ü
ý	ý	y-acute	y (Not on Mac)
þ	þ	Lowercase Thorn	þ (Not on Mac)
ÿ	ÿ	y-umlaut	ÿ

[1] The Macintosh substitutes an unbroken vertical bar (|).

[2] The Macintosh substitutes a lowercase x.

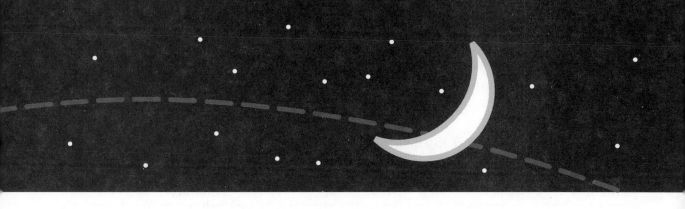

APPENDIX D

Putting It Up on the Web

Now that you've learned HTML, you are going to want to create a Web page and put it up on the Web so that the rest of the world can see your handiwork. There are a few things you need to do before your Web page can set up shop and open its doors on the Web.

Finding a Web Host

The first step is to find a server to host your page. If you are a student, your school might be able to host your pages. If you are a subscriber to one of the online services such as CompuServe or AOL, it also might provide some Web space. Your local access provider that connects you to the Internet might also be able to provide Web space to you at nominal cost (or no cost).

However, if you want to create a commercial Web page, generate a considerable amount of traffic, or access a fuller range of features and services, you might want to find a Web host that focuses on providing raw Web space. For a list of affordable presence providers, see my Web site, the Budget Web Host List, at `http://www.callihan.com/budget/`. It also includes a link to my article "Web Site on a Budget," which was published in the April '96 issue of *Internet World*.

Transferring Your Web Page to a Server

Your Web host should provide you with FTP access to your Web pages. This means providing you with a user ID and a password, as well as assigning you a password-protected directory on its server where you can store your pages. You might also be assigned an account name, although usually not. This allows you to access your directory (and any directories you create within that directory) through FTP, copying files to or from it, while keeping everyone else out.

A Few Things You Need to Know

Before you can use FTP to transfer Web pages to your Web host's server, you need to find out the following information from your Web space provider:

- **Host name.** The host name of your Web host's server. This must identify a fully qualified Internet host name or IP address that belongs to a real server, and cannot be a virtual host name (such as callihan.com, for instance). Your Web host should provide you with this information.

- **User ID.** This is a unique user name that identifies you to your server. If you have received your Web space from a local ISP or a commercial online service, this will very likely be the same as the user name you use to log on. Otherwise, your Web host will ask you to specify a preferred user name when you get your Web space account.

- **Password.** You need to have a password so that only you can access your Web pages on the server. Your Web host will ask you to specify a password when you get your Web space account. As with your User ID, if you have received your Web space from a local ISP or a commercial online service, your password will likely be the same as the password you use to log onto the Internet.

- **Account.** Most Web hosts do not provide an account name—only a user name (User ID) and a password are usually required. If they require an account name, they should let you know.

- **Remote directory path.** This is the directory path to where your files are located on your server. In most cases, you shouldn't need to provide this information—most Web hosts automatically switch you to your own root directory on your server when you log on with your User ID and password. If a remote directory path is required, it needs to be the actual full path on your server, and not your alias.

 On Unix servers, the Host Name and User ID are case-sensitive. So if you have chosen "JBlow," for instance, as your User ID (rather than "jblow"), you'll need to enter it exactly as shown. Windows NT servers, however, are not case-sensitive, so you could enter your User ID in any combination of upper and lowercase letters.

Setting Up WS-FTP LE

To transfer your Web pages from your local computer to your server, you need to use an FTP program. The following examples all use WS-FTP LE for Windows 95, version 4.5, which is on the CD-ROM that comes with this book. Earlier versions of WS-FTP LE should all be quite similar, except the arrangement of the Properties and Options menus will be different. Other FTP programs should work similarly.

If you don't have a CD-ROM drive, you can download WS-FTP LE directly from the Ipswitch Web site at `http://www.ipswitch.com/downloads/ws_ftp_LE.html`. It is free to qualified noncommercial users.

Run your winsock dialer to log on to the Internet; then, after you connect to the Internet, run WS-FTP LE. Figure D.1 shows the opening screen of WS-FTP LE for Windows 95, version 4.5, displaying the General tab section of the Session Properties window (earlier versions of WS-FTP LE might combine the General and Startup tab sections in one window).

Follow the steps outlined in the subsequent sections to define a new session profile.

The General Tab

1. In the Profile Name box, type a name for your session profile. This can be whatever you want. For instance, you might define "MySite" as your profile name. Just make it something you can remember.

2. In the Host Name/Address box, type the host name of the Web host server where your Web space is located. This is a fully qualified Internet host name or IP address—mine is vp2.netgate.net. This is not your virtual host name, if you happen to have one (my virtual host name is www.callihan.com).

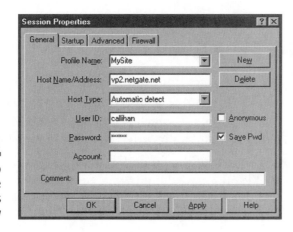

Figure D.1

The General tab section of the Session Properties window

3. In the Host Type box, you should leave "Automatically detect" enabled. If that doesn't work, try "Unix (standard)"—the majority of Web servers are still Unix machines. In most cases, one of these two settings work. If neither works, you need to find out from your Web space provider the actual host type you need so that you can select one of the other options.

4. In the User ID box, type your user name.

5. To disable anonymous login, click on the Anonymous check box so that it is unchecked (blank). To save your password so that you won't have to retype it every time you log in, click on the Save Pwd check box to check it.

♦♦

If you are on a network, you should be aware that checking the Save Password check box will save your password to your hard drive in an encrypted form. It is not difficult to unencrypt for someone who is determined to do so—a hacker, for instance. If you don't save your password here, you must type it in each time you use FTP to log on to your Web server. It's your pick—security or convenience. If you are not on a network, security shouldn't be as much of an issue, as a hacker would have to be sitting at your keyboard to get at your password.

♦♦

6. Type your password in the Password box. If you enabled Save Password, it appears as a row of asterisks. (Don't type a row of asterisks!)

7. Leave the Account box blank unless your Web host has provided you with an account name.

   Refer back to Figure D.1 for an example of how your filled-out General tab section should look (substituting your own information, of course).

8. Click on the Startup tab.

The Startup Tab

1. Normally, you wouldn't type anything in the Initial Remote Host Directory box—your Web host automatically switches you to your root directory. On the off-chance that your Web host should require that you specify your root directory here, you'll need to give the actual full path to your root directory, not just an alias path.

2. In the Initial Local Directory box, type the path of your local directory (folder), such as **c:\pages**, where your HTML files are stored on your hard drive.

3. Click on the Apply button to save your new session profile. (In some earlier versions of WS-FTP, this is a Save button.)

4. Leave the rest of the fields blank. (See Figure D.2.)

5. Click on the Advanced tab section.

The Advanced Tab Section

You need to change the settings here only if the default settings don't work. For instance, if you're having trouble connecting, you might increase the number in the Connection Retry box. You could also increase the Network Timeout entry if you are timing out before you connect. Lastly, a port number other than 21 (which is the standard port number for an FTP server) might need to be set in the Remote Port box, although this is unlikely. (See Figure D.3.)

Figure D.2

The Startup tab section of the Session Properties window

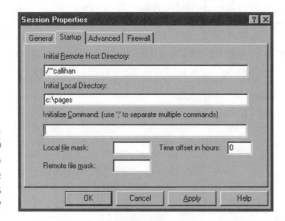

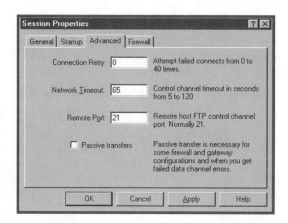

Figure D.3

The Advanced tab section of the Session Properties window should usually be left as is.

The Firewall Tab Section

There is no need to fill out the Firewall tab section unless your Web directories are located behind a firewall, which is unlikely. If you need to fill out this section, find out from your Web space provider the information you'll need to type in here.

Connecting to Your Server

To connect to your server, you need to be logged on to the Internet. In WS-FTP's Session Properties window, click on the OK button. If your settings are correct, you'll see the root directory on your server displayed in the right-hand window. (See Figure D.4.)

If there is a Web directory present, as shown in Figure D.4, this will be the actual root folder for your Web pages. Other directories might also be present, such as an FTP directory where you could place files that you want to make available via FTP (rather than HTTP).

If this hasn't worked, you'll need to go back to the drawing board. You may need to specify a host type (you'll probably have to e-mail your Web host to find out what this is). Make sure that the host name of your Web server is correct. You should double-check that your user ID, password, and account name (if you have one) are correct. If it still doesn't work, under

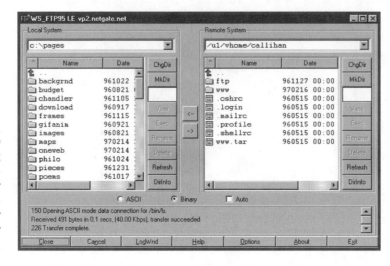

Figure D.4

Once you connect to your server, WS-FTP displays your local directories on the left and your directories on your server on the right.

the same Advanced tab, try increasing the Network Timeout amount or the number of connection retries. Also, make sure you have the right directory path, if that is required.

NOTE The whole battle of being able to use FTP to update your Web pages on your server is getting these settings correct. So make sure you find out from your Web space provider the exact settings you need to provide here. Once you get them right, it is as easy as pie. (But it's pretty much pie in your face if you don't get them right! So be patient if you can't get this to work right off the bat.)

Using WS-FTP LE

Once you connect to your directories on your server, WS-FTP LE's main screen is displayed in the form of two side-by-side windows. The window on the left shows the local folder (directory) on your hard drive that you specified in the Initial Local Directory box under the Startup tab. The window on the right shows the directory on your Web server that you specified in the Initial Remote Host Directory box, also under the Startup tab.

As shown in Figure D.4, the remote host directory that I log on to on my Web server contains two directories, the ftp directory and the www directory. My Web pages are actually inside the www directory. If this is also the case on your server, go ahead and double-click on the www directory—or whatever other directory name that is being used to contain your Web directories. (See Figure D.5.)

You'll notice that I have quite a few directories already set up in the right-hand window. That's because I've been a busy chipmunk and have managed to create quite a few Web pages. In order to keep track of them, I have organized them into separate directories. Because you're just getting started, you might not have any directories or files set up yet, unless your provider has already created some sample directories or files for you.

 TIP You'll also notice, as shown in Figure D.5, that the folders on my Web server match the folders on my local hard drive. When creating Web pages on your local hard drive, you want your folder structure on your local drive to mirror your folder structure on your remote Web server. So, if you have a **c:\pages\images** folder on your local drive, you'll want to have a corresponding \www\images folder (or www/images/, to follow Unix conventions) on your remote server. That way, if you always use relative URLs to link to other files internal to your own site (strongly recommended), you can fully test the links on your local hard drive and then transfer your Web pages to your Web server without having to reset any of the links.

Navigating WS-FTP LE's Main Window

Navigating WS-FTP's main window, you can do the following:

- ♦ Move up or down the directory structure in either window. Double-clicking on a folder will open a subdirectory. Double-clicking on the two periods (..) will move you up one directory level. You can also use the ChgDir button in either window to change the directory.

- ♦ Use the MkDir button to create a directory in either window. You can use the Delete button to delete a directory.

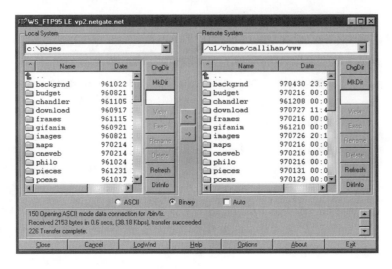

Figure D.5

Your Web page directories may be inside a www directory on your server.

○ Transfer files from the directory on your local PC to the directory on your Web server (you can also do this the other way around). For instructions for transferring files from your local computer to your server, see "Transferring Your Files to Your Server."

○ Of the remaining buttons, the ones you are most likely to use are the View button and the Rename button, which (unsurprisingly) let you view and rename files, and the DirInfo button, which gets information on the files in a directory (such as size and date).

Transferring Your Files to Your Server

Actually transferring your files onto your server is fairly simple. Just follow these steps.

1. On your local PC (the window on the left), change to the folder that contains the files you want to transfer to your server. Highlight the files.

2. Check the radio button of the type of file you are transferring. If you are transferring HTML files or any other text files, you must click on the ASCII radio button so that it is filled. If you are transferring graphics files, such as GIF or JPEG images, you must click on the Binary radio button so that it is filled. (Don't check the Auto check box unless you want to transfer a folder and its contents.)

3. To transfer the highlighted files from the local PC directory (the left window) to the currently displayed directory on your Web server (the right window), click on the right-arrow button. (To copy a file the other way, from your Web server to your local PC, you would click on the left-arrow button.)

Be patient. If you are copying several files, or if any of them are large (such as a banner graphic file, for instance), it might take a minute or so before the files have been transferred.

Forcing Lowercase File Names

One gotcha that is easy to trip over when transferring files from your PC to your server is the case-sensitivity of file names on Unix systems. Thus, **Whacko.htm** and **whacko.htm** on a Unix system represent two different files. To avoid this problem (getting the wrong case), I set WS-FTP to force lowercase file names when transferring files to my server. I then make sure that all hypertext links in my Web pages are also all lowercase. To set up WS-FTP to do this, log on to your server (or any FTP site). Then, in the WS_FTP LE window, follow these steps:

1. Click on Options. Select the Session tab (in earlier versions of WS-FTP LE, you might need to select Session Options here).

2. Click on the Force Lowercase Remote Names check box so that it is checked. (See Figure D.6.)

3. Click on the Set as default button and then click on OK.

Once you've transferred a Web page, and any attendant graphic files, to your server, you can run your browser and then specify the URL for your Web page to open it in your browser. Two errors that are very common when transferring files are transferring files in the wrong mode (ASCII as Binary, or vice versa) and not transferring all the graphics that are included in a Web page. The only way you can be sure that everything has been transferred the way you want it is to check out the transferred Web page or pages in your browser. You don't have to exit WS-FTP LE before running your browser to check out your transfer—that way, if you've sent a file in the wrong mode, you can easily retransfer it immediately.

Closing and Exiting WS-FTP

When you are through transferring files to or from your server, you should always close your FTP session before exiting WS-FTP. To do this, just click on the Close button, wait for the "Goodbye" message to be displayed in the lower activity window, and then click on the Exit button. After exiting WS-FTP, log off the Internet.

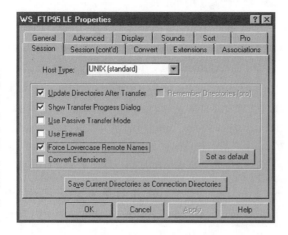

Figure D.6

You can force all files transferred to your Web server to be converted to all lowercase letters, which will keep you from tripping over Unix's case sensitivity.

PROGRAM DETAILS

WS-FTP LE by Ipswitch, Inc.
www.ipswitch.com/
E-Mail: sales@ipswitch.com
Phone: (617) 676-5700
Fax: (617) 676-5710

Other Ipswitch products: WS-FTP Pro (professional version), VT320 Telnet Terminal Emulator (DEC VT320 terminal emulator and Telnet communication program).

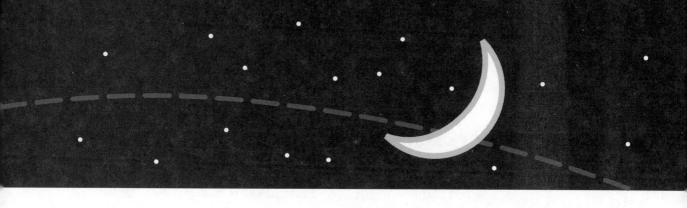

APPENDIX E

What's on the CD-ROM

The CD-ROM that accompanies this book contains all the example graphics and Web pages you use in the tutorials and exercises, plus a good deal more. Here's a rundown of the contents:

- ✪ All example graphics and files for the three HTML tutorials
- ✪ All example Web pages and graphics for the planning and creating sessions
- ✪ A wide assortment of software tools—HTML editors, graphics editors, and utilities for creating forms, frames, image maps, GIF animations, and more
- ✪ A Web art sampler, including backgrounds, icons, graphic rules, and decorative letters
- ✪ A collection of freeware and shareware fonts that you can use to further enhance your Web graphics
- ✪ A selection of Web page templates—two-frame and three-frame Web site templates, a newsletter template, a genealogy Web site template, and more

Running the CD-ROM

To make the CD-ROM more user-friendly and take up less of your disk space, no installation is required. This means that the only files transferred to your hard disk are the ones you choose to copy or install.

◆◆

The CD-ROM has been designed to run under Windows 95 and Windows NT. It will also run under Windows 3.1, but you may encounter unexpected problems. If you run into any problems under Windows 3.1, you may be able to access the files on the CD-ROM using File Manager. All the example graphic and Web page files used in the tutorials and exercises are also available for download from this book's Web site at http://www.callihan.com/create2/.

◆◆

Windows 3.1

To run the CD:

1. Insert the CD-ROM in the CD-ROM drive.
2. From File Manager, select File, Run, to open the Run window.
3. In the Command Line text box, type **D:\primacd.exe** (where D:\ is the CD-ROM drive).
4. Select OK.

Windows 95

Because there is no install routine, running the CD-ROM in Windows 95 is a breeze, especially if you have autorun enabled. Insert the CD-ROM in the CD-ROM drive, close the tray, and wait for it to load.

If you have disabled autorun, do the following to run the CD-ROM:

1. Insert it in the CD-ROM drive.
2. From the Start menu, select Run.

3. In the Open text box, type **D:\primacd.exe** (where D:\ is the CD-ROM drive).

4. Select OK.

The Prima User Interface

Prima's user interface is designed to make viewing and using the CD-ROM contents quick and easy. It contains four category buttons—Book Examples, HTML Tools, Multimedia, and Web Tools—that allow you to install, explore, view information on, or visit the Web site for any of the example files or tools included on the CD-ROM.

Category Buttons

This list describes the category buttons and their functions:

❂ **Book Examples.** All the sample files contributed by the author, including example graphics used in the tutorials, example Web pages used in the planning and creating sessions, a collection of Web page templates, a Web art sampler, and a font library.

❂ **HTML Tools.** A wide assortment of HTML editors and other utilities.

❂ **Multimedia.** A selection of graphics, animation, and sound editors, as well as a couple of additional clip art libraries.

❂ **Web Tools.** A miscellaneous selection of Web tools, including image mapping, forms, FTP, file compression, file management, and other utilities.

Category Options

When you select any of the examples or tools from the category windows, you can execute the following options:

❂ **Install.** Install the example or tool on your hard drive.

❂ **Explore.** Explore the example or tool folder on the CD-ROM.

❂ **View Information.** View any README text file or, alternatively, any Help file that accompanies the example or tool.

❂ **Visit Web Site.** Launch your Web browser (Internet Explorer or Navigator only) and visit the associated Web site.

Shortcut Menu Options

If you right-click on any title in any of the category windows, or on the Prima button in the lower-left corner, you can execute any of these shortcuts:

❂ **Return to Main Menu.** Return to the opening screen.

❂ **Previous Page.** Takes you to the last screen (page) visited.

❂ **Next Page.** Takes you to the next screen.

❂ **Visit the Prima Web site.** Check out some of the other Prima offerings at the Prima Publishing home page. Selecting this option will launch your Web browser (Internet Explorer and Netscape Navigator only) and take you directly to the Prima Publishing Web site as long as you have an Internet connection established.

❂ **Exit the CD-ROM.** When you are finished working with the CD, click on this option to exit.

You can also click on the "<," ">," and "?" buttons in the bottom-right corner of any category window to go to the previous category, to go to the next category, or to access any help prompts for the current window. Clicking on the "<" or ">" buttons in sequence will return you, following any interceding categories, back to the main window.

Book Examples

The Book Examples category window contains all the example graphics and Web pages that are used in the book's tutorials and exercises. It also contains additional author-provided resources you can use to further enhance your Web publishing efforts, including a collection of Web page templates, a Web art sampler, and a font library.

Example Graphics and Web Pages

Selecting the Tutorials title will take you to all the example graphics and Web pages that are used in the Basic HTML, Intermediate HTML, and Tables Tutorials in the book. Selecting the Web Pages title will take you to all the example Web page files and other example graphics files that are used in the book's planning and creating sessions.

You can easily install the example files and Web page examples from the CD-ROM onto your hard drive. I've provided more detailed instructions on how to do this at the start of the Saturday Morning session and the start of the Sunday Morning session.

Web Page Templates

Selecting the Templates title will allow you to install a selection of Web page templates from the CD-ROM that you can use to create a wide range of different kinds of Web pages. You will be prompted for the folder on your hard drive where you want the template folders and files to be unzipped.

○ **Calendar Template.** Use this table-based template to create event and other schedules in a calendar format. To preview the Calendar Template on the CD-ROM, use the Explore button, then double-click on CALENDAR.HTM to view it in your browser.

○ **Frames Templates.** These are two templates, one for creating a two-frame Web site and the other for creating a three-frame Web site that uses "nested frames" (this feature allows you to update the contents of two frames from a single hypertext link without using any JavaScript). To preview either the Two-Frames Template or the Three-Frames Template on the CD-ROM, use the Explore button, then double-click on INDEX.HTM to view it in your browser.

○ **Genealogy Template.** Use this template to create your own geneal-ogy Web site for your family. It includes example photo gallery pages, as well as general instructions on how to use GED2HTML to add HTML GEDCOM files for your different family lines to your Web site. To preview the Genealogy Template on the CD-ROM, use the Explore button, then double-click on INDEX.HTM to view it in your browser.

- ✿ **Generic Templates**. These are an assortment of generic templates that use a variety of different features, such as background images, background text, link colors, font size, color changes, transparent banners, vertical banners, drop-caps, icon bullet lists, and styles. To preview any of these templates on the CD-ROM, use the Explore button, then double-click on any of the included HTML files to view them in your browser.

- ✿ **Navigation Bar Template**. This template includes an image map navigation bar that you can use on any of your Web pages. The template includes instructions for including it in your Web pages, as well as how to use Map This! (a freeware image mapping utility included on the CD-ROM) to edit and create your own image maps. To preview this template on the CD-ROM, use the Explore button, then double-click on NAVBAR.HTM to view it in your browser.

- ✿ **Newsletter Template**. This template allows you to create your own online newsletter. It uses a two-color background image and tables to create a Web page that is laid out like a newsletter, including a masthead at the top, a sidebar table of contents along the left side, and a front page with summaries and links for the articles. To preview this template on the CD-ROM, use the Explore button, then double-click on NEWSLTR.HTM to view it in your browser.

- ✿ **Resume Template**. This template allows you to create your own online résumé. To preview this template on the CD-ROM, use the Explore button, then double-click on RESUME.HTM to view it in your browser.

Web Art Sampler

The Web Art title lets you access a Web art sampler on the CD-ROM that contains many background images, icons, graphics rules, and decorative letters that you can use to enhance your Web pages.

The best way to view the Web art sampler is to install Paint Shop Pro from the CD-ROM and then to use its browse feature to view thumbnail images of all the graphic files in any of the folders included in the \EXAMPLES\WEBART folder on the CD-ROM. To load an image into Paint Shop Pro, just double-click on the thumbnail image. You can then easily save the selected graphic to your hard drive.

Font Library

The Fonts title lets you access a library of freeware and shareware True-Type fonts on the CD-ROM. You can use any of these fonts to further extend the kinds of text effects you can create in your graphics editor. The Installation Instructions option provides instructions on how to install the fonts in either Windows 95 or Windows 3.1. You can also use the Explore option to copy any individual zip files for the fonts onto your hard drive. You will need to have WinZip or another file compression/decompression utility installed to unzip them.

Software

A wide range of different freeware, shareware, trialware, and demoware programs and utilities has been included on the CD-ROM. You are expected to register any shareware programs or evaluation versions if you wish to continue to use them beyond their evaluation periods. Some programs will stop working after their evaluation periods are up (anywhere from 14 days to 90 days), while some will just pester you with nag screens. Freeware programs are free to use as long as you wish, as are some demo programs (although they may have some reduced functionality). Here are brief descriptions of some of the software that you'll find on the CD-ROM:

- ✿ **1-4-All HTML Editor.** A 32-bit, tag-based, shareware HTML editor for Windows 95 or NT 4.0.
- ✿ **Animagic GIF.** A powerful animation tool that not only creates GIF animation files but optimizes them to minimize file size.

- **Aardvark Pro HTML Editor.** An excellent HTML editor from Australia for Windows 95 and NT.

- **Flashview Multimedia Browser.** A powerful multimedia utility that handles most of the common graphic, sound, and video formats.

- **Frame-It.** A great program that allows you to almost effortlessly create frame-based Web sites.

- **GoldWave.** A sound editor, player, recorder, and converter for Windows 95 and NT.

- **HTML Power Tools.** A collection of powerful HTML utilities, including a spell-checker, syntax analyzer, rule-based editor, and more.

- **HTMLed HTML Editor.** A powerful HTML editor with versions for both Windows 3.x and Windows 95/NT. HTMLed Pro, a trialware version of the full commercial version, is also available on the CD-ROM.

- **Map This!** A freeware image map editor that can create both client-side and server-side image maps.

- **Paint Shop Pro.** One of the leading graphics editors, with features rivaling commercial graphics editors, such as Adobe PhotoShop or Corel Photopaint, costing hundreds of dollars more.

- **WebForms.** A great program for creating and managing both client-side and server-side forms. Imports form responses into an MS Access database.

- **CoffeeCup HTML Editor++, Image Mapper++, and StyleSheet Maker++.** A great collection of programs that will edit HTML files, create image maps, and create Cascading Style Sheets.

- **WinZip.** One of the most popular file compression utilities around. Makes working with ZIP files and many other file compression formats in Windows a breeze.

- **WS-FTP LE.** A great freeware FTP program. Use this program to easily transfer your Web pages, graphics, and other files to and from the Web server hosting your pages. You can also use it to manage your files and folders on your Web server. WS-FTP Pro, a trial version of the full commercial WS-FTP, is also available on the CD-ROM.

INDEX

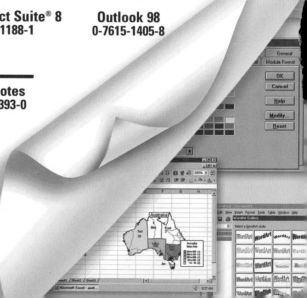